The events in this book are portrayed to the best of the author's memory. While all the stories in this book are true, some names and identifying details may have been changed to protect the privacy of the people involved.

Introduction

Olympia, WA
October 8th, 2013

If you told me when I was in high school that I would one day write about the biggest secret and greatest source of pain in my life, I would have laughed in your face. Even if you'd told me just two years ago, I don't know that I would have believed you. But here I am on a cool, damp, fall night in Olympia, Washington, clicking away at my keyboard— beginning to tell a story I thought would never be told.

It's a story I chose to ignore. A story that I thought couldn't possibly be appealing, helpful, or even redeemable. Even calling it a story seemed like giving it too much credit, because good stories, while they are not always easy, offer valuable lessons. Reading them stirs up all kinds of emotions. We recognize the ways in which we are similar or different from

1

the characters in the story, and we experience, to some degree, the emotions they feel as they traverse whatever challenges lie before them.

Some stories are told and retold. They grow larger than the author ever could have anticipated. People get lost in these stories. Some such stories might even inspire a reader to take a big life step, or to find clarity in confusion. These stories aren't always easy to get through, but at the end, you see with new vision; it all makes sense, and you can feel confident that you finally understand.

For the longest time, I believed a lie: that none of these things could be true for my story, and that they never would be. I knew that my story was meant to be hidden away and suffered through alone. It would only ever be a source of pain, hopelessness, fear, disdain, and confusion. In fact, I felt it would always be a barrier to my relationship with God and the *real* story He had planned for me. To me it seemed like a great chasm that separated us—a chasm too great to cross.

I was wrong. God shows up in those rifts that seem impassable to us and blows our minds. God can and does build bridges over the deepest and scariest of chasms so that we can run to Him, jump into His arms, and hear Him tell us that He was always there—walking with us, crying in our pain, understanding our frustration and disappointment. Always present, even in the silence, God offers a peace and a hope that passes all understanding.

This book will tell the story I'd locked away for so long, hoping never to tell. It's littered with pain, confusion, and ugly stuff; but God calls it good, and that's why I could never call it anything but "good" again. It's tough, and there are moments

I'd rather not revisit, but they all played a part in getting me where I am today.

I pray that as you read, you are able to set aside your preconceived notions and just hear me out. As I've learned, stories are meant to be shared. They challenge and bless us when they're received as the gift that they are. Jesus is our best example of how to hear people's stories—truly *hear* them. He walked with people through the hardest parts of their lives, lovingly challenging and caring for them. He's still doing this today, and I have been a lucky recipient.

God built a bridge in my life. This bridge looks far different than any I would have built, and its assembly was a far from easy process. But it is more detailed and more beautiful than any I could have dreamed of building myself.

Come taste and see that the Lord is good; blessed is the man who takes refuge in him. Psalm 34:8

Growing Up

Olympia, Washington
The First Eighteen Years

I was born on September 6, 1983, in Redmond, Washington. I was raised in an evangelical Christian home, the oldest of three boys. We grew up in our state capital of Olympia, in a house that was next to a big field that we could run around and play in. Beyond the field, there were train tracks lined with trees—perfect for building forts. My friends and I spent our summer days smashing pennies on the tracks. Our tree fort—really just a bunch of awkward platforms nailed on branches—was a never-ending project.

As a young child, I was creative. I loved to draw, and I was good at it. The walls of my room became murals of all my favorite Disney characters from different movies. I would tell people that one day I was going to be a Disney animator. On most weekends, our dining room table was littered with papers, pencil shavings, and colored pencils, as I worked diligently on my next piece of art. My mom called these my "projects," with a knowing and loving smile.

When I wasn't drawing, I was playing with dinosaurs. I was obsessed, and I still am today. I'm thirty-six years old, and to this day my friends still occasionally text me to quiz me on identifying dinosaurs whenever they come across an image or one— I always get it right.

I have never been shy. Making friends always seemed to come easily for me; I like to talk, and I enjoy making people laugh. I've been told that I am easy to be around, that I make people comfortable, that people feel safe when they're with me because I accept them without judgment.

As I got older, though, there was one person that I struggled to love. As much as I may have appeared to others as kind and accepting, the reality was that I was judgmental and unforgiving, especially to this one person. In my eyes, he could do nothing right. His actions, even those that appeared good, had a self-serving motive. He claimed to love the Lord with all of his heart—going to Bible school, spending summers working at a Christian camp, serving as a youth pastor, and going to seminary. Those things were well and good, but there was one thing about him that disqualified him from any kind of love or grace from me: While he claimed to be a Christian, he was also gay. This paradox just didn't work in my mind.

Inevitably in life there are people we can't agree with, and in those cases a natural distance forms. But that couldn't happen with this person. Wherever I turned, he was there. Inescapable. Why? Because this person I hated so much, the person who could do no right and deserved the worst of outcomes, was none other than me. Tyler Krumland.

In order to understand how this came to be, we'll have to back up, back to early childhood—to that home at the edge of a field, where I grew up and where my parents still live today.

My mother and father loved me and my brothers very much, and they always did their best to make sure we had the best they could give, even if it meant they had to sacrifice. They both worked for the Washington State Department of Labor and Industries; my mother was a secretary, and my father was a safety and community inspector. At times money was challenging for us, but they never wanted us to feel like we weren't able to do the things our friends did. They'd get creative so that we could still have fun, and although I hear stories now of how tight money was at times, or the things they wish they could have done differently, I don't remember ever feeling like we had less. There was never any doubt that either of our parents loved us.

My mom is one of the nicest women you'll ever meet. I get my heart for people from her. She cares so much for those around her and genuinely wants everyone to feel special and heard. She is patient. Every day when we came home from school, she would wait for us with a snack, asking about our days. I was a mama's boy. Whenever she ran errands, I went with her, and we had great conversations. To this day, when I go and visit, I still look forward to running errands with my mom. It was our thing, and I cherished it.

From my dad, I get my creativity. He was always working on a project around the house, building shelves, rebuilding the engine of his truck, or putting an addition onto our home. He could fix anything. Like my mom, he always found ways to make special memories with his sons. When I was in fifth grade, he took me to a Seattle Sonics game because they were playing the Charlotte Hornets, and Larry Johnson was my favorite basketball player. I remember after the game, some of the players (Alonzo Mourning and Muggsy Bogues) came out to sign autographs. I was short, and Muggsy Bogues, who was only 5'3", gave me hope that I could one day play in the NBA. I remember reaching out as Alonzo Mourning tried to hand me his sweatband, but another person snatched it away. I cried the whole way home, but I still think of that day when I haven't seen my dad in a while. He wanted to create a special and lasting memory by taking me to that game. I've never forgotten it.

Growing up, people always told me I looked just like my mom, so I often thought we had a lot in common. But in recent years, I've realized I'm a lot like my dad, too. He recently retired, but he is the busiest retired person I know. I am the same way—I can rarely just sit down and relax.

I grew up in the Evangelical Covenant Church (The ECC), which was founded by Swedish immigrants in 1885. "Known originally as Mission Friends," according to its website, "the ECC has its roots in historical Christianity as it emerged in the Protestant Reformation, in the biblical instruction of the Lutheran State Church of Sweden, and in the great spiritual awakenings of the nineteenth century." I loved being part of this denomination. I saw it as the best and right denomination—anyone in any other denomination was missing out, I thought.

Throughout my childhood, we went to church every Sunday morning. One of my first memories of church was with my cousin, Colin. We were playing behind the pulpit—I think I may have been pretending to be a pastor—and being little boys who weren't always the most careful, we knocked it over. As I got older, I was social—never shy. Because of this trait, I typically landed a speaking role in our annual Christmas program at church (and I'm still waiting to receive my Oscar for those performances.)

Before every meal and before bed each night, our family prayed together—for friends who were going through rough times, or giving thanks when things were good. From an early age, and still now, prayer was an essential practice in my life. A time for quiet reflection, questioning, and growth.

Although raised with a strong religious background, my theological questioning started at a young age. I remember somewhere around the age of eight, I was in the backyard on a hot summer day playing with the hose to cool off. I noticed that as I sprayed the water up and watched it fall to the ground, a rainbow would appear. This confused me because growing up in church I learned that the rainbow was God's promise to never send a flood onto the earth—a reference to the story of Noah. I knew this was why we could see rainbows after a rainstorm, but why was I able to create a rainbow on a sunny day, I wondered? My little brain was gearing up for a lifetime of theological questioning.

Most summers I spent a week at a church camp in the foothills of Mount Rainier. I was always excited leading up to it, and then when the day came for me to go, I would get nervous. Being away from home for a week was always kind of scary for me. I struggled even to sleep over at friends' houses, so this was a big challenge.

Once I got into the flow of things, though, I found camp to be such a fun place. While there, we stayed in huge tents on raised platforms that smelled like fresh earth and wood. I always got there early so I could get a top bunk. The long summer days were filled with swimming, big group games, crafts, junk food, and of course Bible study, where each day our counselor would teach my cabin mates and me about Jesus.

Some days, we met up and sang crazy camp songs. Most of them were faith-based, and the people in the Evangelical Covenant denomination know all the same songs by heart. Everyone's favorite was "Pharaoh Pharoah," which was sung to the tune of "Louie, Louie," by The Kingsmen. The song was all about Moses leading the Israelites out of Egypt, and it came complete with silly hand motions.

> *Pharaoh, Pharaoh,*
> *oh baby let my people go*
> *oooh ahhh*
> *Yeah yeah yeah yeah*

All the kids' favorite part was the end, when Moses and his people made it across the Red Sea, and the waters came washing away. "Pharaoh's army was a comin' too / So what did you think that I did do? / I raised my rod, and I cleared my throat / and all Pharaoh's army did the dead man's float." We leaned over with our arms stretched out, like we were doing the dead man's float. At the time it was just a fun song to sing, but I can't believe we were reenacting people drowning. This is common in the evangelical world. We take violent stories and make them "fun" for children. Think of all the Sunday school classrooms and nurseries decorated with Noah's ark imagery. Cute animals protruding from a boat jam-packed full of other cute animals, surrounded by water. Water that doesn't show all the dead men, women, and children from a great natural disaster. As a child, I didn't think much of it.

One summer, after my fifth grade year, on the last night of my week in the woods, everyone at the whole camp sat around a campfire while the leader talked to us about taking our belief in God to the next level. He told us that we could have a personal relationship with Jesus, where we could talk with him like a friend—about the good things in our lives and also the hard things. All we needed to do was say a prayer and invite Jesus to live in our hearts. This was our way of asking Jesus to come with us everywhere, like our conscience. If we wanted to do this, he said, we could go back to our cabins, and our counselors would lead us in a prayer. The Sinner's Prayer. We were taught that saying this prayer—also known as asking Jesus into your heart—was the only way to guarantee a spot in heaven.

I don't remember much of what I was thinking that night, just that all the other boys in my cabin went back to say the prayer. I didn't want to be different, and I was already afraid of going to hell, so I followed them. I later learned that becoming a follower of Christ was more of a process than a moment in time. But that day at camp, and the environment in which I was raised, set a foundation for a consistent relationship with God.

In my evangelical world, we used vocabulary that could be called "Christianese." We asked questions like, "Are they saved?" by which we signaled our interest as to whether people had committed their lives to Christ through the aforementioned sinner's prayer. We wanted to know whether they were just like us. Other people, overhearing us, might not have understood what we meant, and in that way, it was like learning a second language at a young age. We said things like, "It's a God thing," in reference to something unexplained but good. When struggling with faith, perhaps through questioning or doubt, we said, "I'm really wrestling with that." When curious about someone else's faith, we would ask, "How's their walk?" When someone was going through a hard time or struggling with something rough, we'd make sure to "love on them." If I found myself in the midst of temptation to do something I had come to believe was sinful, I knew that I needed to "harness my thoughts." If someone was very invested in his or her faith, they would be described as "on fire for God." I could go on and on, but you get the idea.

I was raised in a world where a particular kind of faith was so interwoven with all that I did that it found its way into my vocabulary—it shaped the way that I saw, experienced, and spoke about the world. Some of these phrases were helpful, but others weren't. One phrase in particular burdened me for a very long time: "God won't let you endure more than you can handle." This claim is taken from 1 Corinthians 10:13, and I found comfort in it whenever I was facing something that seemed too much to bear. I came to believe that God wouldn't have allowed something into my life if I wasn't strong enough to overcome it, so I needed to keep pushing through. This is how I came to think of my attraction to men as something I should be able to endure and overcome.

I don't believe hate is something we're born with. It's a learned condition. I didn't come to hate myself overnight—it grew in me over the years. There were many causes, but the biggest of these was fear.

Many of my friends who grew up in Christian homes weren't allowed to watch certain TV shows or movies. Maybe it's *The Simpsons*, or *Friends*. In my case, it was *The Smurfs*. My parents had heard somewhere that magic was involved with the

Smurfs, so I wasn't allowed to watch. They were doing their best to protect us from the world around us, and in our religion, magic was off limits. My parents—and so many other Christians—were wary of the world, but when it came to the church, they let their defenses down. At church, there were no limits, no questions asked, no caution. If only they'd known.

In high school, a friend invited me to a theatrical performance at church with her family. I don't remember hearing anything about the play beforehand; I just wanted to hang out with my friend. Since it was a church event, my parents didn't ask any questions.

The play was performed by a company that traveled the country from church to church. The show was called *Heaven's Gates and Hell's Flames*. I remember sitting in my seat, chatting with my friend, when suddenly, the whole church fell into complete darkness. A spotlight, shining on a door in the church sanctuary, clicked on. A man dressed as Jesus carrying the cross began to drag his cross on his bleeding back to the front of the church. A narrator read the story of Jesus's crucifixion. From there, it jumped ahead to present-day. The play depicted multiple scenes, each one portraying some aspect of the lives of different people.

The first one started with a spotlight shining on a little old lady as she hobbled along with a cane. An inner dialogue played, of her reflecting on a life dedicated to Jesus. As she was walking, she grabbed her heart and fell to the ground. The lights went dark. Intense music played, followed by silence, followed by bright lights and celestial music. As the light got brighter, it revealed a golden stairway, lined with at least twenty angels in glittery white robes. Standing to the side was an angel at a gold podium with a giant book on it. The little old lady began to sit up. She saw the stairway with all the angels as she got to her feet. Amazed at her ability to move without a cane, she was overtaken with excitement that she was about to enter heaven. With a big smile across her face, she ran to the angel at the podium, yelling with joy, "Angel, is my name in that book of yours?" The angel looked over the page and then with a big smile on his face raised his arms and the Hallelujah chorus began to play. Jumping with excitement, she ran up the stairs as a man dressed as a stereotypical, white Jesus greeted her with a hug.

The lights went dark again. The spotlight shone on a young couple, walking onto the stage. They looked like they were in college, and they were fighting. She was concerned because she was pregnant and didn't know what to do. He didn't want anything to do with her pregnancy and pushed her to get an abortion before storming off stage as the lights went black. In the next scene, the woman was on the floor, crying, while two other women approached. They asked her what was wrong, and she explained that she had just gotten an abortion and that she felt awful and alone. The two women begin to tell her about Jesus, and she ends up converting to Christianity. In the next scene, she shares her newfound love of Jesus with her boyfriend, asking him to also give his life to Jesus by praying a prayer of commitment. But he says no. They get on a fake motorcycle, and as the lights go out, we hear the sound of screeching, them screaming, and a loud crash.

When the lights come back on, the couple is lying in front of the big stairwell. They had died in a motorcycle accident. The woman begins to cry, knowing that even though she tried to tell her boyfriend about Jesus, he didn't listen. He tries to comfort her, saying that everything will be fine. After all, they're together, so he's probably good. She continues to cry, saying, "No, there are no second chances." He walks up to the angel at the podium and says, "We will see about that! Angel, is my name in your book?" The angel surveys the page, and a frown flashes across his face as he raises his arm to cover his eyes. The other angels do the same as the lights dim to a deep red. Then, with a loud bang, the floor in front of the stairs flies open, and lights flickering like flames flash from the open stage. The sounds of people screaming can be heard coming from the hole in the floor. Smoke billows out, and people dressed as demons jump out from below. The man goes running to hide as a Satan figure jumps out, laughing evilly and saying something like, "All you get for eternity is pain," and "I own your soul," and "You should have listened to those who loved you."

Satan then commands the demons to get the man. Wanting to escape, the man came running down the aisle, passing me as the demons ran after him. I watched as they caught him right next to me and dragged him by his feet back to the stage as he screamed in agony and fear, grabbing hold of chairs along the way before Satan wrapped his hands around his neck. Holding the man above the hole in the stage, Satan laughed evilly and said, "You're mine for eternity; this is the last you will see of the land of the living," and kicked him into the hole. We hear his scream slowly fade out and blend in with all the others while the demons and Satan jump back in. Then as quickly as they opened, the doors in the floor slammed shut, and the lights return to normal.

Hardly phased by what happened, the girl gathered her emotions and ran to the angel at the podium, saying something like, "I know I haven't always done what is right, I had an abortion, but Jesus has forgiven me. Angel, is my name in your book?" As with the old woman, the angel smiles and raises his arms once he sees her name in the book. The woman begins to cry as she sees Jesus emerge, carrying her aborted baby down the stairs to her to walk with her into heaven.

Stories like this continued for the next hour or so, culminating in a pastor preaching from the front about how this is real, that time was running out, and we only have one chance. This ultimately led to an "altar call," a time where people are invited to come forward if they want to leave their old lives behind by praying to give their lives to Jesus and convert to Christianity. Although I had converted years before while at camp, I did it again that day because I didn't want to be like those I had seen pulled into hell by the demons.

We stopped at Dairy Queen that night on our way home. I was consumed by what I had just seen. I couldn't get the image of the man running away, then being dragged down the aisle, out of my head. It was violent.

As a youth, these kinds of images and stories are hard to experience or understand in any kind of nuanced way; it was hard to interpret them for myself. What I saw was truth and lies, heaven and hell, angels and demons, right and wrong. For years and even decades of my life, I exercised this binary mentality. If it wasn't good or God-honoring, I needed to do anything in my power to eradicate it, lest I be dragged into hell. Going to hell became an enormous, all-consuming fear. As depicted in that play, I could die at any moment, so there was no margin for error. I was terrified that I would somehow mess up, miss the boat, and end up in hell.

I became very rigid about my faith, and whenever I made a mistake, I beat myself up about it. I learned that we are to fear God. I do believe now that it is good to have reverence for God, but as a young child, I wasn't able to grasp this difference. When I heard "fear God," I thought it meant that I needed to walk on eggshells so as not to upset or anger God to the point where I would be punished. In my mind, God was up there watching what we did, and the moment we did something disappointing, punishment was coming. I always had to be on my best behavior, and I was afraid.

Another byproduct of the environment I grew up in was that I wasn't able to trust my own heart or my desires. I believed that because of sin in the world, or what was sometimes called the "fall of man," my heart was so corrupted that there was no way I could tell the difference between right and wrong. My heart could not be trusted. My brain could not be trusted. I could not be trusted.

There's something else about American Christianity that's sometimes called the prosperity gospel. Although I was not directly taught the premises of this belief system, I lived according to its basic tenets that if we behave ourselves and do our best, God will bless us. This is how I interacted with God. Though I had been told that I should pursue a relationship with God, for me, Christianity was all about not making God mad.

Each time I did anything I saw as contrary to how God would want me to live or not what a "good Christian" would do, I would be overcome with shame. Especially when I kept repeating those same behaviors over and over again. I believed that whenever I wasn't honoring God, I needed to repent, which meant acknowledging the wrong I had done, and then pray to God and ask God to forgive me. I had been taught that once you had completed this process, you shouldn't keep struggling with the same sin. I was supposed to move forward and learn from my mistakes.

This binary thinking also led me toward charismatic Christianity, which is typically characterized by its physically responsive faith, including hand-raising while singing in church, dancing, or speaking in tongues. It can also be characterized by a kind of outspokenness about faith or the gospel. When I was still in junior high, I learned in church that there was a very real spiritual battle between the forces of good and evil, raging around us, and that at some point I would be required to stand up and defend my faith. Christianity was under attack in our country I was taught.

Having to defend one's faith was a badge of honor that I wanted, and I found the first opportunity to do so in my seventh grade world history class. We were learning about the Middle East. The topic for the day's lesson was Islam, and our teacher told us we needed to learn the five pillars of the Islamic faith for the upcoming test we would be having. As a Christian I thought, "I don't need to learn this." So I walked up to my teacher and told her I wasn't comfortable memorizing these "pillars" because of my faith. She was surprised, but she offered me an opportunity to go out into the hall and think about something I would want to do in place of the assignment. As I marched out of the class feeling persecuted for my faith, I also felt like I had won an important battle. This was the kind of public confrontation I thought I needed to be willing to have in my life.

This way of thinking continued into my high school years. Anything that had the power to make God visible in the world interested me, maybe because it helped me to believe God was real and could work miracles in my life. I was intrigued by things like the biblical "end times." I was very much into a book series called the *Left Behind* books, which told the story of a rag-tag group of non-believers who had been left behind after a miraculous event where all Christians in the world simultaneously disappeared and were taken to heaven in an event known to Christians as the rapture, leaving non-Christians behind. The members of this group came to believe in God and had to live through a seven-year period of judgment called the "tribulation," complete with biblical plagues from heaven such as earthquakes, demon locusts, blood rain, and the rule of the antichrist. It all culminated in the return of Jesus. I was obsessed; I knew we just had to be in the end times and that the rapture could happen any day. Once I had access to the internet, I was consumed with research on end-times prophecy, hoping something like what I'd read about would happen in my lifetime. Little did I know that these ideas were not sound beliefs or thinking and were made up by evangelists' misinterpretations of scripture.

Never the less, these ideas about the end times rooted themselves deep within me during my time in high school, especially when I started attending a church youth group and made friends with other young Christians during retreats, mission trips, and at a youth conference led by the Covenant church in Tennessee called CHIC, an acronym for Covenant High In Christ. At these events, I learned more about who God was, and my relationship with Jesus deepened, but my fear also grew stronger. I wanted to please God and make God happy and didn't want to go to Hell.

In the midst of my fixation on visible signs from God, binary thinking, and my belief in a spiritual war between good and evil in our world, everyone my age was starting to date—and I began to notice something. The feelings and attractions that I had toward women were hardly present and nowhere near what I saw in and felt about men. I could tell what women I thought were pretty. As a child of the 90s, I watched shows like *Saved by the Bell* and *Boy Meets World*, where I saw dating relationships that became my model for real life. I needed a woman to be my Kelly Kapowski, and I would be her Zach Morris. (I was clearly disillusioned and thought I was far cooler than I actually was, but that's beside the point.)

The reality was, the very few times I actually started dating a woman, which never lasted more than a week or two and didn't include any actual dates, it was typically because I heard that they thought I was cute and I figured, why not? I wanted to fit in. But the whole time, I felt an inner turmoil that I didn't understand. I didn't want to see them or be around them, I just wanted to be able to *say* I was dating them. It didn't make sense. I would barely give myself the space to explore in my mind and heart what this might mean, because while I could tell what women in my school were cute, I also was very aware of what men I found handsome, even though I didn't acknowledge that, not even in my own mind. I knew what the Bible said: "Homosexuality is a sin." It was an abomination, and that meant that if I was gay, I was an abomination. I would write off my feelings and doubts, telling myself I just hadn't met the right woman and that I just admired those men whom I had feelings for, and that was it.

Homosexuality—or sexuality in general—was never discussed in my family. My mom had only one sibling, her older brother Glen. I don't have many memories of my uncle, Glen, but I do remember that he was a lot of fun and always loving toward my brother, Eric, and me. I really enjoyed him, and I wish I had more memories of him. Glen died of AIDS in the 90s. He was gay. It was such a shameful thing then at the height of a pandemic that many people believed was God's punishment for the sins of the gay community. I don't have many memories of Glen being sick except for one Christmas at my grandparents' house. It's just a tiny moment in time, nothing more, but I remember him wearing a big robe and slippers, and sleeping on the couch. He died when I was in first grade, and I am not even sure I knew he was that sick. My parents told my brother and me that he had died. I mostly remember how upset my mom was.

I didn't know anything about my uncle being gay until fifth or sixth grade. I was wrestling with one of my cousins from my dad's side of the family, and I accidently got a little too rough and hurt him. In anger he said something along the lines of, "Ow, you fag, you hurt me!" Immediately he apologized and said sorry for calling me that and that he had forgotten about my uncle Glen. My uncle? I thought. What about him? But over time I put it all together. My parents had always kept my uncle's sexuality a secret from us, and that was how I knew these must be things you shouldn't talk about with anyone. Looking back, I believe that this secret played heavily in my decision to keep the same secret in my own life.

When I was in high school, the topic of homosexuality was rarely raised in any context. It just wasn't the public hot-button issue it is today, and in my mind, it was clear: the Bible says it's wrong, so don't choose that way of life. Enough said. Let's work on bigger issues. Meanwhile, discussion of sexuality was just starting to make its way into the media in a more prominent way. Before Ellen DeGeneres had her hilarious talk show, she had a sitcom; I don't even know what the plot of the show was. I do remember that in the last few episodes of the series, she came out. This was also around the time that Rosie O'Donnell came out. Aside from them, there weren't many public personalities who had openly talked about their sexuality. I remember that so many of the people I respected criticized these women for coming out—that they'd stopped watching their shows because they didn't want to support their sin, and how sad it was that they had chosen this ungodly way of life.

Around the same time, the movie *Brokeback Mountain* came out and I went to see it with a friend. I was intrigued by it but afraid to show any interest, so I'm pretty sure I played it as if I were doing her a favor by going with her. The night we saw it, I was so scared we'd see someone I knew, and my fears were realized when we left the theater. We ran into a couple I had known since I was young—from church. They were the worst people we could run into. They asked what movie we had seen, and before I could say anything, my friend responded. You could see exactly what they were thinking by the reactions on their faces. Disgust, judgment, and disappointment in us. "Why did you see that?" The woman asked accusingly. I'm not sure how I answered; I just know I did what I could to get out of there as quickly as possible. I was ashamed and feared that they would think I was gay, just because I had seen that film.

At school, one of the worst insults was to be called gay or a fag. I had a lot of girlfriends and was really outgoing, and during my junior high years, I'd been on the receiving end of harsh words a few times. I remember coming home one day in tears—devastated, embarrassed, and hurt—and telling my mom, who hugged me and prayed for me. Today, looking back, I wonder what was really going on in my head and in my heart.

Was I just upset that people could be so cold? or was I afraid that I'd been found out or possibly understood and known before I really knew myself? I'll probably never know.

In junior high, I got in a fight with a girlfriend who lived up the street. I had been teasing her on the bus, and she was mad and went home and told her parents. Her dad immediately called my dad and asked if we could have a meeting. This was so irritating to my dad because it wasn't the first time we had to do this with this friend. After a quick and awkward meeting between the four of us, they left. My dad, in frustration and anger, sternly said, "You'd better be careful; always having fights with girls, you don't want people to think you're gay, do you?" The question was rhetorical, but I believe it had a lasting effect on me. I didn't hear his question, but rather a statement: "You'd better not be gay, because I am not okay with that."

This interaction had repercussions all the way through high school. I made every effort to avoid any behavior or activity that would resemble anything "gay." I made a lot more male friends and was accepted by them, and the usual junior high teasing subsided.

I am often asked when it was that I first knew I was gay, and that's a hard question for me to answer because to be honest, I don't know. I will say I think it was junior high when I started to notice I was different than other boys. In the spring of seventh grade, everyone was talking about the hit movie *Titanic*. All the girls loved it because of the love story and dreamy Leonardo DiCaprio, and the boys loved it for the action and the chance to see Kate Winslet topless. I was more like the girls. I didn't care about the Kate Winslet scene, but I felt so drawn to Jack, Leonardo DiCaprio. I was heartbroken when Rose (Kate

Winslet) didn't make room for him on her door and let him sink. (I mean come on, there was room on that door! Why didn't she try harder?) I didn't think that what I was feeling was attraction or a celebrity crush. I thought it was more of an admiration, like I wanted to be like him one day. In reality, I was compartmentalizing. It was totally a crush.

This escalated more as I got into high school and began to notice this attraction to men growing. It was confusing for me though, because I found some women attractive, too—I even had crushes on some of them. In reality, I think these were more romanticized ideas about hypothetical relationships and what those relationships would look like to those around me and how it would feel to fit in. Wouldn't we have so much fun going to the movies, the mall, dances, and youth group retreats, I thought? It was what I had been taught to want. It's what I saw on TV, in the movies, and at school. So while I struggled with my attraction to other guys, I found myself in inner turmoil feeling hopeless and trapped.

I remember hearing somewhere that maybe it was just puberty—that this would go away one day. Scared it wouldn't, I continued to look for help. During a lecture at school, we had been handed out information for a crisis line, in case we were ever in need of help or struggling and needed someone to talk to. We were told the whole thing would be kept anonymous. This is what I needed, I thought, a place I could ask if I was okay and find out how to change with advice from someone who didn't know me and would never tell anyone.

I saved the number, crumpled up at the bottom of my backpack, until a night when my parents were away. I made sure my brothers were on the other end of the house, and I took the cordless phone out to the garage to build up the courage to call. I took multiple deep breaths and dialed the crisis line. My heart was racing. I could hardly breathe. When the woman answered and asked what I was going through, I tried with all that was in me to say something, but nothing would come out. I hung the phone up and began to pace. Ugh, why can't I just say it, I wondered? It was so scary. After about ten minutes of pacing and trying to build up my courage, I hit redial, but the same thing happened. I hung up and went and hid the number back in its spot at the bottom of my backpack so no one would find it. Afraid someone would accidently hit redial and get the crisis line, I dialed another number and hung up in order to hide my tracks.

I slumped down on the couch, discouraged that I couldn't do it. I couldn't say the words, and as I was learning to do, I shoved all the emotion, fear, pain, and concern deep down, and chose to not think about or acknowledge it. I loved God, and this was most definitely not what God wanted for me, I thought.

Toward the end of my high school career, a student transferred in because he had been severely bullied at another local school for being gay. He'd come to our school, looking for safety and acceptance, but unfortunately, I'm not so sure he came to a safer environment. He was picked on a bit, but found his niche as our only male cheerleader. From the moment he arrived, he never ceased to be the topic of conversation and jokes. This further confirmed to me that it was not acceptable to be gay. I pushed the truth about myself a little deeper each time I saw him mistreated or heard anything negative about him. I felt like he was just bringing it on himself for being so flamboyant.

All of this bottling of my emotions led me to lash out at my parents, both in high school and also later in life. They would often tell me they felt like they had to walk on eggshells around me, and that I was too sensitive. I couldn't tell them why. I was so ashamed to talk about who I was and what I was going through. I would get angry and blow little things out of proportion.

Once, during my junior year of high school, we had a disagreement about something, and I stormed off to my room. They followed me back and asked what was going on. They said they felt like they could never have a disagreement with me without me flying off the handle. I remember crying and saying I don't know why, I'm just always sad and stressed. I now know that it was likely I was struggling with anxiety and depression. We talked about me going to see someone, but nothing ever came of it. I'd like to say that I knew what was going on, that I was afraid I was gay, but I would never admit that to myself. To me, it was all attraction, that was it, and I just needed to pray harder.

One afternoon in my room, I just started crying. I was supposed to meet up with a friend, but for some reason my emotions took over. My parents came in and asked what was wrong, but I couldn't tell them. I just said I didn't know and that I felt sad a lot, but just got good at hiding it. They didn't understand; how could they? We talked again about getting me some help, but I shook it off and said I'd be fine. I put on a happy face. I didn't want to have to go to someone who would force me to talk about my secrets.

A friend had loaned me a psychology book that covered, among other things, topics of human sexuality and the church. I'd hidden it under my bed, planning to read the section one day, but I never found the courage. Some kids my age hid porn under their bed; I hid a psychology book on homosexuality. Every so often, I would stop by the Christian bookstore, and when no one was looking, I'd try to find books on homosexuality. I thought maybe when I went to college and was away from home I could buy a book like that and read it to find help—in a place where no one knew me and where I wouldn't have to be afraid that I might run into someone I knew.

The first time I really talked out loud about all of this was my first year in college. It's hard to think that I kept it to myself for so long, especially as an extrovert, but I'd learned that if you were gay, you were broken, overly sexual, and flamboyant, and that you'd be ridiculed and criticized for these things because none of them were okay. I'd learned in junior high what it felt like to be teased. So I kept it a secret and believed I always would—but God had other plans. I was about to begin a journey that would be scary, sometimes painful, and terribly confusing, but also incredibly rewarding. Had I known it beforehand, I would have run as fast and as far as I could in the opposite direction.

Just "Homosexual Temptations"

Windsor, Colorado—Covenant Bible College
September 2002–Winter 2003
Age: 19

I spent my first year of college at Covenant Bible College in Colorado, a one-year Bible school of just forty-five people. I'd never enjoyed academics, so I wasn't even sure that I would continue with college. But my faith was very important to me, and what better place to strengthen it? Because the school was so small, the students in my class quickly became like one big family that seemed to just accept each other for who we were. There was no need to explain why you liked what you did, or the way you acted; everyone was kind and welcoming. For once in my life, I didn't have to try so hard, as I'd done when I was at home. In many ways I felt like I was finally able to be me—other than that one part I never talked about and would never bring up. I figured that would go away when I met the woman who would change everything.

It had always been one of my biggest dreams to get married and have a family of my own. We'd have a house and a dog, and we'd both have great jobs and serve God together, and this thing that I was tempted with would no longer be there. I'd never have to think of it again. If I just kept it a secret and waited, it would go away.

About two weeks into the school year, a bunch of us were getting ready to drive down to Colorado Springs for the weekend. I was excited but had no idea what God really had in store for me. It was the day I would first feel God calling me to share my story, and I can remember it like it was yesterday. It was cloudy but warm, and one of my friends had just shared with me some pretty heavy stuff she had never talked about. I was honored that she trusted me with this vulnerable part of her story and made sure she knew that I was there if she ever needed a friend.

Walking back to my room to get my stuff, I thought, "Wow, you're so good, God. You use us in ways we never would expect. Thanks for letting me be there for my friend." As I walked up the stairs, though, I fell to my knees as if my legs had been kicked out from under me, and I felt this strong nudging in my heart, as if God was saying to me, "Tonight is the night. You need to start sharing with your closest friends what you're going through." Terrible timing. I was about to get into a car with a bunch of people for two hours, and now I was on the verge of tears. "Why now, God?" I asked. But again, that overwhelming feeling came: "Trust me and do as I have called you."

I quickly tried to plan how it would happen and told God I would obey, but I asked God to bring the words out of me. I grabbed my bag and walked out to the two cars. In one was Sarah and Claudia, two of my closest friends from growing up, and in the other were the four friends I'd just met but already felt so close to. I chose to ride in the latter.

Sarah and I have been great friends since second grade. She's one of the most creative and nurturing people I know. She'd moved to Colorado Springs our senior year of high school, so it was fun to be back in the same place again.

Claudia and I met in high school and became fast friends, affectionately referred to as an old married couple by most of our other friends. We'd been on many adventures together, and I'd learned she was someone I could trust. I could always count on her to tell me the truth about how things were. If things were hard she was also ready with a quick comment or joke to make me laugh.

That night Claudia and Sarah could tell something was up, and they asked if I was okay, which almost caused me to break down. I told them that I thought God had just spoken to me and that at some point in the evening I would tell them about it, but not right then. Knowing and believing in what God had called me to do, I chose to ride in the other car—it just felt like what I was supposed to do.

For the first twenty minutes of the drive, I sat quietly staring out the window. Anyone who knows me knows that I am not one to be quiet unless something is up, but for some reason no one asked. As raindrops hit against the glass, I started to think about how much I hated what I was going through. *Why was this happening to me?* I was so afraid of rejection. These four people had become fast friends, and now they would have no choice but to reject me. I was disgusting, broken, wrong, and I couldn't help it.

One of the people in the car was my friend, Josh, whom I'd gotten really close to. It was one thing to ask a girl to understand this, but to ask a close guy friend? That was another story. He no doubt would not understand and would push me away and never see me the in same way again.

Tears filled my eyes and began to stream down my face as I fell deeper and deeper into hopelessness while a storm outside formed, clouds welling to the point of bursting with a downpour. The more I thought, the more the tears came, and soon I was sobbing. My friends must have been so caught off guard—Tyler, who is always upbeat, smiling, and cracking jokes, is sobbing for no apparent reason. As I cried, I wished they would ask me what was going on, but no one did. Instead they moved me into the middle seat and put their arms around me and hugged me as I cried in shame into my hands, feeling so undeserving of love or anything good. I cried for what seemed like the whole trip to Sarah's house, finally calming down just before we arrived.

Carrying our stuff into the house for the evening was a blur of anticipation and anxiety. I couldn't say no to something God had asked me to do, no matter how scary. I was at Bible school, after all, and from what I had seen in the Bible, I knew it wasn't uncommon for God to ask for something difficult from faithful people. God could see the big picture, when all I could see was what was right in front of me. I knew rejection was coming, but there was no use in delaying the inevitable.

For the next hour, I took my friends aside and told them my big secret. Not everyone, just the ones I felt that I needed to share it with. I started with Sarah and Claudia, friends who knew me so well, yet had no idea of the one thing that caused me so much pain and self-hatred. They received it well and showed me great kindness and love. It felt good to know it was finally out there. Someone other than me knew, and I didn't have to keep it all to myself anymore.

I took Josh aside and told him that I needed to talk. I couldn't make eye contact. I was so ashamed, and I couldn't bear to see the disgust on his face as I spoke. Fear was flowing through me, my throat was tight, and I wondered if I would even be able to get the words out. But I had to.

I swallowed, and with tears in my eyes and my voice shaking, I said, "For a long time I have struggled with something that I am so ashamed to admit. I wrestle with homosexual temptations. I have never acted on it, and I am not gay. I just struggle with attractions. I hate myself for it, and want it to go away. I know it's probably hard for you to understand, but I felt like God had put it on my heart to tell you. That's why I was so upset on our drive down." I just rambled, feeling like as long as I was talking, he wouldn't be able respond and I wouldn't hear what I was so afraid of—that he was disgusted by me.

Even after getting it out, my throat felt tight, and I stared at the floor. The moment between when I finished talking and Josh responded felt like an eternity. But his response was the opposite of what I expected: Josh told me that he loved me, and this didn't change anything about our friendship. He said we all have things we struggle with, and there's no reason why I should feel any more sinful than anyone else or undeserving of love.

It was like coming up from underwater and being able to breathe again. It felt so good to know that I now had people who would walk with me through the pain in my life. Most importantly, it felt good to know that I had done what the Lord had asked me. This was the beginning of a year of me slowly opening up about my "temptations," as I called them then, with my friends at Bible school. I didn't tell everyone, but only shared the truth about me when I felt that God was asking me to. God's requests came to me not as an audible voice, but rather as a nudge in my heart, and an overwhelming desire to share would come over me. It felt like a gift to honor and pursue God's requests, and I found that after first opening up, my "temptations" seemed to vanish.

For months, I thought I was healed. I often wrote in my journals about how I once had this struggle or dark past, as if I had somehow escaped it. I had been so hard on myself about my desires for so long, and I could barely think about it without disgust and hatred emerging from deep within me. I hated who I once was, and there was no way I would talk about it publicly. I knew what it meant to be viewed as gay. I knew how such people were treated. Share it boldly? No way. I used to think I'd share it someday when I was married. I could be an example to all those liberals out there who thought it was okay to be gay or that you couldn't change. I would be the undoing of their arguments and their platform, I told myself. I just had to wait to meet a woman, so she could be the proof that it was all behind me. Until then, I leaned into the freedom I experienced after sharing with my friends.

A New Hope

Windsor, Colorado
Winter 2003–May 2003
Age: 19

My dreams were shattered five months later, when all the feelings and desires about other guys that had somehow "disappeared" came flooding back. For a few months, I had gotten good at ignoring that part of me, focusing on the newness of being in college, in a new place away from home. But I could only suppress things for so long. I was crushed. I thought I had been healed. Did I do something terrible or sinful, and God sent it back(as he had hardened Pharaoh's heart in Exodus)? I told no one that the "old" me was back. I was too ashamed.

Each day at 11 a.m. at our Bible college, there was a dedicated time for students and staff to share their stories. It was called "Story at Eleven." It was the administration's hope that by the end of the year, every student would have shared their life story. Listening to other people's stories gave me hope. It showed me that I was not alone in struggling. It made me feel like I was human and that it was possible for me to relate to my peers. I heard story after story of how God had changed people's lives, and it gave me hope that change could still happen for me. On one particular day, a visitor came to campus to tell his story in our 11 a.m. gathering.

He told us about how he had been raised in a Christian home, but that he had always struggled with his sexual orientation. As each words left his mouth, I felt a jolt of recognition. It was my story. As I intently listened, I had to remind myself to not look too interested as I was afraid I might out myself. The speaker said that he had prayed for years for this temptation to go away, but nothing seemed to help. Then he heard about a Christian-led program they called a "ministry" that changed his life. The program was connected to another larger ministry called Exodus International.

At the time, Exodus International was a "non-profit ex-gay ministry" that claimed it could help those who wanted to change their sexual orientation and live straight lives, void of homosexual desires. This was all done through a process called reparative therapy, a destructive process that has been shown to cause long-lasting damage and little or no actual change. Studies have been conducted on Exodus International in particular, to show that reparative therapy is not only ineffective and a pseudoscience, but also harmful to participants. In June 2013, Exodus ceased its services and offered an apology for the harm its programs had caused to so many. But the day I heard this man's story was over ten years earlier, in the fall of 2003; the ministry was still going strong, and I was the perfect target.

The man shared about how he had been changed thanks to this ministry. He was married and gay-free. I had previously opened up to the college director about what was going on in my life when I heard this man was coming, so the director helped to arrange a private meeting in his office. I didn't want anyone else to know I was going to meet with him, so I was grateful for the privacy. I sneaked over while other students were sitting down for lunch, so no one would know. I entered the building through a rarely used side door. Although I had shared my struggles with some at my school, it was still a secret and would remain one for years. But also, I was nervous, curious, and excited about the prospect of change.

I don't remember much about our meeting. I walked in, and we shook hands and sat across from one another. I remember that the man seemed very distant, closed off, a bit vacant. I'm outgoing, and was hoping for a lot of encouragement and support from him, but I didn't really get that. He was robotic and cold. I believe today that God was protecting me because, for some reason, I never looked into Exodus after that meeting.

The talk did, however, prompt further dialogue with the director of the college. He was loving and kind, and using college funds, he made it possible for me to see a counselor for a few sessions. Sure, I could have talked to my parents about using our health insurance, but that would mean telling them what was going on—not an option for me. I was in a hard spot because I was trying to fix something I had been raised to think was flawed about me. I had to be strategic about finding help.

This was the first of many counselors I would see over the years as I struggled to deal with my sexuality. When I went to see him, I spoke about myself with shame and disgust with a bit of hesitation. I didn't know if I could trust him but I was ready to live my life void of this "thorn in my flesh," as I had begun to call it. The counselor drew a big circle on a piece of paper. In the middle, he drew a little black dot and referred to that as my "homosexual sin." I remember thinking the dot needed to be a whole lot bigger. He then asked me to tell him all the things I am good at. As I began to list my abilities, he wrote each of them in the circle. He then held the paper up and told me that I just needed to realize that my sin was only a small part of who I am and that there was so much more to me than that. He clearly hadn't heard how much pain this "dot" had caused me or how often it was on my mind. I never went back.

For the remainder of the year, I continued to shove the "thorn in my flesh" to the back of my mind. I continued to share it when I felt led, but I really hated thinking about it. Instead, I would dream about my future—someday it would pass, and my perseverance would just make my story more interesting. Although sharing my story was good, every time I did so made it more real to me, and I started to question if I was even a true follower of Christ. I had read the scripture references that deal with homosexuality, and although there weren't very many, they didn't sound forgiving to those who were gay. I had never acted on it, so in my mind, it was still only a temptation. But I still struggled daily.

One day, I received an assignment for my ethics class: to write a paper on an ethical issue that Christians might encounter. It was a no brainer. I would write on homosexuality. But before I committed to it, I needed to talk to my professor. As usual, I shared my story through tears apologetically, but she was kind and gracious. I told her what I wanted to write about but that I was afraid my classmates would make assumptions about me. She just smiled and said, "Well, then, I am assigning this topic to you. If they ask, you can tell them that you asked me for direction on a topic, and this is what I assigned you." I decided to write my paper on whether one can struggle with homosexuality and still be a Christian.

I wish I could find that paper today. Writing it stirred up memories of my uncle, and for the first time, I asked my mom directly about him. This was my way of scratching the surface, getting a feel for how she might react. I knew my mom loved her brother dearly even though he was gay, and there was no doubt she would give that same love to me. But I wasn't ready to tell her the truth.

As my first year came to a close, I continued to suppress this part of me. I kept my feelings out of sight and deep inside me so I could enjoy the time I had with my friends. Although it was hard to not talk about it, I was so thankful for the love and acceptance I had from my friends. I believe now that the friendships I forged at Bible college that year were a gift from God. They were the nourishment I needed for the long road ahead.

Off to the Big City

Chicago, IL—North Park University
Fall 2003–Spring 2004
Age: 20

Since the Bible school I went to was only a one-year program, I had to quickly decide on a next step. I chose North Park University in Chicago, the sister school to Covenant Bible College, and my home denomination's university. It was not an easy decision to move there—if anything, I made that decision kicking and screaming—but I felt it was where I was meant to be. The transition initially went well. Many of my friends from Bible school were there, including a few of the friends with whom I had shared my story. But as the seasons began to change, I slipped into what would become one of the most hopeless periods of my life.

To this day, I still talk about that first year in Chicago as my worst year of college, and maybe even my life. It was the year I began to realize how destructive suppressed depression and anxiety can be. The funny thing about depression, I learned, is that sometimes you may not even know it's there until it has already reached a boiling point. This was the case for me. The hopelessness descended gradually, like a gathering storm.

Although I had friends from Bible school in Chicago, in this new context, our friendships seemed different. I found myself alone a lot. That isolation, paired with the continued wrestling with and exhaustion from my struggles with sexuality, began to raise my anxiety. My sexuality was constantly on my mind—it wouldn't go away no matter how hard I tried to get rid of it. I began to wonder if it was a demon inside of me that needed to be exorcised. I questioned once again if I was really a Christian. I prayed for my desire to be taken from me, yet it wasn't going anywhere—that had to mean that I was doing something wrong. But what? The constant self-analysis and persistent stress roiled inside me. I began to snap at friends, or act out of character. At times, my heart would start to race; sometimes I felt like it might leap out of my chest or spontaneously combust.

Often, I turned to drawing—something I had always loved—to find peace. But one day while working on a drawing of Mt. Rainier in my intro to drawing class, my heart began to race. My hands were shaking. I couldn't draw a straight line. I was afraid my heart was going to explode. As calmly as I could, I got up and asked my professor if I could be excused from class. I did not feel well, I told him. He gave me leave, and I went back to my dorm. As I lay on my bunk trying to fall asleep, hoping that sleep would calm me down, I prayed and prayed again that God would heal me. I just wanted rest, relief, freedom. As I drifted into dreams, I felt a sense of relief that—at the time—I could only access through sleep. But the moment I woke up, I was immediately back in shackles.

Anxiety, sadness, and hopelessness became my new normal. I felt I deserved it. I just had to figure out how to function in the midst of it, wondering where God was or when God might show up. I became more and more isolated, a shell of who I once was. The real Tyler had been full of life, laughter, excitement, and joy—a distant memory. I don't know what I did with all my time. I didn't see how things could ever get better. If I shared publicly what was going on in my head, I would be hated and rejected by everyone I loved. I already felt like I was different than most people all the time; I didn't need to see what would happen if I opened up. What I didn't realize at the time was that I had already rejected myself.

The idea of accepting that I might not be straight was out of the question. In my mind, it was giving up, going against God, and even worse than what I was already experiencing. I've heard it said that oftentimes, the people who are most against homosexuality have unresolved feelings or understanding about their own sexuality, and that was true for me. I was adamantly opposed to homosexuality and the idea that being gay could be seen as okay. I looked forward to the day when I would be healed and could speak out against it, showing that with enough willpower, dedication, and prayer, anyone could be changed. But during that first year in Chicago, the hope that my sexuality would one day go away began to vanish. In its place was self-loathing, self-destruction, self-hatred, disgust, and dejection. I would beat myself up each day. I hated who I was.

But it didn't stop there. At the time, Xanga, a blogging site where people shared writing and poetry, had become pretty popular on my campus. Without sharing any specifics, I wrote a little on my own blog about my sadness. Some of my followers responded with kind words, asking why I was so down, or saying they would have never known based on the smile they saw on my face as I walked around our small campus. I had become very good at putting on that mask. But the comment that really stuck out came from a man on campus I had never even met. He responded to my posts by saying that I was a waste of space—pathetic. His comments were meant to be witty, to draw some admiration from his peers at my expense. Probably stemming from his own insecurities. How could someone be so cruel, I wondered? He had never even met me. What had I done to deserve this kind of treatment?

But I also seemed to know what I had done to deserve it. As much as it hurt to hear what he said, somewhere deep in my spirit, I agreed. I *was* a waste of space. A mistake. He didn't know everything about me, but he was right; I had already been thinking the same things, and his comments just validated my sense of low self-worth.

I couldn't see a way out. Sleep had been my only respite from this constant self-hatred and anxiety. When I slept, I didn't hurt; I didn't have to think about the pain. I couldn't sleep the rest of my life, but *if I were to die, I wouldn't have to hurt anymore*, I thought. Thoughts of death slowly crept in and became a more and more common coping mechanism—the only way to escape reality. Thankfully, I never had a plan to take my life. I still believed that God had given me life, so it was God's choice to take it, not mine. But I began to ask before falling asleep for the Lord to take me painlessly so I could be free of the torment. It was such a scary prayer to pray. In my core, it was not what I wanted. I had seen how good life could be. But I was so far removed from that goodness that it was hard to even remember what good felt like. Fortunately for me, God didn't take me in my sleep, and I know now that God was looking out for me. As had happened many times before, God showed up in a friend. This time, it was my friend Kelly.

Kelly and I had met the previous summer at camp. We had an almost instant connection; I could talk to her about anything. She was always there to offer me a calm and loving listening ear. One night after a campus activity, she asked if we could talk. She was aware of the hurt in my life—the result of my struggles with sexuality. She sat me down and said that she was seeing trends in my life that were not healthy. People close to her had wrestled with depression, and a lot of what I was going through seemed to mirror those patterns. She encouraged me to go and talk with someone, to see if I needed some help. It may sound funny, but I found hope in the idea that I might have had depression. The idea of my pain coming from something I couldn't really control took the pressure off—it wasn't so much my fault as it was (or might be) something that could be processed and dealt with.

The next day, I visited the health center and talked with someone about what I was feeling. They gave me a long questionnaire, and I was told to fill it out and then drop it off to be reviewed. The questionnaire laid out multiple everyday situations, and it required me to check the box that most described how I felt in those situations. I finished on a Friday, so I had to wait until the following week for answers.

When I did hear back, I wasn't surprised by my results. I was struggling with depression and anxiety. But knowing didn't bring the relief that I thought it would. *Now what*, I thought? The health center recommended I seek counseling, but if I was going to do that, I would have to use my health insurance, and that would mean my parents would find out. How would I even begin to explain what was going on? "I'm depressed and anxious because I am attracted to guys and it won't go away and I feel like that means I'm an abomination." No way, that was not going to happen. Instead I just sat with the results and allowed things to continue to worsen as I dragged myself through each day.

One day, I found myself alone in my room, weeping over the hopelessness in my life. I prayed for my life to end; I hated who I was. I didn't want to hurt anymore. Desperate for relief, I called my mom. I began to tell her how bad things had gotten. I can't remember if I had told her about the prayers for death (after all, what parent would want to hear that?), but I know it was hard for her to hear about what I was going through. Then, my fears became a reality. She asked me what caused me to feel this way.

This was it—time to tell her. As always, I started with a defense: "I have never acted on this and have never been okay with it, but I struggle with homosexual temptations that won't go away, and it makes me hate myself so much." The moment the words were out of my mouth, I was flooded with shame and I wanted more than anything to take them back. I buried my face in my pillow on my bed as she lovingly cared for me the best she could, thousands of miles away, telling me how much she loved me. I asked her to tell my dad because I didn't have the energy or the courage to say it again.

After I told her, I didn't feel the same sense of peace I often had when I shared my story with friends. Instead, I felt disgusted and fearful that the next time my parents saw me that this is all they would be able to see.

It would be only a little over a month until I found out if there was any change because my parents decided to fly me home for Thanksgiving that year. I think after hearing how low I was, my parents didn't want me away from home. I felt a mix of emotions going home. I was relieved to get out of the city but afraid to face my parents. I didn't want them to treat me any different than they always had. After I told my mom what I was struggling with, I was filled with disgust and embarrassment. What would it be like to see my dad after she told him? Would he say anything? I should have remembered, Scandinavians don't like to talk about hard things, and when I arrived, it was as if I had never said anything to my mom. I think at the time I was relieved. I didn't want to talk about it, and I was hell-bent on changing my orientation. I simply had to.

In the following months, in order to cope, I did what I had always done—I suppressed it. In order to release the pent-up pain and frustration, that spring I started running, which helped in many ways. I looked forward to those runs. They meant I could be alone with my thoughts. Running became a designated space for processing so the rest of my day could be focused on other things. Life seemed to slowly get better. Nothing went away, but I also didn't think about my sexuality as much.

Year Two in Chicago

Chicago, IL—North Park University
Fall 2004–Spring 2005
Age: 21

Back in Chicago for my junior year, I moved into a new dorm. Within days, I was close with many of the other guys on my floor. I had always heard about how much fun college and dorm life can be, but I figured my experience was just different that first year in Chicago. By the end of the first week, though, I felt like I had a new set of best friends. But that didn't mean I would be sharing my secret.

I still thought about my struggle with sexuality often, but I had somehow found a way to convince myself it was temporary. I truly believed being gay would go away the day I met the right woman. In my mind, sin was something that could be overcome with prayer and by asking God for healing. If my desires were a sin, I just needed to be more dedicated, I thought.

At times, though, my secret was almost too much to bear. I needed relief. All my life I had pictured myself with a perfect family: a wife, two children, and a dog. When I focused on that dream, it helped me to ignore the struggle and temporarily escape the parts of me I didn't like.

I now know that this was part of a pattern. The rush of something new—new friends, New Year, new living situation— helped me suppress my secret. I would convince myself I just hadn't met the right woman, and the relief in believing that was, at times, life-saving. But within months or weeks, routine would set in, and everything would come rushing back. I hated that these desires and attractions were back, and I would try to figure out what I had done to get it to go away, so I could just do that again. As if there were some kind of formula.

That year, I publicly took a stand against homosexuality for the first time in my life. At the time it was common knowledge that one of the students on the planning team for the Sunday night worship service was openly gay. In my mind, this was a paradox—it didn't work. It didn't make sense. He couldn't be both a Christian and gay. After talking with a friend who agreed with me, I made an appointment to talk with two of the staff members in the campus ministry department. I met them for coffee one afternoon, and although I was not supportive of my fellow student, I was as kind as I knew how to be.

The staff explained that this is one of those things in the Bible that is not as clear as we would like it to be. They told me that many people interpret Scripture differently. I could barely hear what they were saying. After all, this was deeply personal to me. The Bible was very clear, I thought. Scripture was clear. Somehow I had to maintain my composure in the midst of inner conflict. I felt that at any moment I might burst. There was no way this was the truth. Look at all the pain I had been through, all because of the very thing we were discussing. If it wasn't a sin, then why had it caused so much destruction in my own life?

I thanked them for their time, but left feeling frustrated that they were not able to see where I was coming from. I wondered how they could be so close-minded. I should have been asking myself that very same question.

As the year progressed, I began to doubt for the first time the hope that I had gripped onto—that the right woman would somehow heal me. (As you read this, it is important to understand that, while I was attracted to men—and I later realized that that attraction was a lot stronger than I was willing to admit—I was also attracted to women. I would later understand that it was more the *idea* of dating a woman that I was drawn to.)

There were a few women that year whom I was interested in, and it was endlessly exciting to imagine the prospect of finding the right one. I could almost taste the freedom as I spent time with them. What I was unable to face at the time was that although I enjoyed their company and kissing them was okay, I still did not feel fully happy with them. I found myself in a routine, where I would immediately find all the reasons we wouldn't work out before we had even been on two dates. I would get more excited about the future as a married man than actually spending time with these women. I lived for that hope. The hope for freedom. But while I was on dates, I had a hard time imagining them fulfilling that hope. For many years thereafter, I believed I just hadn't met the right woman. In hindsight, I know that I had become a master of suppression—of convincing myself that I knew better. But with each woman that I quickly lost interest in, the hope for healing and freedom slowly eroded. Still, for years, I was utterly unwilling to consider any alternative.

The idea of acting on my temptation terrified me. Even being around gay people scared me, as if somehow it would unleash some inner beast within me that I had been holding back. I worked at a local Starbucks at the time, and three of my co-workers were gay. They were very nice, but I am embarrassed to admit that I made little to no effort to get to know them because I was afraid. I remember having to take one of them to a store nearby, to pick up milk for our store. As we drove, I didn't know what to talk to him about—I assumed we would have nothing in common. When we got to the store, I was concerned someone I knew would see me with him and question my sexuality. I made every effort to not stand near him. Now, it saddens me to think that I treated him that way. How was I expressing the same love of Christ that had been expressed to me by so many people with whom I shared my story? The thing is, I wasn't. Even though getting to know my coworkers better may have showed me some things about myself that I did not yet understand, I allowed fear and shame to isolate me.

I continued to share my story with friends as I felt God asking me to. It felt safer to share with my friends who were women, so that's who I spent more time talking to. It felt good—I felt known by at least a few people. It didn't take the pain and anxiety away, but it made the hardest times bearable, knowing I had been honest and open and received love and acceptance. Then again, I was never completely honest: in my mind I was still just a straight guy who struggled with temptations I had never acted on and never would.

Over Christmas break, an adult family friend gave me a journal as a Christmas gift. I had always wanted to keep a journal, but I had never really gotten into it. In the years to come, journaling would become my number one way to connect with God. In journaling, I have found truth, I have confessed, and I have received grace and love from God.

On January 6, 2005, halfway through my junior year of college, I journaled for the first time. In the first few pages, I began to write about my struggles with sexuality, although I didn't name it. I wasn't ready to see it written out on paper. Here is a portion from my first entry, which I wrote when I was twenty-one years old.

January 6th, 2005

One of the hardest things for me growing up has been my many battles with sin. I know that sin is something that no man can hide from, but it is still knocks me down daily. One sin in particular. It's the thing I am most ashamed of. That sin is so disgusting that I do not even want to write it in this book. It is something that at times I have felt that I was on top of, but most of the time it is on top of me; holding me down. I don't understand why it is so hard to move away from. You would think that since I know it is wrong that I would just not do it. But the annoying part about it is that although I know, I still fall into it.

Tyler

Through the rest of that year, my journal was an outlet—a space where I could share what I was going through and how I was feeling. I tried to write as if I was writing something that God would read after I was finished, and in many ways, it gave me peace knowing I had handed something over to God. Although it was a freeing new way to express myself, I would never come close to giving enough information that would name what the "sin" was, in the off-chance that someone would find my journal and read it. Looking over my journal entries from my junior year, it was not uncommon for me to come across entries that mentioned "my sin."

March 7, 2005

Free me from my sin. I hate it so much.

Tyler

To even put words to what I was up against was out of the question. Too scary. Too final. I didn't want that label, and I was not ready to or willing to accept it. Though I treasured the friends who were willing to talk to me about it without judgment, I began to realize yet another pattern: sharing and talking with people would give me great relief and comfort at first, but over time the peace would subside, and the truth would come roaring back. The reality was still there. Sharing didn't change anything.

I found tremendous hope and peace in Scripture. I journaled about how the Apostle Paul writes in Romans 7:14–20 about the sin he no longer wants to give into. I broke it down verse by verse, envisioning how it applied specifically to my situation, as if it had somehow been written just for me. I identified with a line in verse 18, "I know that nothing good lives in me." That was how I felt—that nothing good was in me. I found solace in that verse because I had twisted it to relate to my story, but it was hard to know what to do next.

I wasn't always so critical, only clinging to verses about sin. I also found peace in verses like Isaiah 40:31: "But those who hope in the Lord will renew their strength. They will soar on wings like eagles; they will run and not grow weary, they will walk and not be faint." I came back to Isaiah 40:31 often. When things were hard, I imagined what it would be like to soar away from the pain and self-hatred that I woke up to each morning. I longed for wings like eagles— to run and not grow weary.

As the year came to an end and I prepared to leave for the summer to work as a camp counselor, I began to lose hope again. Although I would be back in the Pacific Northwest, a place that I loved so much, I could sense the familiar depression creeping back in.

May 21st, 2005

There is so much filth in my life Lord. I need your help. Why must I carry this burdening sin? Take it from me Lord. I'm scared it will never be gone. I have met people in the past that have dealt with it and they talked about how they were not delivered from it until they were prayed over by tons of people. Does that mean that if I am not prayed over I will not be freed from it? I've had people pray for me many times. Does that count? This struggle has caused me to be angry, unemotional, and hard hearted. Father that's not me. Change me.

Tyler

As I wrote this, my heart ached for healing and restoration. I was fearful of what my sexuality was doing to me. A week later, I was journaling again, unleashing lashings upon myself for something I was constantly failing to eradicate from my life. I was incapable of stepping back and realizing that the attractions I had were nothing I chose, but in my mind it *had* to be my fault. So I would repeatedly come before God to say I was going to start over.

May 28th, 2005

> *Starting over is going to be more than a journal entry. It's going to take me giving my heart fully to God to take and transform. Transform my heart. Take it Lord. Please!... Lord I'm in need of a major heart transformation. Help me love, understand, and reflect you. God this is the summer I want to overcome it. Help me and be my guide.*

Tyler

Although it saddens me to read these now and see how hard I was on myself or how hopeless life seemed, I am also reminded that God was always present through gentle love I could almost feel wrapped around me as I cried out. Had that not been the case, I would not have continued to come to God, laying down what I was going through. I didn't know why God wouldn't take it away, but I still had to hold onto hope that one day God would. Maybe it would be that summer. On June 18, I begged again for healing in the upcoming summer break. But no miraculous healing took place, and I continued to fight as I went into my senior year. I hoped yet again that this would be the year.

Senior Year

Chicago, IL—North Park University
Fall 2005–Spring 2006
Age: 22

By this point, journaling was one of my favorite ways to connect with God and still my heart. I loved Chicago, but I always longed for the Pacific Northwest, where I was raised. I longed to be deep in the woods or up in the mountains. When I was there, I felt small in this greater story called life. The trees in the Pacific Northwest seemed to stretch into space, and the mountain ranges went on forever. It slowed me down. I could breathe easier while I was there.

During my junior year, I would often drive up to Evanston, a town just north of Chicago, and sit on the rocks next to Lake Michigan. In the quiet on the lakeshore, I felt at peace. I felt like I could think and breathe. I would watch the sailboats on the water and feel the warm air on my skin—the last bits of summer blowing off the lake and washing over me as I sat with the Chicago skyline watching over me in the distance—sun reflecting off its skyscrapers. Closing my eyes, I would picture God's love enveloping me, and for a moment, I would forget how lonely I was—how undeserving I felt of God's love. I spent hours there, journaling, reading my Bible, and praying.

Over time, I had developed an idea that this thing about me, this sin, was a thorn in my flesh. It was a biblical image, from 2 Corinthians 12:7-10: "To keep me from becoming conceited because of these surpassingly great revelations, there was given me a thorn in my flesh, a messenger of Satan, to torment me. Three times I pleaded with the Lord to take it away from me. But he said to me, 'My grace is sufficient for you, for my power is made perfect in weakness.' Therefore I will boast all the more gladly about my weaknesses, so that Christ's power may rest on me. That is why, for Christ's sake, I delight in weaknesses, in insults, in hardships, in persecutions, in difficulties. For when I am weak, then I am strong."

I took what Paul referred to as a thorn in his flesh, and I fit it into my own experience of wrestling wit the fact I might be gay. That's what it felt like to me—a thorn that was always there, sometimes not bothering me, but at other points producing enough pain that it seemed I walked with a limp. I had become very good at twisting verses like this to fit into my story. I had always followed the Lord and served in ministry, wondering if God placed the thorn in my life to keep me from getting too proud. I grasped for some understanding of why He God had not taken it away. I rested in the final sentence of the verse—about delighting in my weakness and hardships— because when I was weak, the Bible said I was strong. I had always thought I was one of the strongest people I knew for having to carry this for so long without most people knowing. In hindsight, I see no strength or bravery in hiding alone. On one of my regular trips to my spot next to the lake, I wrote in my journal.

September 27, 2005

> *I'm dealing with a lot spiritually. It's all dealing with my battle with secret sin. I am obviously longing for a relationship but I understand that in order for me to ever be ready for this I need to deal with this stuff. So I signed up for counseling. Lord let this help me. Give the counselor words of wisdom.*

Tyler

I hadn't seen a counselor since my first year of college—the guy who drew the circle and put my sin in the middle as a dot. But just because that hadn't been a good experience didn't mean I couldn't try again. I put in an application to the health center and was placed on a waiting list to see a counselor. Soon after, I was told that a slot had opened up. *Good*, I thought, *things were coming together*. Hopefully this time, it would fix things.

But, as was the pattern, my excitement and hope crashed quick and hard. The counselor was nice—she was about ten years older than I was— kind and easy to talk to. I opened up fairly quickly about what I was going through, and I shared directly the outcome I had hoped for, as if she were a genie who had just popped out of a magic lamp, waiting to grant my every wish. I shared my guilt for the past, and gave her a detailed outline of what was going to be in my future, so she could wave her magical counseling wand and I would be normal. She listened quietly at first, but in the coming weeks, what she had to share and offer was the farthest thing from what I was open to hearing.

In one of the only three sessions I went to, I sat there frustrated and wanting to leave, as she asked what it might look like to accept myself for who I am, and to ask if God had a plan in all of this. What? A plan in all of this? She had to be crazy! There was no way I was going to accept this sin in my life. What did she want me to do? Walk right out of her office and tell everyone that I was gay and that God made me this way? No way. I wasn't gay. It was just a temptation I faced, and I needed to pray harder or become more disciplined and remove from my life anything that would bring me down. As far as I could tell, that meant no more counseling.

But all these thoughts and feelings had to go somewhere, and I needed to continue to process them, so what did I do? The only thing that made sense—I shoved them down as deep as I could. I wrote about them from time to time in my journal, but mostly I just kept praying and praying that they would go away. My best friend, Erik, and I were living together at the time. He knew that I struggled with depression but didn't know anything more, and at one point he asked why I wasn't going to counseling anymore. I wasn't going to tell him that it was because she was trying to make me be gay and okay with it, so instead, I put on a happy face. I made up some excuse about how things had gotten better, and I no longer needed to go.

Underneath the mask, I was hurting. Though I had some great times with my friends toward the end of the year, the summer seemed daunting—I had no job because at the last minute, the Bible school I had been hired to work at had to shut down due to lack of funding. I still had no girlfriend. And though I began the year, as I always did, with so much hope, I still had this "thorn in my flesh."

At the time it felt like God wasn't really doing anything. But God hadn't forgotten about me. I was already on the road to where I am today, but what a long road it would be—full of bumps and potholes, and covered in loose gravel.

Wandering Like the Israelites

Olympia, WA
Summer 2006–Spring 2008
Age: 22–24

The summer after my senior year, I moved back home to Olympia. Not long after settling in at my new job at Starbucks, I landed a temporary state position. I could make enough to support myself, but I still wanted to serve in ministry, so I started volunteering with the youth group at the church I called home at the time.

I enjoyed being back at my home church, but the all-too-familiar struggle with sexuality was as present as ever. The difference now was that, aside from my friend Claudia, who had also moved home from Chicago after graduating, there was no one else who knew my story. I had slowly shared it with people around me over the four years I was in college, and when I graduated, we all scattered. Wanting to grow in my faith, I came to the conclusion that it was important to find a person I could go to for advice, prayer, and support—a mentor.

For the prior four years, I had known an older man whom I will call Mark, and I really admired him. I asked him how he would feel about getting together on a weekly basis to talk about life, faith, and to pray. He was all for it. So we started to meet weekly.

Life was moving in a good direction it seemed, but as had become the pattern, I often found myself overcome with anxiety. I felt dirty and broken because of my sexuality. Just as had been the case so many times before, I felt God tug at my heart and tell me to talk with my mentor about what I was going through. I was afraid. I wanted to run, and I even somewhat regretted seeking out a mentor in the first place. I was so afraid of what he would say, or worse, that he might tell me he was no longer comfortable with me leading his son's Bible study group. No matter how hard I tried to find a way out, God just wouldn't let up. Each day the need to tell Mark would eat at me like a tugging at my heart. I'd go to bed nervous and anxious and wake up with the same feelings, as if I was on a slow march to my own execution. The only way to remedy to this was to share honestly with him.

Finally, one afternoon, Mark and I met for coffee, and I knew that the time had come. We sat down to talk, and I thought my heart would jump from my chest, but what happened wasn't anything like what I'd expected. I shared, remorsefully, explaining that it was nothing I was acting on, and he just looked at me, offering love, seeing the pain and paralyzing fear that I was in. I had told many friends, but this was one of the few adults in whom I had confided. He looked at me without an ounce of judgment and following the commandment Jesus gave in the Gospels, he loved his neighbor as himself.

It felt so good to know I had someone else to talk to. More importantly, it felt good to do as God had asked. Over the next six months, Mark and I met regularly, and he never held back from asking me tough questions. I slowly started shedding the shame, at least with him. I was more and more comfortable delving deeper into the struggle. I was able to get a glimpse of the grace of God I had always heard about but never quite felt. I had high hopes that this would be it; this would change everything.

That spring, I began to feel that maybe God was calling me to work as a pastor in full time ministry. I loved volunteering, but I knew I wanted to do more. In addition, I wasn't cut out to work a desk job—I'm far too social. I have the most life and energy in me when I am with people. I wanted to love people and care for them. As this calling blossomed within me, I was suddenly and unexpectedly let go from my job with the state. I felt so many emotions: grateful that I never had to go back to a job I hated, but terrified about what I would do for work. But even though it was stressful, this change of direction felt like yet another curve on the path God had chosen for me. That misfortune—and so many others—led me to today.

Freedom from that job made room for me to meet up with friends more frequently On a fairly regular basis, I met up with my friend, Marie. I had felt safe with her very quickly during college, and I shared vulnerably what I had been carrying all those years. She had become a strong part of my support system. She had the ability to not overreact, take what I shared seriously, and to always find a way of putting a positive spin on how I was feeling.

One day while Marie and I were talking, she encouraged me to reach out to her dad about what I should do next in terms of ministry and work. Marie always believed in my abilities and gifts in ministry, way more than I was able to in those early days. Her dad was a great person to talk to and get advice from because he had years of ministry experience and many connections in the Evangelical Covenant Church (ECC), as he was one of the leaders at the time. I contacted him and made plans to meet up and talk with him about my future.

As I prepared to meet with Marie's dad, I thought about where I found the most joy in serving. Hands-down, it was working with students. Their excitement for life, willingness to ask questions, and bold honesty gave me life and inspired me. I told Marie's dad that this felt like the right path. He was insightful and encouraging. It was late spring, and as we talked, the sun was setting, but the air was warm. We sat on their back porch under the shade of towering evergreens. I pictured myself serving in ministry. I could feel my heart swelling with joy and excitement for what could be.

The conversation flowed naturally; I shared everything with him short of my secret sin. The ECC had taken a hard stance against homosexuality. There was no room for it, and even I felt the same way as I battled internally. I figured there was no need to bring it up, since that would put an immediate stop to the dreams being born in me through this conversation. Besides, God was going to take it away, I believed.

Before heading home, Marie's dad encouraged me to pray about applying to North Park Theological seminary. The idea of more school was scary, not to mention leaving the Pacific Northwest to move back to Chicago, but I agreed to pray about it and even just apply to see what happened. I drove home that night with the windows of my truck down, letting the warm spring air blow over me. The future felt bright. I couldn't wait to start my application. As it turned out, I wouldn't finish filling it out for a few years.

Summer flew by, and as fall set in, I once again slipped into hopelessness. I doubted again that there was anything good in me because of my sin. The shame and self-hatred was heavy, and I felt like I was going to have to quit volunteering in ministry. How could I be a leader in a church youth group if I were gay? What was wrong with me? Had I not been praying the right prayers? Was it somehow my fault that I wasn't changing?

Over the coming months I found myself becoming more and more tired. I worried that one day I would try to justify my sexuality and maybe even come to accept it as part of me. In my understanding at the time, that would mean I had turned away from God. I had built up so many walls around me, I had no idea what to do or which way to go. A fleeting feeling would sometimes flash into my head. *What if one day you stand before God, and God says, "Tyler, I wish you hadn't fought against this so much. I never asked you to do that. I made you this way and wish you would have just been content and saw yourself as I do: good.*

Whenever I heard this in my heart, I shoved it as far away as possible because I thought it could only come from one place, Satan. *There's no way God would tell me to accept who I was*, I thought.

I remember being told by a woman in my home church that we can't trust our hearts because they are deceitful. This idea comes from Jeremiah 17:9, which says, "The heart is deceitful above all things and beyond cure. Who can understand it?" I was raised to take everything the Bible said literally, I didn't really question what she said and allowed conflict to stir in my heart whenever I found myself desiring something. In the world I was raised in, Scripture could be understood just by reading it—no need to ask questions about who wrote it, why they might have written it, and who they might have been writing to. No need to wonder about the context. In my world, as for many evangelicals, it wasn't outside of the realm of possibility that Satan would tempt my heart and plant a desire like fruit in the Garden of Eden.

This made knowing what to do almost impossible. I was always grasping and struggling to know if I could even trust my own heart. No wonder I struggled so much, figuring out who I was. As I questioned my desires and who I was becoming and where I had been, I wasn't even able to trust what I had learned about myself. How could I possibly know who I was if I wasn't able to know what voices within me were God, and which ones were Satan?

As the weeks went by, my depression got worse. I did what I always did—kept it all to myself and put on that happy face. In March I journaled about the pain and anguish I was in.

> *"I lift my eyes to the mountains where does my help come from? My help come from the Lord, the maker of heaven and earth." Psalm 121:1-2. I know you can help me, but I feel somewhat alone and hopeless. I know you love me but I can't fathom how. I want forgiveness but I'm afraid that I'll only let you down.*

> *Tyler*

Although I wrote that, I knew God loved me, I wonder if I really believed it though. I found out that spring that I had been hired for a two-year internship as the junior high youth group leader starting that summer. It would be with the church I had grown up in and that I had been volunteering at. It was hard for me to be really excited about it when I was experiencing so much pain and shame. Thankfully, the Lord had provided me with a few friends close by that I was always able to process these things with.

A Tough Pill to Swallow

Bellevue, WA
Spring 2008
Age: 24

On a spring afternoon in 2008, I went up to Bellevue to meet with Marie. We both loved Chipotle, so we often went there to catch one another up on our lives. On this day, my heart was heavier than usual. She asked me about my life. I cried as I had done with her many times before, about the pain I was feeling because of my sin and my struggle. I feared it would affect my ability to serve, and I was so ashamed. "I just don't understand why God won't take the struggle from me," I told her. Knowing that God could but wasn't was exhausting, I confessed.

Then, very confidently, Marie smiled and said, "Tyler, I know this is so hard for you, and I can't imagine what it must be like to go through all of this. But if you didn't have this pain and struggle, I don't think you could be as effective and compassionate in ministry. I believe that the reason you're able to love people the way you do is because of this struggle. I wonder if God hasn't taken it away because he knows how much good is coming from the way you love in spite of it. Look how people are drawn to you, and so many people love you. Everyone considers you as one of their closest friends. You love people so well."

I was rocked. I could see the truth in what she was saying, though I still didn't love the struggle. I'd never been able to fully love myself or see myself as good, and I never wanted anyone to ever feel that pain. Thus, I offered love the way I believed it should be given—unconditionally. That day, I experienced the first blush of self-acceptance, but Marie's theory also raised a new question: If this struggle wasn't going to go away, how would I pray now? If deliverance is beyond my reach, then does that mean God just wants me to suffer for the rest of my life? It seemed pain was my destiny. Others would continue to come to me sharing their heartaches and pain, and I would offer love and grace how I believed God would want me to and I would see a shift in their perspective on life. I'd walk away, thinking *at least they no longer have to ache*. Was I meant to always hurt and hate myself and love others? Was this my calling?

Just as quickly as I began to take in this new perspective, I shoved it as deep down as I possibly could and went back to clinging to the hope of deliverance from it. Sure, I believed that because of my hurt I loved better, but I also knew that to some degree I would always be attracted to men. I hoped that a full attraction to women would grow and surpass that of my "sinful" attractions, so I could still one day speak about how God healed me. I would be starting the internship at my church in August, leading the junior high student ministry program alongside the youth pastor. I thought of that as the perfect deadline for getting my sexuality cleared up. There was no way I was going to enter ministry with this going on.

The Internship

Olympia, WA
Fall 2008
Age: 25

The first month of my internship was a blast. I was finally getting paid to do something I loved—caring for people. And not just anyone, but students. I had so many ideas for things I wanted to do with them, and I couldn't wait to get started. I had mainly worked with high school students up until this point, so working with junior high students was going to be a new challenge. But I was ready. Even in the midst of my pain, it felt so good to know that I could help these students to wrestle with things and still feel God's love for them. I wanted more than anything to feel that love myself.

That fall, I helped lead an annual retreat for the high school students. Together, we journeyed deep into the mountains, where the air was crisp and the forest was quiet and deeply peaceful. I spoke in front of the group about the importance of community and how, in community, we find support and grow closer to God. I certainly knew this to be true—time and time again, my community had and would continue to support me on my own journey to self-acceptance.

On a slow afternoon, I broke away from the group for some quiet reflection with my journal and my Bible. I sat by a creek in the woods under the last bits of warm fall sun and prayed. My heart was both heavy and empty—void of passion and of enthusiasm for life. I was constantly fighting with myself, trying to change who I was, and I was exhausted and heartbroken. Even in the midst of precious opportunities like this, the tension was always there. The self-hatred and self-rejection were always present. It was sad to reflect on the previous years of journal entries and to see how this thing kept weighing me down—day after day, month after month, and year after year. I had been keeping journals for three years at that point, but on the struggle had lasted for so much longer.

The Accident

Interstate 5, Milepost 62—Toledo, WA
September 15, 2008–December 2008
Age: 25

I was home not even an hour from the retreat when my friend, Claudia, and I left for Portland to visit our friend, Kelly, from college. The same friend who had first helped me open my eyes to my struggle with depression and anxiety. We both needed a break, and time with Kelly was just what we needed. Portland was only about a few hours away from Olympia, and we got there as the sun was setting. It was a short but needed trip full of laughter, good coffee, and good food.

Before heading back to Olympia the following night, we grabbed dinner with a few friends and were on the road north to Olympia around eight o'clock. Very late on September 15, 2008, at milepost 62, we got into an accident.

The highway was dark. I remember seeing hazard lights ahead of us. There was a car in the left lane with its red brake lights on. As we approached, out of nowhere, dead directly in front of us, was a giant elk. Claudia swerved to the left as soon as she saw it, but the car that had hit the elk was stopped in the left lane. She quickly swerved again to the left, into the shoulder to avoid hitting the stopped vehicle. That's when it happened. A man had stopped to help the people who had hit the elk, and was on the shoulder on the phone with 9-1-1. When he saw us coming, he started to run one direction, but wasn't quick enough. Our car struck and hit him. I will never forget the sound of him hitting the windshield in front of us, sending spider-web cracks and tiny shards of glass in every direction.

That night still doesn't seem real. Everything happened so fast. We were both really calm initially—in a state of shock. Claudia asked if I was okay. I didn't know what to do. As someone who struggles with anxiety, I would have expected myself to be a nervous mess, but that night something weird happened, and I felt an overwhelming sense of calm come over me. I wanted to stay in the car forever, like I wouldn't have to face the reality of the situation as long as I stayed there in that moment. But as I sat there, I remembered my dad had once told me that if I was ever in an accident on the freeway, I needed to get way off the shoulder in case other cars came through. Wanting to take care of my friend, who was also in shock, I got us out of the car.

As we crossed over to the right-hand shoulder into the grass, I looked back and saw the man lying on the ground and not moving. I tried calling 9-1-1 but I got a busy signal. I kept calling back over and over, panicked. When I finally got through, they were already aware of what had happened and said paramedics were on their way.

Claudia sat down sobbing into her hands. I felt so helpless, and I couldn't figure out why I wasn't crying. What was wrong with me, I wondered? I sat down next to her and put my arm around her. I stretched my arm out toward the man lying on the ground. I closed my eyes and prayed silently. I wanted a miracle so badly. All I could do was recite a prayer my dad had taught me as a young boy, the Lord's Prayer. The man couldn't die. I didn't want his life to end or his family to lose him. I didn't want my friend's life to change or for my life to change. It was an accident; there was nothing more that could have been done. Why was this happening? I began repeating quietly out loud, "We serve a sovereign God," even though at the time I don't know that I believed it.

After what felt like forever, an officer approached us and somberly and gently delivered the news we had been praying not to hear. I believe wanting to provide some comfort, he told us that the man's wife was by his side, and that she had told them the man was probably dancing with Jesus. It didn't make me feel any better. I just sat there next to my friend, my sister whom I cared for so deeply, as she wept.

That's when a woman who didn't look like she was any older than I approached and kneeled down in front of Claudia. Looking Claudia directly in the face, she told her it was an accident. Her husband was a Christian and loved Jesus, and we're all going to be okay, God has a plan. Then she hugged Claudia, and as quickly as she showed up, she got up and walked away. I can't begin to imagine what that must have been like for her. It was a moment I'll never forget.

We sat there on the side of the road for hours. At one

point the officer told me we were lucky. Had we swerved into the right shoulder, we would have missed the man and the other vehicle, but we would have hit the back of a semi that had pulled over. We wouldn't be alive. At the moment, it was too much for me to process, and I hardly thought much about it. I was exhausted. It wasn't until three in the morning that an officer took us to get our statements and then to where we would meet our parents in a nearby town. He had us get in the back seat of the cop car and was so unkind, so unfriendly. We had both just been through so much, and he treated us like we didn't even exist, or as if he was just giving us a lift to another town because our car had broken down. The ride to meet our parents was quiet. I just stared out the window.

When I first saw my parents, I could tell my mom wanted to hug me, but I knew that if she did, I might break down. I just walked straight to their car and got into the back seat. As drove out of the parking lot my mom turned around and put her hand on my knee. That's when it hit me. I saw every moment of the night flash before me as if I was just now experiencing it. Immediately, I began to sob and scream uncontrollably. I couldn't stop, I just rocked in place, wailing and crying as my dad drove us home. When I finally came to, I asked my dad to turn off the radio. I didn't want any music or anything playing. I just wanted to be in silence.

That night, I was afraid to go to sleep. I didn't want to have nightmares. My parents prayed for peace and that I wouldn't have any nightmares before I climbed into my old bed with my dog. It would be a week or two before I'd be able to go back to my own apartment to sleep.

The next day and in the coming months, I found myself

often asking, *How could God have done this?* I was angry because I felt like I had already endured enough pain in my life—why was it okay for me to have to go through this, too? I understood the pain I was experiencing. It was familiar, and I could take it. But why did this family have to lose their loved one, and why did one of my best friends have to carry such a burden?

In hard times like this, it's human to want to say something that will somehow be a balm for the pain, but after this experience I believe most words, although well intentioned, can cause even greater harm. People meant well, saying that it was "God's plan," or, "We don't always understand why God causes bad things like this to happen." I hated those responses because they were the same things I had been telling myself for years about my struggle, and little to no comfort or hope had ever been found there. The most encouraging thing anyone ever said was, "This is terrible, and I know that as you hurt and process this asking why, God is asking the same thing." It was a perspective I had never really thought about: What if God was aching in the midst of the bad things saying, *I don't like this either, but I'm here.* Maybe it wasn't part of God's plan—sometimes bad things just happen. It was too much to grasp.

About a day or two after the accident, a friend came across a blog written by the victim's wife. In it, she wrote about a conversation she and her husband had a few nights before the accident. He was a youth pastor in the Portland area. He had wanted to write a book, and a few nights before the accident, she asked him what he would write about. He responded by saying that he wanted people to know how important it was to live each day with a constant passion for God, taking every opportunity to give God glory in both the good times and the bad.

It was so surreal to read these words. So much of what her husband wanted to write about applied to my life. Just the weekend before, I had been troubled by my lack of passion and excitement. I felt stagnant and dry both spiritually and emotionally. This man's life verse, his wife said, was "To live is Christ and to die is gain." Philippians 1:21. He died, serving, and it really inspired me to serve from that point on with a greater passion, not taking any moment or any relationship for granted. Although it felt good to find some inspiration in this tragic loss, I still wondered, *Why did he have to die?* Wouldn't it have been better had he lived? I was running on empty.

Over the next few months, I had a lot to process. I wondered why God would spare my life. I still thought at times that I was a waste. Did God really have a greater purpose for me? Why did I have to witness this death? More importantly, why did my friend have to go through this tragedy? She did her best to protect us that evening. I was angry with God for so many things. The pain I experienced from the accident, the struggle that was still very real, the pain and hurt Claudia faced, as well as the victim and his family.

I had to find hope and trust that God had a greater plan for me, but what was it? The whole thing was an accident. I kept thinking about what the officer had said. I didn't want to die, but whenever I found myself struggling with my secret sin, this thorn, or whatever I was calling it at that time, I felt like I was taking my life for granted. I wasn't choosing who I was attracted to, but I still somehow believed I should have some level of control over it.

For the first three days after the accident, I would cry so easily. Each time I told the story, tears would come flowing, and it felt good to cry. At any moment, I would break down. But the more time I took to reflect and think about the event, the more this changed. The tears didn't come as easily. I specifically remember a time late on the third day after the accident when hardly any tears came while talking about it. It was as if they had dried up. It was a long time before I was able to cry again. It was as if I had cried all the tears I could, and that was it.

By December, my depression had escalated. The constant pain that had become so familiar, together with the acute pain of the accident, made some days hard to get through. A few weeks before the accident, I had begun to see a counselor to process my sexuality. That was quickly set aside to process the accident instead. By December, I had to stop going because I had met the maximum number of appointments my insurance would cover. I was on my own again.

Outed, Sort Of...

Olympia, WA
Spring 2008–Winter 2009
Age: 25–26

Things were rough, and the youth pastor I worked with could tell something else was bothering me aside from the grief of the accident. He asked me what was going on. I started sharing very cryptically about this struggle I had faced all my life, hoping I was doing a good enough job of sharing details without giving away what was really going on.

He looked at me and said, "Tyler, I have a tough question for you, and I want you to know nothing will change if your answer is yes, but I need to know. From what you're sharing, it makes me wonder if you have been struggling with your sexuality. Is that true?"

It felt like the wind had been knocked out of me. I had

always been the one to share—no one had ever asked me. I wanted to crawl into a deep hole and hide away, never to be found. My skin ran cold and sweat beaded on my brow. I thought I had done a better job hiding. With tears welling in my eyes, I could hardly answer, but I nodded. I was so scared and ashamed. I couldn't even make eye contact. There was no question that I was going to be fired from my internship at the church. I assumed the worst; I was going to have to confess publicly and accept the consequences. I deserved.

But that's not what happened. He gave me a big hug and told me he loved me and that nothing had changed. He asked me questions because he wanted to understand. He could see that I was hurting from hiding my struggle for so long.

That's when he suggested trying something I hadn't really done before. He asked if I had ever fasted about this, in pursuit of answers. It was a practice that is found referenced throughout Scripture. I told him I had tried at one point or another, but that I had always been interrupted or distracted and hadn't followed through. To be honest, I wasn't that enthusiastic about fasting, but I knew it was a spiritual discipline, and not something that was supposed to be fun. It was a way of centering oneself, to seek clarity and to get closer to God.

He encouraged me to fast and pray for God to speak to me about what God was doing in my life and how God wanted me to respond. With the benefit of hindsight, I think now that this may not have been a healthy option. Fasting is not a bad thing; it's supported throughout Scripture. For instance, Jesus fasted when he was in the desert for forty days. But it might not have been healthy for me. Unfortunately, at the time, my mind was in a state of total chaos. I was desperate for a magic bullet;

I would do anything to eradicate my sin. This seemed like the perfect next step.

I accepted the suggestion, which was offered in good faith and out of love, and decided to not eat. Each day instead, I would journal, reflect, and pray during mealtimes. That night, I started my fast with a prayer. Quietly sitting in silence in my apartment, I begged and pleaded for forgiveness because I was attracted to men. I prayed that God would lift me up out of the shame I had carried for so long. I poured out my desperate need for answers and for healing and freedom from my "sinful" desires. Although I was nervous about the actual discipline, I was also excited to hear God's voice telling me what to do. I don't think I had any doubt or fear I wouldn't hear from God. Deliverance *had* to be the outcome, because God wouldn't want anyone to be in sin, as I believed I was.

Therefore confess your sins to each other and pray for each other so that you may be healed. The prayer of a righteous person is powerful and effective (James 5:16). I had confessed my sin and asked my boss and friend to pray for me as I embarked on my fast. Healing was coming—at least, that's what I believed based on what I had seen in the Bible.

By the end of the first day, I was already skeptical about whether God would speak to me. My mind raced; I wanted to make sure I did everything just as I was supposed to. At some point, I had been told that if I told people I was fasting, it wouldn't be effective. Keeping the fast to myself proved to be challenging. I was at my parents' house that first night, and when they offered dinner, I tried to say I wasn't hungry. I believed that because I was fasting, God would finally see that I was committed to getting rid of my secret sin, and God would heal me. I had to do it correctly. I had always leaned toward a sort of legalism—I obsessed over the fine print of salvation from sin; I couldn't see the bigger picture.

It was common for me to stop by my parents' place for dinner, so my mom pressed me as to why I wasn't eating. I took a deep breath, and I confessed that I was fasting, terrified she would ask why. We still hadn't talked about these things since that one time, my sophomore year of college, over five years earlier. I figured if I just said I was fasting but made it seem like no big deal, then everything would be okay. It wasn't like I was posting it to Facebook. She pushed a bit more but could see I didn't want to talk about it.

The fast lasted for about four days, and during that time, I also found myself at a church staff potluck dinner. Deflecting my parents' questions was hard. This was another level. I told people I wasn't hungry. I think I may have even carried around a plate so it looked like I had already eaten something. After a few days without eating, you start to get really bad breath, so I was self-conscious about talking to people. I got out of there as fast as I could.

Late on the fourth night, while lying in bed, I was really struggling. I was so hungry. I didn't feel well. I was shaky and weak, but I still had no answers. What was worse, there was no sign that my secret sin was going anywhere. I tried to go to sleep, but I couldn't take it anymore. I had purchased some grape juice and bread so I could break my fast with communion whenever I felt I was done. At around one in the morning, I poured some grape juice and broke off a small piece of French bread and kneeled down on the cold laminate kitchen floor with my cat. For a few minutes I sat in silence before I began to pray. I reflected on the past four days and shared once again like so many times before about how much I wanted to be made right. I asked for forgiveness for not being able to fast for longer and prayed that God would continue to work and reveal truth to me.

I read 1 Corinthians 11:23-26 which says, "For I received from the Lord what I also delivered to you, that the Lord Jesus on the night when he was betrayed took bread, and when he had given thanks, he broke it, and said, 'This is my body, which is for you. Do this in remembrance of me.' In the same way also he took the cup, after supper, saying, 'This cup is the new covenant in my blood. Do this, as often as you drink it, in remembrance of me.' For as often as you eat this bread and drink the cup, you proclaim the Lord's death until he comes." With that, I took the bread and dipped it in the juice and ate. It tasted so good, and I wanted to eat so much more but knew it wasn't a good idea to go from not eating to filling my stomach full, especially in the middle of the night.

Once I was done, I crawled back into bed and let my thoughts race over all the things I had tried and failed at as I drifted off to sleep. I was back to square one. Nothing was working. I'd seen three counselors at this point, fasted, confessed my sin and been prayed for. In addition, I had prayed daily for freedom. Over the years, numerous times, I got down on my knees and confessed my sin again to God, asking for miraculous healing while rededicating my life to God. I can't tell you how many times while working at Starbucks both in Chicago and Olympia I would go to the bathroom and get down on my knees and cry to God for healing in the middle of my shift. *Maybe I just wasn't praying right*, I thought. Clearly if I had truly repented, my sin wouldn't still be there. What was I doing wrong?

That winter I found yet another thing that I thought would fix me. I had a friend at the time who set me up on a blind date with her close friend. This woman was blonde and athletic with a big smile. She loved the Lord and was artistic. This was it, I thought. We went out, and it was fun, but in the back of my mind something didn't seem right. I couldn't put my finger on it. *Maybe it was just nerves*, I thought. We continued to hang out for the next month or so. We would talk on the phone at night, and honestly, it felt more like an obligation than something I truly wanted to do. The only times I was really excited about it was when I would run into people I knew while I was with her. I was living vicariously through what they saw—the idea of us, two young people dating. It's what I had seen all my other friends do. I figured the feelings would come with time. Eventually, though, we decided to part ways because things just didn't progress. I figured she just wasn't the right woman for me. I know now that I liked the idea of the two of us, but my feelings weren't in it. I was trying to be something I wasn't.

Over the coming months, the topic of the legalization of gay marriage came up in Washington State where I lived. Working in a church, we discussed this topic often. I heard people all around me speaking up, saying that the legalization of gay marriage was wrong. People with whom I was close would share at times how repulsive and wrong it was. An even greater fear began to grow within me of ever accepting or acknowledging the truth about who I was. My church colleagues and friends never meant to hurt people—they were just following the convictions they derived from their understanding of Scripture, just as I had done. The worst part was that I agreed with them. I didn't even begin to ponder on how scary their reactions seemed to me. I thought exactly the same way they did, and that was why this had to go away.

Over the next two years, I continued to invest more and more in the ministry I was a part of. When I was busy caring for the students and the people in my church, I didn't have to think about me and the things I was going through. I continued to hold onto hope that one day I would find the freedom I was looking for. I was committed to finding that freedom.

The next four months were challenging. I beat myself up almost daily for my sin. Each time I began to get up, I would kick myself back down with words of hate and disappointment. I began, truly for the first time, to question if God was even there. If God was, why hadn't my prayer been answered? I was sad to be single; I wanted more than anything to have a woman who loved the Lord and would challenge me, accepting who I was in spite of what I saw as a great failure. That January, I saw what I thought was a light at the end of the tunnel.

Healing on the Horizon

Olympia, WA
January 2010
Age: 26

On a dreary winter day in Olympia, I came across a website that offered sixty-day-long Bible studies, each addressing a specific issue—gambling, self-injury, lust, drinking, and even homosexuality. The promo video seemed so promising. Each day, you would sign in and complete a daily devotion, which was always followed by the same questions: *Have you been feasting on God's word? If so, when was the last time, and how did you feast on it? Were you free from thoughts that were not God-honoring?* I was familiar with this kind of language, and it spoke to me. "Feasting on God's word" meant studying and praying over Scripture. I longed to be "free from thoughts that were not God-honoring"—that freedom was all I thought about, day in and day out.

Each day after completing the devotion, you would submit your lesson, and an email version of it would be sent to a leader who had gone through the program before you. That leader would then mentor you through the sixty-day program. He or she would send you feedback, check in with you, and pray for you along your journey. I was beyond excited. This *had* to be what would fix things—the people in the video seemed to have found freedom! It was the first time I had come across anything so specific to what I was going through. I began the program, excited for the outcome.

Throughout each lesson were bits Scripture and commentaries on how they applied to my exact experience. Unfortunately, the lessons twisted Scripture, ignoring the historic and literary context, presenting the passages as warnings of eternal punishment that, if not followed, would ultimately happen to me if I ever embraced being gay.

"The wrath of God is being revealed from heaven against all the godlessness and wickedness of people, who suppress the truth by their wickedness" (Romans 1:18), and "Or do you not know that the unrighteous will not inherit the kingdom of God? Do not be deceived; neither the sexually immoral, nor idolaters, nor adulterers, nor men who practice homosexuality, nor thieves, nor the greedy, nor drunkards, nor revilers, nor swindlers will inherit the kingdom of God" (1 Corinthians 6:9-10).

We were challenged to memorize these verses to recite to ourselves when we were tempted. Scripture went from being this book of stories that inspired and encouraged me with hope to a book full of razor blades meant for self-harm designed to keep me from ever accepting myself just as I was. I bought into all of it because it was masked in the rhetoric that we were so lucky that we in our depraved nature were being rescued by God's love.

After a few weeks, I was encouraged to start over by my accountability leader because the thoughts and attractions I struggled with had not seemed to diminish as expected. His email was harsh—he told me he thought that I wasn't taking it seriously and that I needed to really think about my sin because I didn't want to go to hell. I felt terrible. I was such a failure. I cried out to God, apologizing for failing so badly, even though I still wasn't making a conscious choice about whom I was attracted to. I still had hope that this would work—I really liked the lessons, even though they made me feel bad about myself at times. I didn't ever want to be okay with being gay. So I started over, requesting a new leader since the one I had was so critical of me.

The second time around, things really seemed to click, and I started to see freedom—or at least that's what I told myself. Whenever I noticed any thoughts that fell under the category of homosexuality, I would quickly push them away and try to think about other things and utilize techniques suggested from my mentor and the online program—techniques on suppression as well as how to administer emotional verbal lashings through Scripture. I figured that if I did this enough over time, I could will away my sexuality. In some ways, it seemed to work, but in the midst of the program, I felt like I was losing a part of me. With that, my depression came back. I felt dishonest, but I tried not to care. This way was the only way, and the pain was worth it. Besides, I would be leaving in five months for seminary. If I was going to be a strong youth pastor, there would be no room for this kind of struggle.

As the months went on, I slowly allowed myself to believe I was free once again. *This time is going to be different than all the times before*, I thought. Like working out—just because it doesn't feel good doesn't mean it's not working.

The only thing I didn't like was emailing back and forth with my accountability partner/ mentor—he was a nice-enough guy, but it made me uncomfortable that he was so adamant about knowing what was going on in my life when I never had met him. To be honest, he seemed creepy. From what I knew, he was an older guy, maybe in his late forties or fifties; I believe he was married. He was a leader because he, too, had gone through the program, and was now helping out by being a "mentor."

He checked in with me regularly and asked me strangely personal questions about my life and attractions. I had been in mentor relationships before, but those were with people I knew and trusted. This guy was assigned to me, and it felt like he was working as a mentor to fill a void in his own life. I know now that it's likely he was living in deep suppression of his own sexuality, and he was trying to guide another person who was struggling as he did. He taught me effective strategies for destroying my self-worth through skewed Scripture readings.

That spring I signed up for eHarmony. I felt like I was getting to a place where I could start dating. *Maybe this will help the online program to be more successful,* I thought. For weeks, I would look through my matches and struggle to find anyone who really jumped out at me. Then one day, I found a woman named Ashley. Once I was able to convince myself that she would be a good fit for me I sent her a note and we began emailing back and forth. As time went on, our emails got longer, and eventually, we exchanged numbers and made plans to talk on the phone. I was excited and nervous.

That first phone call went on for two hours. It was fun and exhilarating. But while I enjoyed how it felt to talk to this new person, something still didn't feel right. It was almost as if I was just acting. I chalked it up to nerves and made plans to go out with her the following day. Driving northbound from Olympia to meet her, I had a bad feeling. This had happened before. Whenever I was preparing to meet a woman who might be the right fit for me, I would be excited at first about the prospect of being in a relationship, but then when it came to actually being in one, I felt unsettled. Like something wasn't right. *But wasn't this what I wanted?*

As I neared our meeting place, I began to panic about what it would mean to be in a long-term relationship with this woman. I felt like I was resigning myself to some kind of prison. I was terrified that I would be trapped. *Where was this coming from,* I wondered? She was sweet, not bad looking, and she loved God. Surely what I was experiencing was just nerves.

The date was okay. She was really kind, but to be honest, I was bored the whole time. I figured it was because we had talked so much the night before. Maybe we had talked too much too quickly and we had run out of things to talk about. At the end of the night, we agreed we should go out again, and over the next few days, we called each other every day. Before long, it became clear again that the phone calls were becoming more and more of a burden. Ultimately, I ended things. I used the excuse that I was moving back to Chicago in a few months for graduate school, and that long distance wasn't a good idea.

That spring, there was a retreat for the high school

students at the church where I worked, and I was scheduled to speak. For this retreat the young men and women would be on separate retreats. One would be "The Manly Man Retreat" while the other was called "The Girly Girl Retreat". It was a tradition that went all the way back to when I was a student, and back then, I hadn't ever even thought about the name of the retreat, but this weekend, as a leader, I began to see things differently.

The Manly Man Retreat was centered on competition. It was designed as a one-size-fits-all, testosterone fest, as if all young men liked the same things and had the same interests. I was excited to be there, but I also wondered about some of the young men who were coming—guys who were kind, sensitive, and artistic. This weekend just didn't seem like it would interest them, and yet there they were.

At a past Manly Man Retreat, I remember playing a paintball game called Juggernaut. According to the rules, there was one person, the juggernaut, who could not be "killed"—he could take unlimited hits. However, if *he* shot *you*, you were out. Whoever volunteered to be the juggernaut knew he would leave the weekend covered in welts and bruises. That year, the last person I expected to volunteer to be the juggernaut, did. He was like me—more overtly sensitive than a lot of the other guys, more artistic. This whole competitive thing seemed a bit forced for him. I watched as he ran through the woods getting shot left and right by the paintballs, but he didn't quit. As he walked away from the field, he took off his mask, and I could see he wasn't happy; this wasn't his thing. Why had he volunteered, I wondered? Years later, he came out as gay. I learned that he had been put into a program to find "healing," and like me, he was encouraged to do stereotypical "manly" things. No surprise, It hadn't worked.

When we got to the retreat, we were divided into four teams and given makeshift kilts from old flannel shirts—a bunch of Braveheart warriors for the weekend. The first challenge was to get into teams and line up and link arms, while another team tried to throw Frisbees between our legs to get a point. No one wanted to be the reason the Frisbee got through, so you'd throw your leg in front of a hard-thrown Frisbee, or squeeze them together to deflect it, leaving a gash or bruise. Although I didn't like it, my online courses taught me that I needed to do "manly" things. Get dirty, get hurt, play rough, and disregard my emotions. Each time my shin got bruised or split open spilling blood, it seemed necessary. It meant I was becoming manlier. Less gay.

Later that morning we hiked up to an open bluff in the shadow of Mt. Rainier and had a time where the students could write down questions anonymously that the leaders would answer. One of the questions was about gay marriage, and I watched as multiple students that I cared about recited the same close-minded, brainwashed thinking I had been raised with, about how being gay was a choice. I agreed with them that gay marriage was wrong, but calling sexuality a choice hit too close to home. I tried to challenge their thinking. "Why would someone choose something that would cause them to be judged daily and treated like an outcast?" I asked. One student in particular, who was raised in a very conservative home, pushed back against everything I said. A few other students backed me up, but he continued to push.

Later, at lunch, I ended up at the same table as this student, and he brought it up again, with a few other students there to support him. Deep inside, it hit a nerve I didn't even know I had. I ached. I knew this student looked up to me, but the way he was responding—how cold and shut off he was—told me that I was not safe with him, or with the students who agreed with him. I lost my cool and told him that was enough, and that the topic needed to change. I was visibly upset, but I don't believe the students could tell why.

I left lunch frustrated, but I told myself I didn't need to worry because I was finding freedom in the online program I was pursuing. That afternoon I journaled with joy and excitement about the healing work God had done in my heart and in my life. My sin was gone and had been for months, I thought. I'd felt this way a few times before and was crushed when it eventually came crumbling down, but I wanted to believe that this time was different. I was excited for what was coming next, even though I still felt somehow like things weren't right and that I wasn't fully me. Likely because nothing had changed. I had just gotten better at suppressing my feelings. I just continued to distract myself by throwing myself into ministry as much as I could.

As the summer of 2010 came to a close, I felt lost. I loved my job, the small group I was leading, and the ministry I was a part of. Why did it have to end? I didn't want to move back to Chicago. I had applied for a scholarship that would give me a full ride to seminary, and I allowed that to be the deciding factor of whether I would really go. I prayed that if it was what God wanted, I would be awarded with a scholarship that would make it possible for me to go to school. When I found out that I had been selected as a full-ride scholarship recipient, a flood of emotions washed over me. I was excited, and I was also afraid. Could I really pursue studies and serve in this way if I hadn't yet reconciled my sin? At the same time, I knew I needed to go in order to grow into my chosen profession as a pastor.

Around this time I met up with my friends, Marie and Alex, as they were driving north from Portland. Alex and I had been close friends since my junior year of college. We were on the same floor in our dorm my second year in Chicago and had many adventures together over the years. I love Alex for many reasons but one of the biggest is his loyalty to his friends and to his beliefs. He cares for his family and doesn't worry about what people think. I admired that he didn't seek anyone else's approval for the decisions he made in his life. I had always felt the need to change myself for others—why couldn't I be more like Alex?

While in college, I never would have dreamed of telling Alex my story, knowing he was raised in a household like mine—conservative in politics and in faith—so it was a surprise to find myself telling him what I had been going through that day over burgers and fries. It was something Marie had known for a long time, but they had recently gotten married and it only made sense to bring Alex up to speed as well. It was embarrassing for me still, and I worried that things would be different between Alex and me, but God surprised me yet again. Alex was amazing. He asked questions and just wanted to understand. He explained that he thought it was an issue that we Christians haven't been so great at dealing with. Alex and my relationship has only grown stronger since that day, and for that, I am so thankful.

My last few months in ministry were a blur. I went on a mission trip to Mexico as one of my final commitments to the youth group. The trip was amazing and only made me want to stay in Olympia even more. I preached a final sermon and even got to help baptize a few of the students in the youth group. Before I left, I was scared and sad about what was coming, but

I knew that it was going to be good. God had provided me a full scholarship, so not going was out of the question. God had also brought about what I saw as healing in my life, so I had to be obedient to the call God had given me.

Packing up my life in Olympia, I said goodbye to the church, my friends, family, and the students, and I boarded a plane for Chicago. It had been exactly four years since I last lived there, and I was thankful to be returning to a familiar place. I was going in order to become a more effective pastor, but God had bigger things in store, too. Had I known about God's plans for me in Chicago, I may have never gotten on that plane.

Old Habits Die Hard

Chicago, IL— North Park Theological Seminary
August 2010
Age: 26

I was picked up at the airport by one of my new roommates, Carlos. We had only ever chatted over email. On our drive I shared a little about what I had been doing in Washington, and Carlos shared with me what had brought him to Chicago from Texas and why he was in seminary. The thing that stuck out to me the most was where he was currently working.

As we drove, he shared how he was working at Caribou Coffee. I had worked for Caribou in the suburbs of Chicago for a short period of time in college. He told me how he had chosen the specific coffee shop he worked at because of its location. His store was on Halsted in Boystown, the gay neighborhood in Chicago. Carlos told me that he had chosen to work in that area specifically because he had seen over the years so much negative stuff between the LGBTQ community and the church, and he wanted to be an example of someone who believed the two could coexist. Carlos wanted to embody the love of Christ to the people with whom he came in contact while he was working, so that they could see that, although they may have heard otherwise, God loved them, too. I could've cracked open right then and there and told Carlos everything I'd gone through, but I felt no need—my struggle was all in the past.

My first week back in Chicago was hard. I missed being in Washington and the youth group I had worked with there. I missed the mountains. On one of my first nights as I was getting ready for bed, I began to think about all I had learned in the last year. Out of nowhere, the old thoughts and fears flooded my mind, and I realized in an instant that I had been fooling myself for months. No healing had taken place in that online study. I always had the same attractions and desires; I had just chosen not to acknowledge them. I had been living a lie. My hope was shattered.

Reflecting on the months leading up to that night, things began to make a lot of sense. I had done every lesson of the online study except the last one. I could never bring myself to do it. Why? The final lesson asked me to write out my story, sharing in depth the sin I once engaged in, and how God had freed me from it. I didn't want to finish the lesson. Deep down, I think I knew that I was lying to myself. I just kept putting it off, getting frustrated when my "accountability partner" emailed me. It was all a fraud.

I began to cry and I felt like nothing was ever going to change. I felt like the worst follower of Jesus. How could I struggle with this for so many years and not overcome it? There was no way I could ever be good enough.

In Chicago, no one knew what I was going though. My other roommate, Sam, moved in a few days after me. Like Carlos, he was very easy to talk to: comfortable and safe. Sam had gone to Purdue for his undergraduate degree and had been really involved in campus ministry there. I was so thankful to know that I had ended up with two roommates who were down-to-earth and easy going. I was going to need that when school got tough and my anxiety got the best of me. Who knows, maybe one day I would be able to share more of my story with them, but not yet. For now, once again, I was alone.

The weeks leading up to my first day of school were challenging in many ways because I began to feel like I was in the wrong degree program. I had come in with the expectation of getting my Master of Divinity but had just recently learned about a different program that had a greater focus on Christian formation, which refers to the lifelong process and practice of nurturing one's faith and spirituality. That degree seemed more like me because it had a greater emphasis on ministry, rather than teaching. I struggled though, because both students and faculty pushed the Master of Divinity program pretty heavily. I was torn and didn't know what to do.

One day while in the library, I ran into Elise, a friend from Olympia who I was an intern with my first year at my parents' church. She told me she had been praying for me the night before, and she felt God wanted her to tell me to trust the voices of those who know me. I would cling to that advice in many difficult situations to come. It was the direction I was looking for: everyone who knew me well told me to switch to the Christian formation program, while those who did not know me as well told me to stick with the Master of Divinity program. I decided to take a leap and change programs. God had not called me to seminary to be a follower and do what others were doing, but to go where God had called me to go. I wanted to do that. I felt peace with my decision, even in the midst of my inner turmoil.

During orientation week, all new students had to take personality tests to help us understand ourselves better as we prepared for ministry. Each of us was required to be evaluated by a counselor who would talk through what they saw as potential obstacles in ministry based on our tests, as well as offer advice and counsel on how to get ourselves to the healthiest place to serve. They had all of us new students in one of the basement classrooms. It was so quiet, you could hear a pin drop. The only noise was the air conditioning unit, providing relief from the intense August humidity in Chicago.

As I looked at that test, my head and heart flooded with anxiety. I could barely get through filling it out. Looking around, I wondered if anyone else was as anxious as I was about this test. Was I going to be found out somehow by answering all of the random questions? *None of you know about me*, I thought. *Would you still love and accept me if you knew? How can I go into ministry with this terrible sin?* I wondered. I filled out my test and immediately went to the dean of students to talk. I had to tell her. I needed to tell someone and hoped she would be safe.

I sat down and started to talk, beginning as I always did with the caveat that I wasn't acting on my desire. I was afraid I would be asked to leave the school if I didn't make that clear. She offered kind words and encouraged me to continue seeking

God, trusting God's plan, and she let me know that if I ever wanted to talk, she was there. Talking with her felt forced, disconnected, distant, and uncomfortable. She didn't offer me the pastoral care or kindness I was hoping to receive, and I left still feeling terrible and regretting sharing with her. I had to find a friend to talk to. Elise came to mind—the same friend who advised me to listen to people who knew me. My one friend from home. Over the years we had gotten very close, but I had never told her my story. I called her up, and we went for coffee. I don't think she knew what she was getting herself into.

Elise and I met while living in Washington and working together during the first year of my internship back at my home church in Olympia. We had the same sense of humor, and we shared a love for coffee. Elise was one of the smartest people I knew with a vocabulary that made me feel like I only spoke at a second-grade level. But she was kind and open, and she loved serving people. How have I not told her yet, I wondered?

As we sat and made small talk, I felt my heart trembling. With tears filling my eyes, I looked at her and said, "Elise, I'm not doing very well." I began to tell her everything. More than I had shared in a while. Not only did I share about how much I hated this struggle, but I shared about how I hated myself. How I felt like I was such a failure, a mistake, tainted, wrong; a letdown to my family, friends, and the church.

She listened, asked questions, and over and over again reassured me that she loved me and thought nothing less of me. She then encouraged me to talk to a mutual friend of ours who was a Christian but also gay, she thought it might be good for me to have someone I could relate to so I wouldn't feel so alone. I couldn't accept her suggestion. Even with all the pain I had carried for so long, I still did not even want to entertain the idea of being okay with—me. I told her how one of my biggest fears was that I would one day try to justify my sin, and meeting with gay Christians felt like just that. She didn't push it too much more, but she wanted me to know above anything that whenever I needed to talk, she was there. It felt so good to have shared with her. Before parting ways that day, she told me a story that gave me great encouragement. It had to do with her older brother, Casey.

When we both lived in Olympia, her brother, Casey, moved there. Up until then, whenever anyone would tease Elise, she would always respond, "You better stop, or I'm going to have my brothers beat you up!" Hearing this for so long, I was curious about meeting one of these brothers. I immediately liked Casey and felt safe around him. He was hilarious and always able to come up with some clever retort to things Elise would say, leaving me laughing until it hurt. Even though Elise and my friends were different than he was, he still hung out with us. We were all youth workers at our church; Casey didn't attend our church and was a few years older than we were. He and I seemed to have a connection that I never understood. I always thought he was cooler than I was, but he never looked down on me. While Casey was in Olympia, he apparently had shared with Elise a few times that he felt like I was carrying something really heavy inside. He wished he could help me know that I was okay—that I could talk to him and he wouldn't judge me. He never got that chance—he tragically died not long after—but it was nice to know that he had seen me, and that he had wanted to help. It felt like a sign that God was looking out for me.

Later that weekend, I hung out with my new friend Rebekah, whom I had met the night before at our friend's apartment for a get-together after our first week of classes. Rebekah was from Oregon, and she loved nature, just like I did. A big group of us had agreed to work on homework together, and Rebekah and I were both struggling to get through the same boring book. After they all left, we got sidetracked as we often did while in each other's company and we began to talk about life. I felt the familiar nudge to share my story. I shared how hard life was at times, and how thankful I was for the place I was at, but how scary it was at the same time. Bekah opened up too, about things she hadn't found anyone to talk to about. By the end of that conversation, it was as if we had known each other for years, and since then we have been by each other's side no matter whether we are living in the same place or have hundreds of miles between us.

The first semester of school was a blur. I didn't know it was possible to be assigned so much work. Academics never came easily to me; I never even wanted to go to college, and now here I was in a Master's graduate program.

During that first semester, in pursuit of support and friendship, I learned how much I needed to be able to process verbally, as I opened up to a few other friends. In doing so, I discovered something new: a lot of people were okay with my sexuality, or were at least willing to process it with me without judgment. This was curiously paradoxical to me—on one hand, it felt good to be understood and heard, but on the other hand, I didn't see how it was possible to accept something like this. After all, there was no way *I* would ever accept someone who was gay. Being gay was a sin—it would never be okay.

My first semester came and went, and I went home to Olympia for Christmas break. It felt good to be away from the books and the constant pressure to study. As always, I felt at home in the mountains, with the pines and the low winter sky. I felt free. When it came time to head back to Chicago, I planned to drive there with one of my best friends from college, Erik.

I first met Erik in a Swedish class during my sophomore year at North Park University. Erik and I only said a few words to each other the year we met, but in the following years we developed a close friendship—we became roommates, and went on adventures all over. We were different in many ways—he was tall, and I wasn't; he was from Alaska and loved the cold, while I hated it; he was mellow and relaxed, while I was often stressed and needed a detailed plan for everything. Erik also liked women, and well—I liked men, but that wasn't something I was ready to tell him.

I could talk to Erik about almost anything. I had never shared with him in depth what was going on in my life; he only knew of my depression and anxiety from when we had been living together in college. I never felt the nudge to tell him about my sexuality, but we had become so close over the years, and it felt wrong to keep it a secret. Knowing we would have plenty of time to talk on our road trip, I had to find a time to tell him.

We left just a few days after celebrating the New Year together with friends. Packed tight in my 1999 red Toyota Tacoma, we were ready for adventure! We explored so many incredible places on our wandering way to Chicago—the Redwoods, Santa Barbara, Joshua Tree National Park. In the back of my mind, a constant nagging feeling fired off reminders that I hadn't yet told Erik my secret. Voices clamored in my head, one constantly insisting that I share, the other reminding me of the risks: what if our friendship was never the same? what if I ended up rejected and alone?

Over and over, I planned to tell him. Tomorrow. When we get to our next stop. At dinner tonight. But I never did. I couldn't muster the courage.

Breaking the Silence

Chicago IL—North Park Theological Seminary
January 2011
Age: 27

It's my opinion that Chicago is one of the hardest places to be in the winter, especially in January. The months leading up to winter are fine; you have Christmas to look forward to, and the weather seems to heighten the excitement of the holiday season. But what's exciting about bitter cold in January? Nothing. The city is relentlessly beige with dirty snow lining the sidewalks, and the air is sharp and thin. At the center of the city, on the small campus of North Park University, I began to fear that the foundation I had been standing on was about to crumble.

It started with a blog written by a few people who were a part of my denomination, the ECC. It was called Coming out Covenant. It was about gay people who had grown up in the

ECC, and how they fit in the church. Reading their stories, I once again felt the familiar paradox of hope and self-hatred. I related to so much of what people shared on the blog. It gave me hope to feel like I might fit somewhere, too. But my hope was equally matched by my disgust and judgment—being gay was not okay, and homosexuality had no place in my denomination or my faith. These lessons and beliefs had been deeply ingrained in me, and I needed them in order to know myself. Though I had actively grappled with my own sexuality at this point for several years, my beliefs about homosexuality and faith ran deeper. I tried not to think about it, but the blog got to me. I started to wrestle in a way that I hadn't before.

January 26th, 2011

Lord it has been so so long. I said it on my drive today, Lord. I am sad, empty, frustrated, lost, confused, angry, breaking, and upset. Why must I hurt from a struggle you can take away, but won't? Is the guilt I feel all for nothing? I know you don't give guilt! Should I not think that what I struggle with is wrong?

Is this blog good or is it another step down a slippery slope? I worry we have become too concerned with acceptance that we are beginning to make things that used to be black and white, gray and hazy. Maybe I am just too judgmental. Help me release to you my struggle. I truly feel I am in a place of anguish. It feels hopeless, and you are the giver of hope. But even in my brokenness and hopelessness I have to be strong for people... I need you now more than I ever have. You know my needs and you are the provider. Help me trust.

Tyler

As the cold and brutal winter wore on, more than ever in my life, I began to question if God was even real. How could a loving God let something like this ravage my life for so long, leaving nothing but destruction in its path? Didn't God care about people? When would God come to my rescue? Though I was not ready to fully let go of the belief that God was there— too much had happened that told me otherwise—my journal entries became more raw and honest. I was in excruciating emotional pain.

February 8th, 2011

> *Lord I feel so empty and done. I ask you why? Why the continued struggle? Why the loneliness? Why allow me to be attacked so frequently and in such a big way? Lord I ask and I know you don't owe me any kind of response. But Lord why must you allow these deep longings that can't/won't seem to be filled? I long to have a family of my own. I know you're a great God. A God who works in amazing ways. You are to me a beautiful mystery.*

Tyler

Around this time, a group of students and leaders in the area started a weekly discussion on campus called "Breaking the Silence." It was their hope that through meeting together, the denomination could start a conversation about how to better respond to homosexuality. The leaders of the group knew that everyone would come with a different opinion. The group wasn't about debating or fighting, but about sharing and hearing stories, and grappling together.

When I first heard about it, I was frustrated. No matter

how far I ran, I could not avoid this issue. I had already been fighting for so many years internally—now this? As if the blog wasn't already challenging my thinking enough, here was more food for thought. I didn't have to go, but how could I miss it? I had to admit, I was curious. Maybe I'd find some sort of healing. Maybe I'd see that this really *isn't* me, and be freed. Maybe, maybe, maybe.

I went to the first event. It was on a weeknight in the seminary building. I was surprised by how many people showed up. I made a point to not seem too interested but more curious, not wanting to give myself away. The night was led by a panel of people—both gay and allies who would share their thoughts and beliefs on the topic. One panel member was an older man who was a pastor and affirming of LGBTQ marriage, which was new to me. I always thought older people were against marriage equality, so this was something unexpected. After I left, my mind was racing, and my heart felt like lead in the center of my chest. I couldn't keep the truth from my roommates any longer; the time had finally come to tell them.

We had made a weekly commitment to meet together in our front room on Sunday nights and share what was going on in our lives, and then pray for each other before we went into the week. That Sunday night I told them I had something to tell them. I let it fly and poured out my heart, my struggle, my pain, even that I was questioning if being gay was wrong in the first place. I tried to be as transparent as I could while resisting the fear that, as usual, was trying to get the best of me. Like so many times before, sharing brought me closer to God. Carlos and Sam asked questions, withheld judgment, and shared how they too had wrestled with what they actually think about homosexuality.

Sharing with them that night made that apartment a sacred space for me. They now knew all of me, and when the burden was too great to bear, I wouldn't have to run away. I could call it what it was. I could live in my own apartment with no secrets.

One of the many events for "Breaking the Silence" was a screening of the movie *For the Bible Tells Me So.* The documentary depicts in a series of vignettes the lives of a handful of people who are either gay or who have a gay friend or family member. It documented the different ways people responded, based on their various experiences in the church and with the Bible. I was skeptical of what I would see, assuming the movie would push a one-sided agenda—likely one I wasn't ready to get behind. But as I watched, my heart broke in a million places. I related on such a deep and personal level. I was terrified. The movie humanized people who were gay, gave them faces and names, and made sexuality more than just an issue. Little did I know at the time that years later I would go on to be in a small scene in the sequel documentary *For They Know Not What They Do.*

From my perspective at the time, the movie seemed to demonize the church, which was hard for me—I agreed that the church had not responded well, but I felt it was also important to understand that churchgoers were raised to think and act in a certain way. After all, *I was—and am—one of them.* It was not entirely their fault. Regardless, I was thinking differently than I had in the past; I believed that the church's response had to change.

This was a big step for me. I still saw homosexuality as a sin, but what was once so clear to me began to fade to gray. I suddenly saw valid arguments from people I had once disagreed with. Those that believed homosexuality was wrong, who wanted to act lovingly while still believing that homosexuality was a sin, and those who argued that there was a mistranslation in the Greek—that what was being referred to in Scripture is nothing like what we see today in gay relationships that are committed and loving. What was I supposed to do with that?

Even as I was becoming slightly more accepting, I still saw it as me accepting "them"—the LGBTQ community—as if I was not included in the "them." I didn't believe that God would create people gay, but I also did not think they would choose to live in a way that would cause people to hate them. Who would really want that?

Most importantly, I was beginning to see that God's love was bigger than even I could have comprehended. It seemed for the first time to be for everyone—even gay people.

Love Him Well

Chicago, IL—North Park Theological Seminary
Spring 2011
Age: 27

While in seminary at North Park, students were required to go through what is called "degree candidacy" before graduating. Each student met with two seminary faculty members, and for an hour or so, these faculty members asked the student questions about their life to gather a better understanding of who they were and their philosophy of ministry. The Staff members would decide whether or not they felt you were ready to go into ministry.

Each student was instructed to bring another person along, one who knew them well. The idea was that, if for some reason the student didn't represent themselves well, their colleague or friend could interject. There was no question whom I would bring. Bekah was coming, as she had become my rock, the person I shared with almost daily about my pain and my process.

One of the faculty members I met with was someone I had never met but always felt safe with. His name was Richard Carlson. It wasn't until getting to know him better that I'd find my assumptions about Richard to be true—he was a kind and open person who cared for people and was not afraid of the pain or mess in their lives. He acknowledged the humanity in each of us and believed that no one should ever feel like there was any reason why God couldn't love them just as they were. He was also unafraid to speak up for what he felt was right. If he saw an injustice, no matter what the repercussions, he stood up to be heard.

During the Civil Rights movement, while a pastor in the Chicago area, Richard marched with Martin Luther King Jr, and challenged the church to live more fully into its responsibility and role in the community to be Jesus for all people. The world needed love, and for Richard, that came with no conditions or restrictions. He wanted all people to see the beautiful creation they were and how that was rooted in Christ. Richard passed away in the summer of 2013. Like so many before me, I was blessed to call him a friend, pastor, and mentor. I believe I have the best image of who Christ is today because of Richard.

In the middle of my interview with him, I felt my chest getting tighter and a pit developing in my stomach. My eyes began to fill with tears. I couldn't hold them back. I knew what was coming. Richard looked at me and gently asked how I was doing, not wanting a quick "I'm fine" or a brief "things are hard." No, Richard wanted to *really know* how I was doing. I began to cry harder than I had in a long time, and through my tears, I shared how broken I felt, how hard it was to try changing the way I saw myself. For so long, all I could see was a messy mistake of a human full of guilt, deserving of everything that had happened in my life. Richard and Bekah listened. Bekah, through tears, shared words that were so kind, I struggled to believe them that day. She said, "I have never known someone who was willing to wrestle so honestly with God, desiring only to make him proud and serve him well. I have seen Tyler struggle and hunger for truth, not wanting to justify himself, but truly be where God wants him. I have also seen him hurt in a way no person should ever hurt, and I want more than anything for Tyler to know what it feels like to accept the love of God. He is so loved by so many and is an amazing pastor to so many. I just wish he could see it."

The words were almost too much for me to take. I excused myself to use the washroom. It wasn't until several years later, while reflecting together on Richard's life, that Bekah shared with me what he said when I left the room. He looked at Rebekah with a sense of urgency and said, "We have our work cut out for us Rebekah. We are going to love him well." I can barely get through typing those words without tears filling my eyes. He had only just met me, and he didn't just want to love me, but wanted to love me well. This all while I had never even been able to love myself.

I was sure, because of what I shared that day, that I would not be allowed to move forward with my program. But God had other plans, and I was given the go-ahead. The best thing that came out of that meeting was what happened after— Richard came to me and gave me a hug. I can still remember the smell of his cologne. Anyone who has ever been with Richard knows that smell. It smelled like comfort, safety, warmth, and love. He grabbed both of my arms, looked me in the eyes, and said, "You are a good man, and I want you to know that if you ever need to talk or a place to vent, cry, get angry, or wrestle with God, my door is always open to you, but please feel no obligation." *Obligation*, I thought? No way. I was honored, and for the remainder of my time in seminary I would go to Richards's office to talk, to vent, to cry, and to process what I was going through.

That spring I took a big step. I got together with a friend of mine who was both gay and a Christian. His name was Andrew, and had already finished seminary. I had never been comfortable being around other gay people because I didn't want to be challenged to change my thinking. I figured I would listen to his whole story, but not tell him mine; I had no obligation to, I thought. Andrew was one of the people who started the "Coming Out Covenant" blog, as well as helped organize the "Breaking the Silence" discussions that had challenged me in new and important ways. He was very intelligent and bold about the love of Christ.

Listening to him talk, I related to so much of what he had gone through, and in the end, I opened up about my own struggle. At the time, I still thought I was dealing with so-called dual attraction—attraction to both men and women. Talking with him was good, and it gave me great peace and comfort to have someone else to relate to. Still, his outcome was not going to be mine, I told myself. My story was going to be different. Over the next many years, he continued to check in with me, knowing well that the process of coming to grips with your sexuality is not for the faint of heart.

I continued to grapple with my thoughts on sexuality,

but I finished the year off strong, and I was excited for the summer. I was going to be co-pastoring with Rebekah at the camp where we both had worked for many summers (but never at the same time). It was the same camp where I first dedicated my life to God—Cascades Camp. It was one of my favorite places on earth, and I was going to get to spend the summer there with one of my favorite people on earth.

In my first year of seminary, I went to Rebekah countless times to vent, cry, and process my thoughts on sexuality. We had the same conversation over and over and over. Rebekah didn't just listen, but she often wrestled and cried with me. I sometimes felt like she hated the pain in my life more than I did. She had gone to seminary to prepare for ministry, and God handed her a tortured, wounded man who desperately needed a friend. She was thankful for the challenge and met it with astounding openness, love, and empathy. She loved me and was honored to be my friend and sister in Christ, and she made sure I knew that. There was no doubt in my mind that God had big plans for her; she was and is an incredible woman.

Camp Pastor

Yelm, Washington—Cascades Camp and Conference Center
June 2011–August 2011
Age: 27

Being back at camp that summer was everything I hoped it would be. When I finished my second summer as a counselor, I never dreamed I'd be back, much less in this context. Bekah and I worked well with one another, supporting and caring for the staff, and it was so great to have her with me.

But it wasn't all perfect. On one night in particular, I hit a new low. Bekah and I were walking the mile back to the two trailers we lived in for the summer, and I began to share once again how much I hated myself. I had been doing so well, but this night I was angry. It came over me almost out of nowhere, and it was so strong. I was angry about what I had been through—that things had yet to change—that maybe they never would. Why would anyone ever love me? I figured she must have been exhausted from this conversation, the same one we had had so many times before. But no, through tears, she continued to love and care patiently as she always did, helping me see things I couldn't when I got like this. She asked if she could pray for me. I told her no, I don't want that right now. She looked me in the eye and said, "Okay, well I won't right now, but when I get to my trailer I am going to be praying whether you want me to or not."

I climbed into my trailer, slamming its flimsy door. I hated living in there. It smelled constantly of must and mold; it was dark and dank and depressing, and to top it off, on its front was the name "The Hitchhiker." Why would any company name their product that? My anger continued to rise, its sharp edges pushing at my head and my chest. I picked up a sweatshirt and threw it across the room as tears began to fill my eyes. I was fed up, disgusted with myself, tired of my story. Why couldn't I just struggle with something else that was more acceptable to talk about? I was raised to know that God hears us when we pray, but why hadn't anything changed in my life? I had been praying for years and years. I'd fasted, gone to counselors, what else was I to do? What was I doing, working as a pastor, I wondered? I threw a notebook and a sunscreen bottle. It felt good to release the anger I had bottled up inside.

Outside, the sun was setting. The sky was filled with brilliant colors, and the evening was quiet and still. *Deep breaths*, I thought. I serve a God who pursues me no matter how much I fight, how far I run, or wherever I try hiding, I reminded myself. God always finds me. Slowly the anger began to slip away. I could sense just a little bit of light. God was still with me.

Over the next few weeks I became determined to no

longer be defined by this struggle. Sexuality was not the single most important thing in my life. I had been taught that I should *always* be defined by my relationship with Christ, and the love that Jesus had given me to share with the broken world around me. That was what I was determined to do. During one of our morning devotions as a camp staff, we talked about grace and mercy and what those virtues can and should look like in our lives. It was perfect timing for what I was going through. I had always been taught that grace was something no one deserves, yet God offers freely.

Mercy was different; it was something we all deserve but are not always good at sharing. Although I had been taught these things, I didn't know how to go about living them. How could I accept God's grace while I still continued to find myself attracted to other men? I couldn't think of how to extend mercy to myself, but extending it to others was something I could get behind. I strived to never withhold grace or mercy from anyone who was brave enough to be honest in sharing their story with me. How could I, with the tattered, messed up story *I* had? But what made me think my story was somehow different?

Toward the end of the summer, I was approached by one of the staff members who oversaw eight high school students there for a counselor-in-training week. They were all young women, except one. The young man, who was likely around sixteen years old, had asked his staff leader about her views on homosexuality, and she didn't feel comfortable talking about it. She was curious if I would, since I was one of the camp pastors. *Ugh*, I thought. I really can't get away from this. Why did she not ask Rebekah? Maybe it's because the student was a guy? I smiled at her and told her I would love to talk to him, but that in all honesty, it's one of those issues where I have a hard time knowing what I'm supposed to say.

I met with the student and listened to his story. I really didn't want to focus on what was sin and what wasn't, but most importantly, as I learned from Richard, I wanted to help him understand that God loved him, and there wasn't anything that could change that. Taking a cue from a pastor I had talked to in the previous year about how she responds to the topic, I also asked him what it would mean for him to be a Christian who is also gay.

Hearing his story broke my heart. His family had rejected him because of his sexuality. I knew from experience that no family ever wanted to reject a child, but like most, I assumed they were confused with how to care for their child while he was living in what they viewed as "sin." It was further clarification for me that the church desperately needed to re-examine how to care for people who were gay. Regardless of whether being gay was sin, I knew that God would never ask families to turn their backs on their own children. But when you're a young Christian wrestling with your sexuality, as I was, as this boy was, that's what you're most afraid of.

Our conversation went really well; he wasn't looking for me to answer any big theological questions. What he wanted was what anyone wants—to be heard and loved. I wished I could have been honest with him about what I had been facing. I felt like it would have been helpful for him to not feel so isolated and alone. But there was no way I could share that while I was working at camp.

It made me sad to hear his story, and it was a harsh reminder of all that I still had bottled up inside of me. Sure, I had shared the truth with many of my friends and mentors over the years, but my family didn't really know, and my sexuality was something I still wasn't comfortable being public about. Even entertaining the idea of sharing my story brought up horrible anxiety.

I thought about all the people who would potentially reject me. Or the assumptions they would make about me. What about the churches and other ministries I had worked with? What would the parents of the students I had worked with think about me? Or even worse, what about all the students I had worked with who saw me as their mentor? What would this do to them? I couldn't bear the idea of being looked at as disgusting and wrong by them. *No way, never going to happen. I can still love people who are going through this struggle without sharing*, I thought. *Besides, I was one day going to be married and my sexuality would be a non-issue*, I told myself. Then, when I had found freedom from everything, I could share publicly about how God had delivered me.

The summer afforded me the time I needed to reflect and process. I started to see healing in a new light: Maybe it didn't mean that all my problems would magically disappear, but just that I would no longer be consumed by pain and self-hatred while focusing on all the good things going on in my life. Perhaps healing meant trusting in God's work and God's plan for my life without questioning. Maybe I'd have to walk with a limp, but when I looked at the examples of people in the Bible who struggled, I saw great promise. Rahab the prostitute, David took advantage of a woman and then arranged to have her husband killed, Paul the murderer. They had all been redeemed. Why couldn't I?

Then, on the last week at camp, during devotions, I read

Hebrews 10:26-31. It says:

> If we deliberately keep on sinning after we have received the knowledge of the truth, no sacrifice for sins is left, but only a fearful expectation of judgment and of raging fire that will consume the enemies of God. Anyone who rejected the law of Moses died without mercy on the testimony of two or three witnesses. How much more severely do you think someone deserves to be punished who has trampled the Son of God underfoot, who has treated as an unholy thing the blood of the covenant that sanctified them, and who has insulted the Spirit of grace? For we know him who said, "It is mine to avenge; I will repay," and again, "The Lord will judge his people." It is a dreadful thing to fall into the hands of the living God.

I was thrown into a tailspin of anxiety and depression. It felt like this was my destiny, that this is what was to come for me if things continued as they had. Still living in secret, I hadn't completely eradicated "it" from my life, and so I was doomed. I had just spent a year learning about the importance of knowing the context of each verse and that the Bible was not written to us but for us. This had been new to me as someone who was raised in a church where we would sometimes "gift" verses to one another in hard times or when some accomplishment had been achieved—like spiritual greeting card messages. I would read stories in the Bible as if they were written about me or to me and use those verses as a guide in my own life. It was a subtle difference to think of the Bible as for us instead of to us, but it was one that made a lot of sense to me. At least it made a whole lot more sense than seeing it written directly to Tyler Krumland. And yet, I still figured somehow that this verse must apply to me. What was I going to do? The all-too-familiar feeling of hopelessness began to once again seep into my day-to-day.

On the last night of camp, while walking out to my car to drive down to the main gathering area, I started to ponder the year ahead: my last year in seminary. All at once, softly and peacefully, I felt like I heard God speak to my heart. It hit me in the chest in a way I couldn't ignore what I heard "Tyler, this is the year. We are going to face all that you struggle with together. It won't be easy. You are about to enter a year of pain, but I need you to trust that I have gone before you, I am behind you and I am with you. Trust me."

I can remember exactly where I was when this happened; the sun was low, and I was standing in front of the horse pasture that rested in the shadow of Mount Rainier. I wish I could remember more clearly today how I felt at that moment. I'm sure I was skeptical. *That can't really be God*, I must have thought. *Let's see how things go when I get back to school, and then I'll know.* Still, I wanted to be ready. I had tried so many times to come to a place of healing. Maybe this was it. I had had dreams of what it might feel like to be free, and I was so excited for the day it would all come true. This must have meant God had heard my pleas and was going to take this from me. All my prayers would be answered. The truth was, I had no idea what lay ahead, but I knew one thing: I was tired of running, so no matter what pain was ahead, I was ready. Pain and hurting I was familiar with.

The Year of Pain Begins

Chicago, Illinois—North Park Theological Seminary
Fall 2011
Age: 27–28

I was flooded with emotions as I flew back to Chicago for my final year in seminary. I was excited to be back with my friends and to start a new job at my church, but I was also scared of what this "year of pain" might look like. My friend, Katie, whom I had known since Bible school, picked me up at the airport. On our long drive to the north side of Chicago, we filled one another in on our summers. I told her about this message I had received, about a painful year.

Katie had always been there for me, from the night I first told her my secret under a lamppost outside of our small Bible college in Colorado, in tears from feeling so ashamed and broken; to the many conversations we had in college about how hard it was; to now, while I was in seminary, wrestling with what would become of me. Katie never claimed to have the answers, but she is stubborn and loyal, and she was a great ally and friend. Katie wasn't afraid to ask tough questions or put forth an idea or perspective I hadn't considered. I had no idea how thankful I would be in the coming months for Katie. I was so glad she had moved back to Chicago. No matter how low things got, Katie was always there to remind me we are all in desperate need of God's love, and we are only trying to do our best.

As school got into full swing, the year of pain began to come into focus. The same questions I had been asking came up more frequently in my head and heart. It seemed wherever I went, the topic of sexuality went with me.

September 15th, 2011

> *The church has not done a good job in raising people to know how to deal with their sin in a way that is not self-destructive. I wonder at times if as I struggle through pain and ache and feel rejected, if you are standing there with your arms open waiting for me to get up and receive your embrace. Or worse, what if you're not really there? I don't think that's the case, but I worry at times. Why this thorn in my flesh? I get that allowing it helps me to love others who suffer in a better way. What if it isn't a thorn and that's just what I have been taught? David cried out to you in the Psalms; Job ached and mother Theresa served you in the midst of pain. I want to do the same.*

Tyler

Each day things seemed to get harder, and I was so busy, I didn't have time to process. To try describing how this felt seems impossible. It sucked. My life was like a pond with crystal clear water and a sandy bottom. The water was clear and clean to the eye, but as soon as someone messes with the sand, the water goes from clear to cloudy. Only time can clear it up again while the sand slowly settles back on the bottom. That's how my life felt—cloudy, gloomy, empty, and hopeless. Something had stirred the bottom and was continuing to do so. The emotional pain was so strong, I could almost feel it in my bones. Yes, God had told me things were going to get tough, but God also said we would struggle together. I had to trust that God already had something in the works.

At the time, I was taking a class on spiritual direction and solitude—two things I didn't know much about. While in the class, each of us was assigned a spiritual director to meet with over the course of the semester. I knew that a spiritual director was not a counselor, but someone who helps us see God in our own lives, through prayer and reflection, whether we are struggling with something or looking for clarity or even wrestling with our sexuality. The moment I heard that I would have a spiritual director, I thought, *Wow, God always pulls through when I am least expecting it.* I needed spiritual direction—badly.

I was assigned to a director named Eva. I had never met her, but I knew who she was. In the previous year she had posted her story on the Coming Out Covenant blog about coming to terms with one of her children coming out to her family and how God had been present, offering healing and a new perspective. I was happy she shared, but I didn't want to meet with someone who would encourage me toward something with which I wasn't comfortable. I was going to ask to be switched to another director, but before I did, we were all told that a few of us had been reassigned. I was one of those people. *Dodged a bullet,* I thought.

My first meeting with my director was good. I came in and sat across from him. He lit a candle symbolizing Christ's presence in the room and asked me to take some time to still my heart. When I was ready, I was invited to share what I was thinking about. I took a few deep breaths and looked at my director and began to share about what life had been like for me growing up, bottling up so much. I gave him the rundown about how I had gotten to where I was that day. I shared with him the questions I was asking, as well as what I believed God had told me before leaving camp about the year of pain. I felt hopeless and in need of rescue, and I boldly shared that. He offered his perspective on where God might be working even in the midst of the bad. He reminded me of how I had experienced God's love in the years past, encouraging me that nothing had changed. God was still the same. I was excited for spiritual direction as well as the day-long solitude retreat we were going on soon for the class.

Days before the retreat, I finally admitted something to myself I had avoided for years. I was watching *Glee,* a musical dramedy that tells the story of a group of high school students who feel like they don't fit in, but who find friendship and express their truest selves in show choir. I was watching the show with my roommate, Sam, and when a character named Blaine performed, an unexpected realization hit me like a ton of bricks. I saw myself in him. Blaine was a confident guy who had a lot of friends and was very outgoing; he had good fashion sense, and he was also gay. He had an energy and a love for life like I had seen in me at times when shame wasn't getting the best of me. The main difference was that he was out, and he was not ashamed of who he was. That's where we differed. I immediately texted Bekah and asked if we could get together. She wasn't feeling well, but she could tell something was up. She asked me pick her up so we could talk.

We parked in a lot at the mall nearby. Shaking, I told her what was going on as tears filled my eyes. I knew what was coming, what I was about to admit to.

I looked her in the eyes and said, "Bekah, I have to face it, this struggle isn't just a struggle, it's not just a temptation. It's more a part of me than I have realized. I don't know how it fits into my story, but Bekah, I'm g-g-g I'm bisexual or gay," tagging the bisexual on as I didn't know what to do about my desire to marry a woman.

I could barely get the words out of my mouth. It was as if something jumped into my throat to hold the words back, because I knew that the moment I heard them, being gay would become real, and I wouldn't be able to take my words back.

She looked at me reassuringly and said, "It's okay, I'm not going anywhere. We will figure this out together, and God is good. He knew these things before you did. It's good you're being honest." I cried and cried. One of my biggest fears was becoming a reality right in front of me, though we laughed at the absurdity of the situation—how *Glee* had been the catalyst for this moment, the first time I faced reality. I knew I had to talk to Eva. I needed to get the perspective of someone who was the parent—someone who had faced this before.

God Has His Eye on Me

Winnetka, IL
September 23, 2011
Age: 28

I still remember driving with my friend Cathy, out to my church where the retreat would be held. It was the end of September and fall was in full force. It was overcast, with a breeze and just a little chill in the air while leaves of all colors began to find their home on the streets and sidewalks. I was tired, and I felt like I would not be able to make it through the day, not because I hadn't slept, but because of the weight on my shoulders.

I had told Cathy about my story the year before, and she, like many others, was always there with smiles and love. Cathy has a heart that loves just like Jesus, always looking for a place she can serve others. With a tender heart, she ached with those who were hurting. I told her how heavy I felt that day and that frankly, I was no longer looking forward to the retreat. I was already in a bad spot: why would I want to spend an entire day in complete silence with only God and my thoughts? If anything, I needed a break from that. She gave my arm a squeeze and told me to hang in there.

As we drove, a song called "I Will Lift My Eyes," by Bebo Norman, played over the stereo. I looked at Cathy and told her that the lyrics explained exactly how I felt. The lyrics were about crying out to God in the midst of feeling hopeless, asking for God's presence and love, knowing that God had gone before and was present with us then. *Save me God*, I thought.

Pulling into the church parking lot, I was not ready for the day. I wanted more than anything for it to be over. We were given the freedom to sleep during the day, so maybe I would just sleep through the whole thing—whatever it took to get through. I had no idea what God had planned, no inkling or expectation that it would be a day I would always look back on fondly, even with the pain.

We all met upstairs in the church to get instruction for the day. Our professor, my spiritual director, and Eva, the spiritual director I had originally been assigned, were facilitating. With excitement and expectation, they told us of the different spaces that were available for contemplation, prayer, and reflection for the day. It was our day with God. Spiritual direction was also available with both my director and with Eva. I knew what I had to do. I had to sign up with Eva; something inside me was pushing me to do it. I signed up for the first slot she had open that day.

I sat down in the chair facing Eva, and like my meetings in the past with my spiritual director, she lit a candle representing

Christ's presence with us in the room. When the time was right, I poured out my heart, perhaps more than I ever had. I had always struggled with something I called a temptation, I told her, but I had never called it what it was until earlier that week. I said it again: I was bisexual or gay. It still wasn't easy for me to say. But I said it. I shared how hard and confusing it had been—my fears of sharing it publicly, as well as with my family. The more I shared, the heavier I felt. But Eva wasn't afraid. She sat with me and listened. She extended an open invitation to meet with her if ever I needed support, to talk, or feel loved just as I am. I was once again brought to tears. God had provided amazing friends to talk to, mentors and teachers, and now a parent figure to support me. She didn't care if I was straight or gay; she was going to be there for me.

Before I left, she looked at me and said, "Last year I didn't know you from Adam, but when I saw you in your spiritual journey class the first week of school, something told me that I needed to pray for you. I didn't know why, but I did and have continued to do so since that day over a year ago. God has his eye on you, Tyler."

That afternoon I journaled about all that had happened. Eva had encouraged me to lament, which meant to cry out about the grief, pain, and sorrow that ha been such a big part of my life. She encouraged me to name it for the first time, both in my journal, and in my prayers. For years I had called it everything from "my secret sin," to "my struggle," to "the thorn in my flesh," "temptation," and even a "demon." I had never wanted to write it because doing so made it more real. But I was done running. For the first time, in ink on paper, I was honest. Pouring my heart into my journal as sun filtered through colorful stained glass warmed my back.

September 23rd, 2011

I need to lament. I thought I had. I mean, this is my third journal. I can't imagine on how many pages I have poured out my pain. Calling for your help God. But today I realized I have only alluded to what I am bound by. I need to name it. I need to be transparent here. Lord I know that I am fearfully and wonderfully made. That you look at me and don't see a mistake. You have loved me in so many ways. I love you Lord and I want to make you proud but Lord, I think I might be gay. Maybe bisexual. I'm not entirely sure. Maybe I want to be straight so bad that I have created some delusional attraction to women because then it doesn't seem so bad.

Even today I am so confused about where I stand. Isn't Scripture so clear about this issue? It's wrong, right? This part of me that I can't help is a terrible sin and I should be punished by people's hate and judgment. It makes so much sense... I should change who I am so it is easier for everybody else. Because after all, according to the church, it is just a choice. These are all the things I have felt from the church. A church that follows you. But it doesn't line up with the God I know. I would not say, even in my journal, that I am a gay or bisexual man. As I wrote it on the previous page I found my heart racing as I slowly approached the part of my sentence where I would write those words. It seemed like it was so final after I wrote it. I found myself procrastinating as I wrote.

Scribbling fillers as I got to that part of my entry. But now it's out. You already knew though. Now for my lament.

What do I do Lord? Where do I go? Do I come out completely? I fear that if I do so, many will walk away from me. What about the pain it will cause my family? Will they ever be able to treat and love me the same? What about the church? Will I be abandoned by them? Where are you in all of this, God? Won't you come to my rescue? Maybe all of that is too much too carry. Maybe I should just continue to keep it to myself. They don't need all that pain from frustration, betrayal, disappointment, and sadness from this "choice" I have made to struggle with, something so lonely and painful. I should just continue to let it eat away at me from the inside out.

Lord I won't ask for you to take this from me because I've done that so much already. I don't even know where I stand on the issue either. I know what I was raised to believe. I know what the words in your book say. Are they clear Lord, or is there more to them?

Please Spirit, speak to my heart, my life. Wherever it is that I will see it most clearly. I have to ask God, if you are as loving as I believe that you are, a God whose love is not even fully understood by our little hearts, then what is so wrong about two people loving each other? Two men or two women? Why would you allow me to be created this way but expect me to hide who I am? It's not fair God! It doesn't match up with my ideas and understanding of you.

You're a God of surprises, though. I have felt so far from you God. Like you weren't there for me, but today you showed up through Eva. I sat there for an hour and cried and poured out my frustration and pain. She sat and listened. She has a child who came out a while back. It had to be hard for her and her family. But she allowed her ideas and thoughts on the issue to be expanded. She took a stand. She asks with her child the same questions I do today! I didn't want to talk to her because I was sure that homosexuality was wrong— I wasn't gay, and I just struggle with same sex attraction issues. I just needed to avoid the issue as I have always done.

I started my class on spiritual direction and solitude expecting to drop out of it. But then I realized, if I took the class, I would also get to meet weekly with a spiritual director who would help me to see where God was at work in my life through prayer and time together talking. So that made it worth it to stay in the course. So be with me, Lord, especially now as I am making huge strides to finally face my issues with my sexuality.

Carry me God and reveal in a clear way what it is I should do. Spirit, speak to me the words of truth in this cloudy, hazy time. You who were tempted in every way and resisted. Is it wrong? Do I ever want this for me? Will I be alone forever? Answer these questions for me and help me keep my head above water. Be the comforter and healer I need now because only you make sense to me anymore.

Tyler

Although the retreat took an enormous weight off my shoulders, I had only scratched the surface. In the coming weeks, I spent a lot of time trying to rebuild the faith that had broken down the year before. God doesn't scrap things that aren't working and start over completely; God makes broken things new. So far it had been a year of discovery, growth, and a lot of pain. Just as I expected.

My Life the Paradox

Chicago, Illinois—North Park Theological Seminary
October 2011–Dec 2011
Age: 28

Over the next few months, the pain continued, and that murky pond that had been briefly so clear was being stirred again. Although it was almost unbearable at times, I felt God's presence when I least expected it, giving me encouragement. For years people had been telling me to give myself a break, to ease up and not be so hard on myself. For the first time, I tried to put this into practice. "Tyler, you are not alone. I am always here for and with you," I felt God saying to me. Times were tough, but it was God who gave me the energy to continue moving forward no matter how scary and hard it got.

I had never been much of a *Lord of the Rings* fan, but that year I got lost in Middle Earth. I felt the story was relatable to what I was going through. I was Frodo, and the ring was my sexuality. I was on a mission for Mt. Doom. Sam who went with Frodo on his incredible journey was symbolic of all the friends I had in my life who were on the journey with me. It was a long and scary one, but it had to be done because I was the only one who could truly carry this burden.

I had started meeting with a counselor, the fourth counselor I had ever seen. This time was different than the others. This time I was willing to hear a different perspective for a change, rather than going in expecting to hear what I wanted to hear. Her office was in downtown Chicago, and although I had never really enjoyed taking the "L" (elevated train), I began to look forward to my weekly trips. I was able to listen to music, drink coffee, and people-watch. My counselor was kind and easy to talk to. I appreciated that she was a Christian, always keeping God present in our sessions.

The majority of our conversations dealt with my sexuality. I had slowly been getting to a place where I was more comfortable naming what it really was, but I was still afraid I would come to the conclusion that I was gay. I often reminded myself to be open-minded; I had been closed off for so long, and that clearly hadn't gone well. *Take it one day at a time*, I told myself.

It was becoming more and more clear that I was going to need to talk to my family. At that point, telling them in person was out of the question, so I started to think about giving them a letter. *A lot has to go into that*, I'd tell myself, and I procrastinated on actually doing it. Fear was the perfect roadblock.

In early October, sitting on a bench on a crisp sunny fall day, I met with my theology professor to talk about some things we had been discussing in class. I ended up telling her about my story. I wanted to know how to read the Bible in order to find truth. As many other professors had said while I was in seminary, she told me that the Bible is a narrative that transforms us, not a bunch of rules about how to live our lives. As she spoke, I began to cry. I'd always seen the Bible as a book of rules that I could never measure up to. I shared how hard it was for me to accept God's grace, even though I had no problem offering grace to those around me. I wanted more than anything to be angry with God. If I could just be angry, maybe I'd find some closure and relief.

As I cried, she looked at me and suggested that maybe I needed to demand the blessing of God like Jacob did when he wrestled with God by the river. The idea sounded good in principle, but I didn't know how to do that. She agreed to be praying for me as I figured it out. Before our meeting came to an end, she looked at me and said, "I see God in you Tyler. You are right where you should be."

Later that day, I met with Eva for coffee. I shared how I was coming to grips with the things she and I had discussed during the retreat. I had experienced growth, but I also still felt an overwhelming sense of pain and confusion. Eva reminded me of Psalm 139:14: "I praise you because I am fearfully and wonderfully made." They were good words to cling to. I felt that God was present in the midst of the chaos I had grown accustomed to calling life.

As October wore on, I felt like I was finally beginning to let go of my desire for control. For so long I had been fighting for a specific outcome that I saw as good and right. In reality, I was limiting what God could do in my life. I had put God in a box. I think of the section in *The Lion, The Witch, and the wardrobe,* by C.S. Lewis, where the children ask the beavers if Aslan, the lion, is safe. Mr. Beaver responds by telling them that no, he's not safe, but he's good. He's the king. This was exactly what I was learning about God and would continue to learn.

My biggest fear had always been that I would think that being gay was okay, and although I wasn't there yet, I was at least facing the facts. I wondered if God had been trying to get me there for a very long time, but I was too stubborn to hear. Rather than listening, perhaps I had assumed I could do it myself, that my way was best and then would find myself shocked when things didn't work out. Thankfully, God is patient and is willing to wait. I was reminded by what had already taken place that although I may be afraid of abandonment from the church, God would never abandon me.

By late fall, I began to fall into a low once again. At this point, I was so sick of this back and forth of my emotions. One minute, things seemed to be looking up, and the next, I was hurting beyond belief—all while I was trying to give my busy schedule adequate attention and serve at my church to my full potential. As I was in the habit of doing, I beat myself up emotionally, feeling like I let God down, that I had failed.

But friends like Bekah wouldn't let me stay in that mindset for long. One day she said to me, "How I wish I'd seek God like you, Tyler. Daily you go to God with this pain, wanting to honor Him." I had never thought of myself as someone who was so devout. I felt like I had fallen into this hole, and it was filling with water. I desperately wanted out. Each time I felt I had gotten a good enough grip to pull myself out, more water would pour on me and knock me back into the mud. I feared I was going to drown.

Many times I found myself retreating to old ways of thinking. *Homosexuality has to be wrong since I can't find any positive examples of it in the Bible,* I thought. The familiar seemed less scary. I had already come out to myself, but I started to backpedal. I again wanted to refer to what I experienced as "same-sex attraction," as if that's somehow different. But as quickly as I came to one of those conclusions, the next day or week I'd find hope on the other side, like a swinging pendulum. It was exhausting.

This back and forth continued in the months leading up to Christmas break. As much as I acknowledged that God was in charge, I wasn't willing to wait. I wanted to have it all figured out and behind me. I wondered again if meeting the right woman would change everything. Not that the "same-sex attraction" would go away, but that it wouldn't matter because I would be in love. I began to pray more and more to the point of pleading that God would bring this woman into my life. I was once again desperate for control, and in seeking it, I was in fact losing control.

I began to develop unhealthy habits to deal with the stress of still carrying my secret and self-hatred. I had interviews for job placement in my denomination coming up after Christmas, and I didn't need my questions about my sexuality to ruin my future. I began to exercise a lot to try and release the stress and pain. In college, I had run my way out of depression, and during my internship, I had gotten really into fitness to distract myself so I started down that road again. I wanted to look more fit, to give off the impression that everything was okay. My physical appearance was something I could control. Without making a conscious decision to do so, I began to limit how much I ate as well. Sometimes I would skip meals due to my busy schedule, but I wouldn't make up for it when I had time—I saw not eating as an opportunity to get my weight down so I was more comfortable with my body. Most days I barely ate more than one meal.

As usual, there was Bekah, and one night she pulled me aside wanting to know what was going on. She had noticed how thin I had gotten. Up until then, I had ignored things that other friends and my family said when they saw pictures of me. When Bekah brought it up, I suddenly realized I might have a problem. I was ashamed and embarrassed all over again. I didn't want to look sick and unhealthy. It had gotten to the point that whenever I stood up I would get light headed or I would lose track of what I was saying while in mid-conversation. I truly didn't know whether the struggle with my sexuality was related to this. I just knew that whatever the cause, it had to stop. I started to make the necessary effort to get healthier, but it was easier said than done. Christmas break was coming up, and I was planning to tell my parents. But how?

The Most Wonderful Time of the Year

Olympia, WA
December 2011–January 2012
Age: 28

I flew home just before Christmas. As usual, I was beyond excited to get back home to the Pacific Northwest—visiting all my favorite spots in my hometown, drinking Christmas coffees while catching up with friends, and not having to worry about homework. On the other hand, I was anxious about telling my parents. What would they say? How would they respond? Would it go well? The more I thought about it on my flight home, the more overwhelmed I became. I shoved it down and tried my best to think of other things.

It was so good to be home, but the looming fear of telling my parents was ever-present. I was so afraid. I didn't want them to look at me differently, to be disappointed or disgusted by me. I reminded myself that, if anything, they would know me better. It was good to be honest with them, even if it hurt. Besides, it couldn't have been that big of a surprise. I had alluded to being gay while crying to my mom my sophomore year of college—eight years earlier.

This fear of telling my parents began to take over my thoughts, always in the back of my mind, robbing me of the joy I typically found in the Christmas season. I was sick to my stomach, couldn't sleep, and felt so trapped by a story written about me that I had no say in. How would I bring this up with them, I wondered? I played a million different scenarios over and over again in my head, hoping one would feel right. But nothing did. I prayed and hoped that the time would present itself to me.

The opportunity to talk to my mom arose when I least expected it to. I had just had coffee with an older friend from my parents' church. I was on the way to meet my mom to go Christmas shopping, and I found myself discouraged by the conversation I had just had with my friend. I couldn't get away from it—the topic of homosexuality was always coming up. We were not on the same page in our understanding; my friend was concerned about my theology because I shared that I no longer am sure what I believed on the topic. I still wasn't fully okay with being gay, but I was more open to wrestling with my sexuality than I had once been.

As I drove to meet my mom, my heart dropped as I felt the strong and familiar nudge in my heart. Now is the time, I felt the Lord say to me. *No*, I thought. *Not now*. But the nudge continued, so I prayed that the Lord would give me courage. I knew I couldn't bring it up on my own. I needed God to provide an opportunity for me to talk about it. I prayed for our conversation and how my mom would receive it. This was no new prayer; I had been praying for months that God would prepare my parents.

I met up with my mom so we could drive together to the mall. Immediately, she asked how it was to see our friend. She was in a good mood. She had no idea what was coming. My hands were sweating as I gripped the steering wheel. I told her that the time with my friend was fine. Normally, my mom wouldn't pry, but today was different.

"You don't seem very happy, did you not have a good time?"

This was it.

"Well, it was fine; it's just really hard coming back from seminary and sharing what God is doing in your life because if you think slightly differently than what people are comfortable with, they get nervous that you are on the wrong path," I told her.

"I don't understand, what did you talk about?" She asked.

Prepare her heart Lord; help me say this well, I prayed silently.

"She just brought up homosexuality and didn't understand how someone would think it could be okay. I know she wasn't saying it directly, and she doesn't know my story, but by saying that she was not okay with it, it was as if she was rejecting me."

My mom was silent for several seconds, looking straight ahead. Then she bravely asked me a question I'm sure she was terrified to ask. "Tyler, are you telling me that you're gay?"

I took a deep breath and said, "Yes, or bisexual. I don't know. Remember I told you about this in college? We haven't talked about it since, but it never went away. I just didn't know how to talk about it."

I wanted more than anything for her to tell me it was okay and that we could go on with our day not talking about it, but that was not fair. Instead, she sat there silently cradling her face in her hands as she began to cry. I felt awful. It had to be said though; I just wished it didn't hurt her so bad. Me hurting because of this was one thing, but not my family, not my mom, who had always been so loving. I wondered what she was thinking. Was she mad? Sad? Disappointed?

I looked at her and said, "Mom, I'm sorry."

Through her tears she said, "It's okay, I'm not crying because I'm mad at you. I am just worried. I don't want people to be mean to you or treat you differently. I don't want life to be hard for you."

"Mom, don't worry about it. People are already mean to me when they don't realize it, and I am fine. For years I have had to listen to some of my closest friends make gay jokes or speak about gay people in a negative way—in the church, in school, everywhere."

As we continued to drive, she asked me questions. She wanted to understand, and I knew I needed to be patient. This was something I had been processing for years, and I had not come this point easily. It would not be fair to expect her be right where I was without the time to process things.

She wanted to know who knew. She wanted to know if I had felt loved and supported by people after I told them. I assured her that I had yet to receive a negative response, and I think that gave her a little bit of comfort. She told me that for the last few months she had been asking her small group to pray for her because she felt like God had been preparing her for something big. She hadn't known what it would be, but this had to be it.

What an answer to my prayer, I thought! I had been hoping that God would prepare my parents' hearts. I wanted to burst forth with excitement, to show her that God was present, but I needed to be respectful of her emotions and all that she was processing. She was still in shock. I gently let her know that I had been praying that God would prepare her and my dad for what I was going to share. Again, I think she found comfort in seeing how God had been at work in the midst of it all.

Then she asked me when I was going to tell my dad. I think that whenever someone comes out, it's always hardest to tell the parent who is the same gender—at least that was the case for me. I told her how I had only ever shared about my sexuality when I felt God nudging me to do so. I was going to tell my dad, but I had decided to do it in a letter so he could have time to process it. She encouraged me to tell him in person, but I wasn't going to do that. I needed to come out the way that made sense for me.

For the rest of the day, the air was heavy. I felt like I had shattered all of my mom's dreams, ruined her day, and even stolen her joy for Christmas. She said she was happy that I had told her, and I am sure many things started to make sense as she pieced together my struggles with depression and anxiety over the years. She finally had an answer for all the pain she saw in her son. I just kept hugging her and making sure she was okay. I was fine, I told her. She told me she was concerned about my future in ministry. I made it seem like I wasn't concerned, but I was.

That evening, I went and stayed the night with Claudia. I had always felt safe around her. I knew she would be honest and up front with me, but also loving and kind. Our night together was just what I needed. Whenever the two of us get together, whether we had just seen one another, or whether it had been months or even years, something strange and fun always happened. We feed off of each other's energy, and it doesn't matter if we are in public or not—we just get ridiculous. We talked for hours, and I caught her up in greater detail about what had been going on that semester over cocktails. She offered her perspective in her usual smart, gracious, and clear-headed style. We had been through so much together already—we could weather this storm, she said.

While staying at Claudia's that night, I got a message from someone on Facebook with whom I had gone to high school. I had never even talked to him and barely recognized him. Out of nowhere, he messaged me to tell me that he thought I was cute. He said that he had realized he was gay but that he wasn't yet out. I panicked. What had I done that made him wonder if *I* was gay? Claudia encouraged me just to let it go; it wasn't as though I would see him again. But I couldn't.

I wrote back, "Well man, I hope your journey goes well. I'm sure it can be a scary road. I have friends who are walking it. I'm not on the same page, but know that I hold no offense from your message."

I felt terrible. I was a liar. Why couldn't I just let it be and not respond? Who cares what he thought? I was so concerned with how I would be perceived that I lied. Clearly, I still had a long journey to self-acceptance.

The day before I flew back to Chicago, I wrote my dad a three-page letter. My hands were shaking as I put my thoughts on paper. Once it was finished, I sealed it in an envelope and put it in my dresser drawer so no one would find it before I left. I had a plan: We'd pack up the car to go to the airport, and as we were backing out of the driveway, I would pretend I forgot something and run inside to put the letter on his dresser. That way there was no way he would read it while I was still there. My plan worked brilliantly, and I felt so free as my plane took off for Chicago. I was afraid of what was to come but relieved knowing the secret was off my chest. Now to pray and wait.

Although I was excited to be back in Chicago, I was nervous because of how hard the first semester had been. Was my final semester bound to be full of pain? I had interviews for job placement within the ECC coming up. How would I get through those without sharing my story?

My new mantra I repeatedly said to myself went something like this: I was only *attracted* to other men, but I didn't really want a relationship. I just needed to meet the right woman, and even if I wasn't super excited about it, that's okay, because that butterfly feeling doesn't last anyway. My identity is in Christ, not my sexual orientation, and this semester I was going to figure out what that meant. Living in this gray area helped to assuage my fears. If I believed a half-truth such as this, then I didn't have to fully face myself. Dressed in the lies I kept telling, I went into my final semester of seminary.

I settled back into life in Chicago—my apartment, classes, preparing for interviews. But I was anxious about the letter I had left for my dad. By then he had to have read it. What did he think? Would he call me, or would I have to call him?

One cold, clear day, when I was buried in school work, my mom called. I knew what it was about. I picked up with trembling hands. She told me that my dad had read the letter and that it was very hard for him, but he was going to be okay. She reminded me again that she felt bad for me and for what I had been through. She told me my dad would call that night—that he wasn't mad.

As promised, my dad called and asked about the letter. We didn't have a history of open communication on difficult or emotional topics. Almost immediately, we had a hard time seeing eye to eye. I was defensive, but it felt like he was speaking without thinking—out of fear in his lack of understanding. He was afraid I was going to come out publicly soon, but that wasn't what I was saying—all I wanted was for my parents to know where I stood so I wouldn't have to be alone. Still, we argued. It was one of the most challenging and painful conversations of my life, and it didn't end in resolution.

After we hung up, I was upset. I had had an unrealistic expectation, and when it didn't all happen the way I wanted, I was crushed. I didn't feel understood or heard. My parents were being held captive by what they church had taught them on the topic of homosexuality. I knew my family loved me, but they were also still processing what that meant. I wish I had taken the time to look a little more into what it's like for a parent to have a child come out, so I could empathize. To me, this was something about *me*, and me alone, but to them my story was so much more. Parents want the best for their children and will do whatever they can to make sure that happens. My parents were no different. They had dreamed about what life would be like for their child, and me being gay shattered those dreams and expectations. They needed time to accept this new information they had about me— to come to grips with the truth. Their dreams were shattered, and they needed time before they would be able to dream new dreams. I was no longer a little boy, but an adult capable of making my own decisions and drawing my own conclusions, I thought. I had been expecting things to happen in fast-forward.

I called Claudia, crying. She made me laugh and helped me put things in perspective, reminding me of all the important interviews I had coming up. I was so grateful to have her by my side, even though we were 2,082 miles apart.

Whenever someone was nearing the end of their seminary career and had interest in finding a pastoral role within the ECC, it was a requirement that they go through multiple interviews with denominational leaders. In each of these interviews, the applicant goes before a panel of three to five leaders and is asked questions about their life, faith, theology, and heart for ministry. It gives the interviewers an opportunity to get to know you better. From there these leaders recommend you to churches across the country that have open roles, and they help you find a job. The process is pretty intense and requires a good deal of preparation.

Over the next week I dressed up in my suit I had bought just for this occasion and went through my interviews, trying to figure out where God was calling me for the next year while keeping my secret tucked as far away as possible. All the interviews went well, but something didn't feel right. It seemed like many of my colleagues had a good idea of what they were being called to do and where they were called to go. But that wasn't the case for me. I'd always said I wanted to be in youth ministry, but I wasn't sure that I enjoyed it the way I once had. I needed a job, though, so I stated youth ministry as my passion and desired area of service and was thankful to get through the interviews without my secret ever coming to light.

In the midst of this process, I found solace in Richard's office. Surrounded by mountains of books, tucked away on the second floor of our seminary building, I would cry to him about the hurts in my life. Together we would get angry at the injustices I was experiencing and had been through. It was one of the first times I was able to get angry out loud about what was going on, and Richard gave me the freedom to do this. He never let me leave our time together without a huge hug and a reminder that I was good, important, and loved by him.

Just before classes got into full swing, my dad and I picked up our conversation again. It had been some time since we had last talked. We still had a hard time discussing my sexuality, but in the end, my dad and I both apologized for the things we had said.

He said, "Tyler, I am sorry if I did not meet your needs. I just don't understand, and I want the best for you. How can I support you? I love you."

I told him I needed him and my mom to listen. I wasn't making some grand statement just yet; I just needed to be fully known by them and for them to let me be an adult and make my own decisions and trust where God was taking me. It was still so fresh for them, and they were terrified of me sharing about my sexuality publicly. Not out of embarrassment, but to protect me. They knew how cold and cruel people can be, and they didn't want to see me go through that. My mom had seen that first-hand with her own brother. I would be lying if I said I wasn't scared, too. Coming out publicly was terrifying, but it felt like I might have to one day. Not yet, though. I still had a long way to go.

Building a Bridge

Chicago, IL—North Park Theological Seminary
Late Winter 2012
Age: 28

In the following weeks I let my anger get the best of me. I was mad about what I had been through, for the fight with my dad, everything. I was sick of the hurt. Why had I ever thought it would be a good idea to face all of this? Life continued to get more confusing and frustrating. Whenever I prayed to God it seemed I would look for distractions so I wouldn't hear something I didn't want to or worse, I didn't hear anything at all. It began to feel like every time God spoke, pain followed..

February 6th, 2012

I love distraction when there is something to be done. Especially when it means facing tough or challenging realities. Why do I look for distractions even when I am coming before you? I think it's because I'm scared of what you may say to me. But amidst the fear and confusion I come. Wanting to hear your voice speak truth to me. Yet more fear enters. What if I don't hear you? What if I don't listen well? What if you don't speak?

But I am at a point where I feel there is no place to go except you. How many times I have been here, where I am right now. Brought to you on my knees feeling hopeless, confused, alone, and void of peace. But even in this, I trust you will meet me in this place. That you are mighty to save.

So now I ask, why have you allowed me to be created in a way that has caused me self-hatred, fear of rejection, and to desire a life that seems to be sinful according to your word? How do I hear? Listen? If you're speaking God, and I am not listening, you know I am a skeptic and stubborn. Can you speak louder to me? But when you speak, can I also know why? Why me? Why this? How do I exercise patience? What about next year? I know you are big and you are present. Be with me now and help me to see you in this hopeless season that is littered with question and fear.

Tyler

Three days after this journal entry, on a Thursday evening, I was feeling fed up and frustrated. I felt like I was on one cliff, and God was across from me on another. I couldn't reach God, and I was being pushed to the edge, ready to fall to my death. I couldn't take it. I needed a break. I knew that that night there was a student-led campus worship service called

Vespers, and I decided to go, praying that I'd get some time away from everything to be still and quiet. I had always enjoyed that service. I knew that no matter what the circumstances, it was good to worship God through song, prayer, and reflection with all my heart. I bundled up and made my way over to the chapel. It was an hour-long service, and for that hour I enjoyed a clear head and a calm, peaceful heart—a cherished state that was so difficult for me to achieve.

When the service came to an end, I began to bundle up again to walk over to Bekah's as the weight of everything I was going through found its familiar place on my shoulders once again. That's when I was approached by a girl I had never seen before.

She said, "This may sound crazy, but when you walked in tonight God told me to pray for you."

I smiled and thanked her. "I could use all the prayer I can get," I told her.

She smiled and told me that while she prayed she had a vision. I wanted to be respectful and hear her out, but this was not something I had ever experienced and really didn't believe anything she was saying.

She said, "God wanted you to know that he is there as you wrestle and wait. He is working in the silence. He is building a bridge in your life to him, and you need to be patient to wait for him. In the vision the bridge was more immaculate and beautiful than you could have ever imagine, and when it was all done, you saw that it was so much better than you ever could have hoped."

Wow, I thought. I almost had no words. What she shared with me was so in tune with what I had been feeling, you would have thought that she had been reading my journals or listening to my prayers. She described exactly what I had been feeling earlier that evening. I told her that it was just what I needed to hear and hurried over to Bekah's to tell her what had just happened.

By the time I made it to Bekah's place, I had already begun to feel like this must have been a wild coincidence. But Bekah encouraged me to just let it be, to rest in the peace that this stranger had just offered me, no matter the source. What that stranger had said to me was eerily aligned to what I had been feeling and thinking earlier. I was alone and in the silence, wondering where God was, as I felt like I was slowly being pushed toward the edge of a cliff. I was on one side of a vast canyon with no obvious way to the other side where God was. All these years I had been trying to make my own way, but I wasn't sure if it was even possible to cross. That night, I began to hold fast to the belief that God was building me a bridge; all I had to do was wait.

It would have been very easy to speculate what that bridge God was building might look like and what life on the other side would be like. I dreamed about it that night. Just two days before, I asked God to speak louder while journaling, and it felt like God had spoken loud and clear. I was in a season of transition—I was figuring out who I was and where God was in the midst of that. In any transition or change, there is a mix of adventure and excitement, as well as grief, sorrow, and pain. Like anyone, I wanted to walk the road that has the least amount of pain. After hearing this word of encouragement, I was given a new perspective and a renewed willingness to face the day ahead.

I wish I could say that in the following months life got easier and the pain subsided, but each day graduation was getting closer, and I had no idea what was next. I had applied for a permanent job at the church I had been working at, even though I wasn't sure it was where I was supposed to be. It made sense for me to stick around because I already had good relationships with the students, their parents, and even the pastoral staff.

As I grappled with what to do next, it became more and more apparent that I needed to somehow learn to embrace all the pain I had been through and give up control to God. I was a control freak, and for years I had been going back and forth from giving God control and snatching it back for myself. At the same time, I was already growing impatient about this supposed bridge that God was building in my life. Even with that hope that came with the prospect of this bridge, life continued to feel hopeless, and hurt still ran rampant in my life. I continued to ask questions like, *Why God? Why this story? Why this pain? Why this hurt? How God? How does this play out? How is my sexuality ever to be reconciled? How do I know what is right?*

Then, at Vespers on another Thursday evening, while sitting with my friend Joey, I found my heart breaking again and I began to cry. He knew life had been hard for me, although I hadn't shared with him what specifically was going on. Joey who was always quick to show love to his friends put his arm around me and prayed for me. I felt so terrible and worthless, awful and unlovable. He began to encourage me, sharing the joy he had found in our close friendship, but I found myself putting up a wall. I wanted to believe what he was saying was true, but I was not going to let his words into my heart. Joey and I had made a connection pretty quickly after I started seminary. In many ways, we were very similar.

Then he looked at me and said, "As I have been praying for you tonight, the words that kept coming to mind from God were this: 'This is my son, whom I love. With him I am well pleased.'" That sent me into another tailspin. How could God not only love me but be well pleased with me? Even if I was gay? Doesn't it say in Scripture that people like me do not inherit the Kingdom of God? I wanted so badly to believe those words but wasn't quite ready, so I held them close to my heart and thanked Joey for being there.

During March of that year, my best friend Erik was visiting, and I didn't want to miss out on another opportunity to tell him what was going on in my life, as I had when we road-tripped out to Chicago the previous year. I knew he cared about me and wanted to know what was going on in my life. I wanted to be known by him, and I was sick of lying when he would ask me how I was doing. So one night we sat down for some beers and began to talk about our lives and what had been going on. It had gotten a lot easier to share my story at this point, but I was a little nervous to tell him.

Even with the nerves, I jumped right in. "Erik, you know I struggle with anxiety and depression, and you've seen me go in and out of bouts of it over the years. There's a reason for why that has happened," and from there, I shared the rest of my story.

I shared about the confusion I had been struggling with about my sexuality. I was not entirely honest—I down-played how much I had actually struggled and positioned being gay like something I was on the verge of getting over, as if that was even a possibility. I figured in time I would be married to a woman, and my sexuality would be a non-issue. No need to make it bigger than it needed to be. I was so afraid of losing him and his friendship. He was one of my closest friends. I could tell he didn't know what to say or how to ask questions, but that didn't stop him from caring. He wanted me to know that he loved me, and nothing could change that; he'd always be there for me. I was relieved. Now when things were tough, I could actually let him know why. But because I hadn't been completely honest, I didn't find the lasting freedom I was looking for.

I found myself often begging and pleading for that freedom. I had always found false comfort in denial, and I dreamt of what life would be like in the future when I finally met the woman who would embrace all I had been through and help me to love those who needed to feel love. Always avoiding the present and living in the future, I dreamed of one day having a ministry with a woman as my partner, where we could love people like me who were going through this struggle and felt abandoned by those around them. We would show them that no matter what they were going through, we would love them as Christ does. A wife was the perfect fix to my problem. I believed marriage was the thing that would bring me healing. I so desperately wanted to love myself but still couldn't. I could only dream of loving people *like* me rather than just loving myself. I was still attracted to other men, but I tried with everything in me to will it away. I was too afraid to face it. Still.

During my final few months in school, in the midst of the continued pursuit for healing, I could not shake an overwhelming desire to be in Seattle. At the time, I was still in the running for the job at the church I had been working at, but when I ended up not getting it, I was relieved. It felt like Seattle was calling me. I'd always wanted to go home. I wondered if it was so I could continue to process all these things closer to my family since we had not talked about my sexuality much since I opened up to them.

Excited about what was next, I called my friends Alex and Marie who lived in Seattle. They had told me many times before that if I ever needed a place to live, their door was open. I couldn't wait. It wouldn't be until September, which was perfect timing, since they were expecting their first son that summer. That would give them time to get into a groove as first-time parents before I moved in. I didn't know what I was going to do for work, but there was still time to figure that out. Alex and Marie had always supported me, and it was comforting to know that I was going into a situation where I was known.

One Last Attempt at Healing

Chicago IL—North Park Theological Seminary
Spring 2012
Age: 28

"Is anyone of you in trouble? He should pray. Is
anyone happy? Let him sing songs of praise. Is anyone
of you sick? He should call the elders of the church to
pray over him and anoint him with oil in the name of
the Lord. And the prayer offered in faith will make the
sick person well; the Lord will raise him up. If he has
sinned, he will be forgiven. Therefore confess your
sins to each other and pray for each other so that you
may be healed. The prayer of a righteous man is
powerful and effective" James 5:13-16.

Over the years, I came back to these verses again and again.
This passage in particular offered what I viewed as practical
advice: It said that if the elders of the church prayed over a

sinner and anointed him with oil, he would be well. *Perfect*, I thought. I asked a few of my friends if they would anoint me with oil and pray over me. They had all been there for me throughout seminary and were honored to fulfill my request.

We met at Cathy's apartment. I had worried before about treating God like a genie, who could grant my wish of healing, and again I was anxious about doing this the right way. But I didn't know what else to do, and I was surrounded by women and men training to be pastors, so I thought, *why not take advantage of that?* In tears, I shared with them how I was feeling. I explained the best I could how desperate I was for change.

There wasn't a dry eye in the room when we were done. I knew I was loved by them and by God, but I just didn't know why God would let this go on for so long. One of my friends looked me straight in the eye and told me not to give up yet and to keep on fighting. Ugh, I was sick of fighting. When was the bridge going to be finished? Graduation was not that far off, and I was a wreck.

In my last month of school I had to write a prayer or psalm of lament for my Old Testament class. It was not hard to pick something to lament about. I sat down to write and was surprised at how easily it came together. I made sure to write it in a way that anyone who read it would have no idea what was going on since I was required to post it online for our class. This is what I wrote.

April 4th, 2012

Guide me, O God,
For you alone know my path.
I can see you have guided me thus far,

And you have yet to lead me astray.

If I trust in myself to guide my direction,
Could I miss what it is you have for me?
No God, you are in control and guiding my destiny.
In my fear, pain, and anxiety, I trust in you.

You have shown me my call and made it known to me,
No doubt I will be blessed by where you take me.
Whenever that may be and whatever it may look like,
To you and you alone I will give honor and praise!

No matter the difficulty of what has been before me,
I have sought you and will continue to do so.
Because you are my God, who has redeemed and loved me,
Your lowly servant.

Therefore, with my unknowable future I lift with praise
My heart and eyes to you;
My soul rejoices in how you have worked,
Because you are the Alpha and Omega, and even in the silence
You are working,
Building a bridge in my life to where it is you are
Taking me.
It is in that I find comfort, rest, and peace.
You desire to bless me with the hope you offer
That is far greater than anything I could imagine.

Now in the knowledge of that truth, enable me
To live in your perfect peace that passes all
Understanding!

May 12, 2012, was the day I would graduate with my master's degree. I couldn't believe it. The guy who said he didn't even really want to go to college was about to walk across the stage and get a graduate degree. During our commencement ceremony, Richard Carlson, who had meant so much to me during my time in seminary, received honors upon his retirement. I was so thankful to have been able to get to know him as a mentor, teacher, pastor, and friend. I believe that because of my time with him, I began to grasp what Christ's love really looks like when we fully let it into our lives. When I was with him, I believed him when he told me that Jesus loved me unconditionally.

There and Back Again

Seattle, Chicago, and Everywhere in Between
May 2012–September 2012
Age: 28

That summer I traveled more than I ever have in my life. I went to Ecuador as an adult leader for a service trip through North Park University, and was back and forth between Chicago and Washington to finish my commitments and get myself situated in Seattle. That summer more than any other time in my life, I became fixated on finding that woman who would change everything. Almost every journal entry was about that. I asked, I pleaded, I begged. I could sense that a change and awakening was coming—but what kind?

While in Washington, I reconnected with a friend with whom I had worked at camp the summer I was the pastor. I'll call her Hayley. She and I had a great connection serving alongside each other. We planned to get together to hang out and share what had been going on in our lives since we had last seen each other. It had been almost a year since we had talked, so there was a lot to catch up on. She shared very vulnerably that the year had been one of the hardest she had been through, but she wouldn't change that because she had learned so much. I could relate. As we talked and laughed together I noticed that there seemed to be more there between us. She was fun, excited about her faith, and very pretty.

As I went away from our time together I couldn't help but wonder if there was something there, but at the same time I remember thinking, *if we have so much in common, why am I not more excited about this?* She's great company, but I'm not leaving bursting with excitement for our next hangout. I called Bekah on the way home and talked to her about it, coming to the conclusion that it must have just been nerves and I had been caught off guard.

In the weeks to come Hayley and I continued our conversations each day, and I made plans to get together with her again before I went back to Chicago to finish things up at the church I had been working at. Before parting ways, we talked about how we both wondered if something more was there between us. I'd be back in Washington permanently in just over a month, so until then we agreed to take it one day at a time and see what happened.

I went back to Chicago, ready to take my youth group to our denominational youth rally in Tennessee, called CHIC (Covenant High In Christ). It was my last big thing with Rebekah and the students we had grown to love. As a high school student, this trip had been so foundational to me. I was excited to see how it went for this group of young adults.

The week went well in general, and I had some really great conversations with my students. But one night, a speaker named Francis Chan, whom I had been excited to hear, and who wrote a book that I had really enjoyed, told a story that felt inappropriate, hurtful, ignorant, and just plain wrong.

He shared how he felt that God had called him to say something different than he had prepared for the night. He began to tell a story about someone in his life who was struggling with sin and how that person wasn't fully honest about it. He pointed out that some of us were the most miserable people on Earth because we were holding onto old sin—that the sin in our life was getting in the way of us fully loving God.

He told about a conference he spoke at where some leaders asked him to let students come up and confess their sins. "The Bible says we need to confess but doesn't say we have to broadcast it to everyone," he said. But he agreed and he held the microphone and he said, "Does anyone feel like they have been lying and they want to confess to God?"

He shared what happened next:

"The first one was nervous, grabs the mic, and says, 'some of you don't know that sometimes I cuss,' and I thought, 'meh, that one's easy.' Then the next one comes up and admits that they have been looking at pornography, and they are feeling sick about it, and I think alright, this is getting deeper, Francis says. Then a girl comes up and shares that she started dating a guy and at the beginning of the relationship it was fine but they've crossed boundaries and began sleeping together and she needed to go home and end it cause it was driving her crazy.

"Then this guy comes up who is a senior in high school.

A big ol' kid from Texas. He comes up and grabs the mic and says, 'when I was a freshman I was a leader of the youth group leading Bible studies and while doing that I was looking at pornography all the time and you didn't know it. Then during my sophomore year I had a girlfriend and we began to sleep with each other but none of you guys knew that, you just thought that I was a leader.' Then he began to share about his last year, and he starts crying. 'I started dabbling in homosexuality. I was just curious and then I fully indulged and none of you guys know this about me and it got so bad I tried to force my little brother—' and then he couldn't even talk."

After he shared this story, Francis very flippantly said, "Everyone started confessing their sins, and you can imagine that after a guy shares something like *that* you're like 'ok well, I killed a few guys,'" cracking a joke to the whole convention center. I worried for all the students who were listening to this. As he shared this story, my heart broke for the students out there who were struggling with their sexuality or gender identity, hearing him crack jokes about it so carelessly.

I know his intention wasn't to be harmful, but it was language like he was using that originally made me think that being gay was the worst possible sin. As if sin was somehow on a spectrum, and nothing was as bad as saying you struggled with your sexuality. Not only that, but he, like so many in conservative Christian contexts, put being gay side by side with incest and sexual abuse. Although I had struggled with attraction to men over the years, never once had it been anything more than that. He made it sound like being gay was a slippery slope that only leads to greater depravity. *Fine*, I thought, *call it sin, you're entitled to your own understanding of things, but at least take the time to talk to more than one person who had been wrestling with that before sharing one man's story as if it were the reality for everyone—before making a blanket statement and using this one kid as an example.*

He finished off by reminding us that Jesus said, "If you love me, you would obey my command." The frivolity of this statement upset me, too. Had I not obeyed? For years and years I prayed in anguish for this to be taken from me. Was I just not obeying? I hoped that the thousands of people in there who had heard his message would not hate themselves like I had for so many years. I worried that the damage had already been done; it was messages like this that I heard when I was young that bore the unhealthy, negative ways of thinking about myself. I had been looking forward to hearing him speak, but left repulsed, unable to respect him anymore.

On the last night of the week, Chris Tomlin, a well-known Christian singer, led us in worship music. One song in particular—"I Will Follow"—became somewhat of a prayer for me in the year to come. I didn't know what was ahead of me, the pain was still there, and I prayed and wished for peace in the midst of my circumstances. Everything about the song was true to how I wanted to follow God, what I wanted to do, and what I felt called to do. "Who you love, I'll love," Tomlin sings, and the words resonated with me. After all I had been through, I wanted more than anything to love people as I had been loved—to love people regardless of their circumstances or struggles.

Back in Chicago, I had a little under two weeks before my youngest brother, Timmy, and I would meet our other brother Eric in Belgium, where he and his wife had been missionaries for the past year. We were going to go on a two-week trip together, with a friend, through Europe. For the first two days, it would be just my brothers and me, and I wanted to find a time to tell them everything.

Timmy was going into his sophomore year of college and was going to be staying in Europe to study abroad in Sweden for the fall semester after our trip. They were both old enough to hear my story, I thought. I just didn't know how to bring it up. So I began to think about how to go about that.

Before I left, I continued to talk with Hayley. I enjoyed talking with her, and sometimes I felt bad because of all the baggage I was carrying. Was it fair to bring her into my mess? She was so kind. She also knew my story, as I had been very transparent with her.

Although I loved how things were going, there was that same nagging feeling that had been there in the back of my mind every time I talked to a woman I thought I might be interested in. *Come on*, I thought. *Why can't I just let this happen?* Hayley, in particular, made more sense than any of the women I had dated in the past. I told myself it was just nerves, and I tried to take it one day at a time. *No need to overthink it*, I would say, as my anxiety nagged at me in the background.

Before leaving for Europe, I had been praying about the two of us and what was to come, and I felt that it might be best to not communicate while I was on my trip in order to be fully invested in the time with my brothers. When I went to talk to Hayley about it, she told me she had been feeling exactly the same way. It was great to see that we were on the same page.

So off I went to Europe. I still look back on that trip with great thankfulness and joy for all that my brothers and I experienced together. It was the first big thing the three of us have done together as adults. I had big hopes of talking to my brothers about my struggle with sexuality, but I never found an opportunity to do so. I had always shared my story when I felt like God was nudging me to, and there just never was a point during the trip that seemed like the right time. I realized later that this was the calm before the next big storm.

Ever since the previous summer, it felt like my faith had been slowly slipping through my fingers. No matter how much I tried, I couldn't shake it. With all the time spent on trains in Europe, I had a chance to think and pray a lot, and I wasn't sure I liked what I saw. The day I boarded my flight home, I had the worst feeling in my gut. I was ready to be home, but nothing felt right. I felt helpless, fearful, disgusted, and exhausted from all the fighting. I was disheartened, dissatisfied, tired to the bone, but I couldn't sleep. As the hours ticked by on the plane, I began to panic. I felt like the anxiety and pain were sucking the life out of me, and I was trapped on a plane, forced to somehow stay calm. I went to the only place I could to try and calm myself— my journal.

August 23rd, 2012

> *Brussels to Dublin: Before you, father, sits a broken man who can't see how you could possibly forgive or love me. I know somehow deep down, though, you do. Why does it have to be so hard? Homosexuality. All I can do is throw my hands up. Maybe I keep walking into a battlefield without any weapons. I don't think that homosexuality is what you desire for your creation, but what if that is the most natural response for me, and it would be a changing of myself to deny it? Maybe who I become by denying it is who you have always planned for me to be.*

Sometimes I feel like I'm set up for failure. Like you're not there to help me. It's so hard God. I want to honor you so much. When does the pain and hardship stop? When do you come in and heal me? I'm begging and pleading! I've been reading Matthew, and today was all about how you healed through Jesus. Some merely asked you to heal their servant who was still at home, and you did it without even going. Or what about the woman who had been bleeding for twelve years? All she did was touch your cloak, and she was healed.

I've been wrestling with my sexuality since I was thirteen, and I am almost twenty-nine. That's just under sixteen years. Should it continue? I know I've not always done what is right, but I try. I wonder why it's so hard. Did you create me this way? I know you hear me and that you are here now. I need you now more than ever. Where is my hope? In you, yes, but what of me and my sin? I'm an adulterous lover.

Please don't give up on me. As I cry out time and time again I find myself longing for someone to support and love me in the midst of all of it. Thank you for the people you have used to shape me. Thank you for taking me back to Washington. I don't have any idea what to expect from this year, but you've provided a place to live with Marie and Alex who are a great blessing. Today I prayed to you through the song lyrics of "Getting Into You," by Reliant K, and "Time Takes its Toll" by Bebo Norman.

God have mercy, grant me peace and faith, remind me that I am Tyler who you love and created

*this way, give me strength and endurance in this battle,
protect me, my mind and heart, mend my wounds, draw
me deeper to you, and bind away anything that comes
from the evil one. God this is me reaching for your cloak.
Will you heal me?*

Tyler

Just a few hours later, in the midst of another panic attack I
wrote another entry:

August 23rd, 2012

*Plane from Dublin to Chicago: Two journal
entries in one day. God, so much on my heart and mind.
So much fear and questioning. Maybe I'm buying too
easily into the lies sent by the evil one. God I call. Will
you answer and come to my rescue? I just want to be
where you are. I need you, God. Present and front and
center in my life. What have I done? How could I have
let something sent from the pit divide me and my calling
from you? Even then as I let this go you blessed me.
School scholarships, great friendships, family, mentors,
work, ministry and the list could continue. God, I feel
like I am once again getting a glimpse of what it means
to be falling in love with you.*

*God, as I sit here and write, I see myself
getting excited more and more and the fear and anxiety
leaving. You are the key. How could I think I would
not find freedom when close to you? Thank you for the
gift of music. Thanks for calling me. Continue to excite
me for you, and use people around me to draw me deeper
into relationship with you. Be present in the days to*

come. God I'm both excited and anxious about this transition.

Prepare for me community that is rich, challenging, and good. Give me discernment as I search for a worship community, as well as listen for your call in my life. You know what I need. Thanks for loving me in way that I will never understand, but show me how to love others in that manner and to love myself.

Tyler

Familiar Place with New Perspectives

Seattle, WA
Fall 2012
Age: 28–29

I landed in Washington, and the next day I went up to Seattle with Claudia and Kelly, two friends who had been by my side throughout college and beyond. I felt good compared to how I felt on the plane. Pouring my heart out on paper must have been the release I needed. Now I was home in Washington, about to spend the day with two friends who were so dear to me. They were getting their noses pierced. The place we went was in the neighborhood called Capitol Hill, a place that was known as the "gayborhood" in Seattle. I had never really spent much time up there, and to be honest, I was a little uncomfortable. It stirred up some confusion about my own sexuality.

That afternoon we went to a Starbucks to meet our

friend Elizabeth, better known to us as Shrub, because of the abundance of ringlet curls that sat upon her head. I had wanted to be close to Shrub the moment we met. She has an admirable confidence; she sees potential in things most would cast aside; and she has a warmth and wit that could always lighten any situation.

While the four of us sat at the table sipping our coffee, I felt my heart beginning to get heavy. I tried to shrug it off, hoping it would pass. But then Shrub looked at me to ask how I was doing. Before I could even begin to explain my plans for the year, my eyes began to well with tears. "Not good," I said. I'm sure Kelly and Claudia were surprised—we had been together all day, laughing, and now here I was starting to cry.

I sat there looking at Shrub and told her about finishing up school and that I was planning to move to Seattle but to be honest, I was struggling with my sexuality and maybe coming to grips with the fact that I was gay. I quickly tagged on "or bisexual" at the end because it still made the pill easier to swallow.

I was hurting. Despite my many supportive friends, I still felt lonely and afraid. The following day, I was supposed to hang out with Hayley. We hadn't talked since before my trip. How was I to act excited and invested while I was a wreck?

Kelly, Claudia, and Shrub were great. They asked questions and wanted to know what they could do to support me better. They told me that it didn't matter what conclusion I came to; in the end that they would love me for me. It felt good to hear those words, but it didn't change what I was feeling. Even as we drove home, my anxiety and despair continued to grow.

The next morning when I woke up, I was exhausted. In my last journal entry I seemed to be in a good place, but I was still struggling. It was the day Hayley and I would meet up. I had been so excited for that day, but that morning, something wasn't right. I went to church and put on a smiling face, while inside it felt as if a battle was being waged against me. My heart was clouded, and I didn't want to be there. No one there knew my story, and as I looked around, all I felt was fear of condemnation. Skepticism ran through my veins as I sat in worship unable to even utter the words outlined in the bulletin. I didn't want to be there or anywhere near there. Never in my life had I not felt safe at church. It scared me. What was going on with me?

As soon as the service was over, I went straight to my truck not talking to anyone, kicking up gravel as I left, as if I couldn't get away fast enough. My heart was racing. I hadn't felt this low since I was in college. Life really felt hopeless. This wasn't ever going to go away I thought.

As I drove down the street, the song "Perfect" by P!nk came on. The lyrics were what I needed to hear—the song is about being perfect and unique just the way you are—but I couldn't let those words into my head or heart. It was too hard. I wanted more than anything to love who I was, but it just wasn't an option, not as long as I wrestled with my sexuality.

That afternoon, while spending time with Hayley, I felt like I was in a haze. I couldn't help it. I had gotten so good at putting on a happy face in hard times, but it didn't seem to be working anymore—at least not that day. She had to be able to tell there was something going on with me. I tried my best to be engaged in the conversation, but in reality, I didn't want to be there. I wanted to run as far away from my feelings, struggles, and everything. It was probably good for me to try getting my thoughts on something else so I wasn't so focused on the downward spiral I seemed to be in. But more than anything, it was emotionally exhausting, trying to be present when my mind was elsewhere. I just blamed it on jet lag so she wouldn't think it had anything to do with her.

A few weeks later, I moved in with Marie and Alex in Seattle. It felt good to know I was going to be settled for a bit. I loved traveling, but I had done plenty of that over the summer, and it was time to just relax and transition into my new life in Seattle. The change of scenery helped with all that I was processing, not to mention having Marie and Alex right there.

I moved to Seattle without a job and figured it wouldn't be long until I found something temporary while I waited for a church position. But finding a job proved far more difficult than I expected, and I ended up splitting my time between trolling Craigslist to submit my resume and hanging out in coffee shops journaling and processing all that was going on in my life.

As time went on, I continued getting together with Hayley. I found it extremely difficult still to be fully engaged in the midst of all that was going on, which made me a poor communicator—something that was not common for me. I also was struggling spiritually more than I had let anyone know. I hoped it was a phase triggered by the lack of certainty about my future.

Understanding a part of myself that I had never taken time to get to know—a part of myself I always saw as wrong—was disheartening. I just kept pushing the doubts and feelings down and denying them. My despair was accelerating, and frankly, I was angry. I had books and books full of pages of my cries for healing, and nothing. I continued to find myself pushing away from God more and more. Anything that remotely reminded me of who I once was in my faith repulsed me. Songs that had lyrics that once touched me no longer had the same effect—all because of the brokenness from a sexuality I didn't choose—no matter what anyone said. To quote Lady Gaga, "I was born this way." But I needed the freedom to process my sexuality more openly, so I could figure it out.

Thankfully, I had Marie and Alex. Not long after I moved in with them, while I was in my room, which was right next to their son's nursery, I overheard Marie say to him while changing his diaper, "Someday, you're going to make some woman or man very happy." *Did I hear her correctly,* I remember thinking? I got up and went into the nursery and asked Marie if I was correct in what I had heard. She confidently said, "Yes, that's what I said. We love him and want him to be happy and be with someone someday that he's committed to and loves. If that's a woman, awesome, and if it's a man, that's just fine, too." Although I was angry with God for everything that was going on, I knew I was in the right place.

During high school, I had a friend named Kaylin. Her mom was the one who gave me the journal that got me into the discipline of writing. She and her husband Blake lived in Seattle, and over the years while I was in Chicago, we lost touch, but one afternoon I got a text from her inviting me over.

Driving over to their house, I knew again what was coming. It had been years since we had caught up, but we were always close. How could I hide what had been going on? If I did I wouldn't feel honest; plus I had no fear that she would respond negatively. I had already told her that I struggled with these things while home for Christmas during my first year of college.

Kaylin had always been very outgoing, like me. She loved music, and like me, often spoke way louder than necessary when excited. Kaylin also had a great memory, and when she asked what's going on, she wanted to know the good, the bad, and the ugly, and was more than excited to talk about all of it.

Summer was still hanging on, so Kaylin poured us each a glass of white wine, and we sat out in the grass and caught up while basking in the last bits of summer sun. There was so much to talk about, and we didn't hold anything back. I let Kaylin go first because I wanted to ease into what I had to share. When the time came, the conversation was good and rich. I shared transparently all the ways I felt God's presence over the years, as well as my frustrations with the church and its response to questions of human sexuality. I also shared about how I was struggling with my faith. In my sharing I was able to see the ways in which I grown.

Although her husband Blake was inside, I knew he could hear me. But I didn't care. Blake is nice to everyone. I knew he loved me and would be great when I was able to talk to him, which I did a few weeks later.

As I shared, I noticed I didn't apologize as I once had. I wasn't excited about my sexuality just yet, but I was accepting it and was willing to answer whatever questions she asked. The night was such a blessing. One of my favorite parts about it was that although we did talk about my sexuality, that wasn't the focus of the evening. Most of it was laughing over good food and wine, reminiscing about when we were younger, and rekindling our friendship.

Hard to See the Light at Times

Seattle WA
Fall 2012
Age: 29

Toward the end of September, Katie came to visit, along with her son. She, Marie, the two baby boys, and I were going on a hike together. I was so looking forward to this time because both of them had been so supportive over the years. It was just what I needed.

Katie asked me how things were going, and I shared about my inner conflict with dating woman while I was attracted to men. That's when Marie stopped and looked at me and asked, "Tyler, I have a hard question for you. Do you really think you are attracted to women or do you think that they are just aesthetically pleasing, and you like the idea of it because that's all you have ever known?" The question, as well as the moss-covered evergreens that we were standing under, made me feel so small. *Wow*, I thought. My immediate reaction was to shoot it down, and even though I spoke as if I was willing to ask the question, I knew I wasn't ready to go there yet. Katie offered up her thoughts, reminding me that she supported me wherever I ended up. I came to no conclusion that day, but it was good to be with them, and although I may have shrugged off what they said, their words lingered in my thoughts.

As the days passed with no job and tons of free time, I continued to let myself wonder what life might be like if I saw things a little differently than I always had. I wished sexuality was something I could have talked to my parents about, but I understood that it was a hard topic for them, and I wasn't sure I was entirely comfortable doing that anyway. I still wasn't even close to talking about sexuality publicly, but I did find myself wishing and praying that I could meet someone like me. Maybe if I did, it would give me the courage to share a little more boldly or at least to accept myself. To have someone who could look at my life, what I had been through, and say, "I get it." So I started to pray that God would bring a person like that into my life.

At this point, I had all but forgotten about that bridge God was supposedly building. During some free time I went and visited my friend named Sarah, and as usual she gave me the encouragement just when I needed it that helped me to keep pushing forward.

Sarah was just leaving the seminary as I was coming in, but we had connected the summer I was the camp pastor and that she came as a guest speaker. Although we hadn't known each other long, we made a quick connection. Sarah has a huge heart and a huge personality to match. Maybe that's why I was so drawn to her.

While sitting at a food co-op, drinking coffee, I asked for her perspective and counsel. After all, she was a pastor! She was very encouraging, affirming, and supportive of whatever conclusion I came to in terms of my sexuality, reminding me that although I was raised to think a certain way, it didn't mean that God wasn't going to stretch that thinking. She also encouraged me to hold onto the vision of the bridge. "God didn't say it would be done in a year; it sounds like he's still building it. You just have to be patient," I remember her saying.

The time with her was yet another blessing, while I was still not very open to talking to God. I had not turned my back on God or even given up on my belief in God; things were just hard. I felt abandoned and basically asked God to not stand so close to me. It was too painful to be close and to not feel supported or at times loved—to know that God could rescue me from my pain but wasn't.

Before winter, I wanted to make it over to Eastern Washington to visit my friends Julie, Aaron, and Jodeana, who lived in Spokane. Growing up, I always loved the drive from Olympia to Spokane because the scenery changed so dramatically along the way. The drive started with lush green trees growing up into the clouds and mist as you entered the mountains, with the occasional waterfall to the side of the freeway, then scattered, long-needled pine trees in Central Washington, and rolling hills after that. Eventually, there came a wide expanse of rocky plains as you crossed over the Columbia River, followed by rustling cornfields that turned back into trees, different than those found in the western part of the state.

On my drive over, at different points, even though I

was not great at being quiet by myself, I turned my music off and sat in silence, fuming with frustration about my life. No job. God was silent. I felt alone. I was slowly accepting my story more than I had but didn't know just yet what that looked like in my future, especially with ministry. I saw my sexuality as something that was there and not sinful unless I acted on it. I felt trapped and suffocated by all the stipulations that would come with living my life this way, and I began to scream out to God. No words, just screaming until it felt as if the anger in me was draining out. It was a temporary release that softened my heart to be able to pray. Just a little. I didn't like being angry at God or trying to keep God at a distance. In many ways, I missed God, but there was something getting in the way of our relationship.

Just a few weeks earlier, I had one of the hardest conversations ever with Rebekah. I missed having her within walking distance. So I called her. I knew I was not in a good place, and I was concerned because I really didn't care anymore.

"Are you angry or indifferent?" she asked. That was a hard question to answer because I knew she was not going to like my response.

"I'm indifferent about my faith right now, Bekah." Indifference was one of the things we both believed to be destructive. At least in anger there's emotion, working toward or against something, whereas indifference was just not caring. This brought her to tears. She cared about me so much, and deep down I could feel it breaking my heart that I was not more affected by her tears. What was going on? Had my heart become stone? She told me she would continue to be praying for me and pleaded with me to not be okay with my indifference. I told her

I would keep pushing forward.

Screaming out was one of my many attempts to work through things. It didn't change everything, but it was a push in the right direction. My mind was always running a mile a minute, so being secluded in my truck for the drive across the state was good for me. It meant I couldn't distract myself from what was going on.

I began to think about meeting up with my friends that night. I hadn't seen them for a long time other than briefly for lunch that summer while driving through, and I knew they would want to know what was going on. Where I was working? What kind of job was I looking for? They'd no doubt ask if I had a girlfriend. My sexuality was going to come out because there was no way I was going to lie, not to them, not anymore. So I began to think about where and when I would share with them. So even in my anger at God, I said a prayer and figured I would know when the time was right.

Julie and I had known each other since I was about five years old. We grew up together. No matter the time in between talking, we would just pick up where we left off. She cared about her friends deeply and never hesitated to ask hard and direct questions if it meant understanding someone better and letting them know that she was there for them no matter what.

In the years before going to seminary, Julie and I both lived in Olympia and hung out often. Both of us really wanted to meet someone and decided to give online dating a try. I never had much luck with it, probably because I wasn't being honest about what I really wanted. But it worked out for Julie, and that's how she met her husband Aaron. I didn't know him super well yet, but in the little bit of time I had spent with him, I could tell he was a very kind, easy-going guy.

I was going to stay at their house that weekend, and although I was excited to spend time with them and my friend Jodeana, I was a little nervous because of what I knew I had to share. I didn't think that they would turn their backs on me for sharing what I had been wrestling with, but I did worry that since Julie and I had been raised in the same church with such conservative thinking, she would not be able to fully understand. That was expected and understandable to me—heck, it had taken me countless years to finally begin to listen to other perspectives without the fear of fire and brimstone?

Not long after arriving as the sun was setting, leaving the sky a glowing orange, we all left for dinner. I was nervous but excited to finally be honest. I had met Jodeana through Julie when I was in college; we became fast friends. When I was with Jodeana, life always seemed a little easier. Every time we got together, we broke into at least one fit of laughter that left our abs feeling sore for days. We also had lots of deep conversations about life and faith.

I could tell very quickly that it wasn't going to be hard to find the right time to share. Since I had been away for two years, there were lots of questions to ask. When dinner was done, I looked at them and told them I really needed to talk to them about something. No tears this time, I told them the truth, to the extent that I had accepted it. They listened without interruption and waited until I was done to ask questions—a simple kindness I experienced over and over and for which I was so grateful.

First and foremost, it was most important to all three of them that I knew I was loved. Aaron shared about his uncle who was gay and had been with his partner for so long and how awful he thought it was that they weren't able to get married. Julie shared how she just wanted me to be happy. She had met Aaron's uncles, and although she was raised thinking one way, she no longer saw human sexuality in the same light she once had. "Whether being gay was sin or not, we all have things we will struggle with, and God still loves us and is with us," she said. Jodeana echoed their thoughts, sharing how a few years back she would have had a stronger opinion against homosexuality but recently had come to know more people who really wrestled with it, and after hearing their stories she couldn't approach sexuality the same way anymore.

I wasn't asking them to become allies for the LGBTQ movement; I just wanted to be heard, to somehow put into words what the struggle had been like, and to be listened to, understood, and known, which is exactly what happened. It felt good telling them. As I look back though on some of those conversations in the earlier phases of learning to accept myself, I realize now that I left things fairly ambiguous, which had to be confusing for many of my friends. They must not have known where to go next in terms of supporting me, yet they were great. If I'm being honest, I don't know that I even knew what kind of support I needed.

Later during the weekend, while I was hanging out with Jodeana and catching up on life, I shared with her in a little more depth. I talked about my faith and how it seemed to be in crisis. Like Bekah, her heart broke that because of all that I had been through, I was feeling like I had been abandoned. She also shared some vulnerable things with me, hoping it would be a reminder that God is still with me even when I can't see or feel God's presence.

Jodeana told me that a few months before I had moved home, Julie asked her if she thought I might be gay. Jodeana said she had not been expecting the question, and they began to talk about it. Apparently, Julie was worried about me. She told Jodeana that the next time she saw me, she was going to ask me about whether I was gay because if I was, she wanted me to know that it changed nothing about our friendship. *Wow*, I thought. During the time she was worried and praying for me, I was in the middle of my second semester, when things were so rough. Maybe God *was* there, I thought.

On my drive home that weekend, my heart was a little softer toward the Lord. I felt a glimmer of faith when I heard that my friend had been thinking of me, unprompted, that past year while I was going through so much. *You are good, God, I can see that, but still this is so hard. What's it going to take to no longer have to feel all this pain and anxiety?*

October 2nd, 2012

> *Where am I currently? The very beginning. I think I expected the "year of pain" to only last a physical year, but when it went longer, I gave up and threw my hands up. I wanted to quit, and in some ways I did.*

> *I'm scared God. I want everything to look and happen a certain way. But that has only brought me to an empty, lonely, hopeless place. It's scary to say, but I'm ready to say it. I want your will, no matter how scary it might be, no matter how I fight and wrestle, don't let me go God. You desire happiness for me and know what that looks like for me and in its perfect form. Maybe it's a wife? A boyfriend? Singleness? I*

need to give myself a break, not care about what my family would say, but follow you. Take on your love, your approval.

So many things have been on my heart and mind for years. I remember when I was in high school and wrestling with my sexuality alone what I only acknowledged as "temptations." I used to fear that someday I would give up and accept that it was just who I was. Now, even as I read that, I see how wrong that was. Why would I fear accepting myself? The question was always there in the back of my mind. What if God created me this way? But for so long I thought, no way! I've always seen myself with a wife, and I think I still want/desire that. But what if you have something else? Are you wanting to use me as an example?

I've wondered many times since I am seen and respected by many, what if in opening up about my sexuality I could help be a catalyst for change? Does that align to your will? Do you think it's alright? Okay? Is it a sin or an abomination? Why would you create me a certain way but ask me to always wrestle and try to change who I am?

I know my family will have a hard time accepting and understanding this. Even as I think about following whatever direction you take me, I fear all the parents of the students at the church I worked at, not to mention the students themselves. But I can't worry about all of them. I have to think about Tyler. What about the bridge, God? It can't be done yet, right? Maybe my way of helping with the "construction" is by taking time to process all of this. I seem to remember being told by that girl who shared the vision with me that when it's all done, it will be better than I could have imagined. Please help me stay out of the way. Lord, as I move forward, I need your support and presence more than ever. Help! God. Take my hand and lead me to wherever you're calling.

Tyler

Same Love

Seattle, WA
October 2012
Age: 29

In the early afternoon of October 9, while looking over jobs on Craigslist, I got a text from Kaylin telling me I had to look up a song and watch the video she had just seen. It was by Macklemore and Ryan Lewis, a Seattle-based rapper and producer duo. They had just released the video to their song "Same Love." I had never heard it, but Kaylin said it would really resonate with me. I looked it up and began to watch.

In the song, Macklemore shares his thoughts about homosexuality and the lack of love and rights that are available to people who are gay. He saw this firsthand, the song says, having gay uncles who were not able to be get married. I, like many other people, found a lot that I could relate to in the lyrics. The song put words out there for others to see what it was like for someone like me. The chorus talked about how changing someone's orientation isn't possible no matter how hard they try.

The video follows the life of a boy that reminded me a lot of myself. It starts when he is young, wearing a Cub Scout uniform. I was in scouts as a young boy. As the video progresses, it follows the boy into high school where he is at a dance having fun, but you can see in his eyes as he looks around at all the couples that he isn't happy. He isn't being himself. That was me, too. As the boy grows up, he comes out and meets a guy that he really loves. Even though it was just a music video, watching it changed the image I had in my mind of gay relationships. It showed gay people doing things that any couple might do— hanging out in their apartment looking over old records, cliff-jumping out in the woods. I admit that the only images I had seen up until that point were stereotypes.

In the video, the couple goes to the home of the main character's parents, and the relationship between the two men is initially not well received by the parents. But in the end, the two men get married, and their family is there for the wedding. The video finishes in a hospital room, where the two men hold hands as one passes away. It's a beautiful love story. It's what everyone wants and should be allowed to have; it's what I had always wanted. It's the same love that all heterosexual couples experience—that was the message of the song. The song and the video called people—called *me*—to realize that being gay is not this distorted, weird thing. Instead, it's nothing different from what people experience every day with their own loved ones.

I have always been someone who has connected with

lyrics, the song and video stirred something inside of me. I found myself wanting to accept myself more, and I realized that even though I sometimes said I was okay with who I was, deep down I wasn't. I was fighting against myself. It was torture, and I needed to stop. But how could I love me and also honor God? It was so confusing. Why wouldn't God just say to me audibly what he wanted me to do?

October 11th, 2012

I'm kind of down tonight. I'm single, unemployed, lacking full vision and call in my life. God, what would you have me do? In some ways I really miss ministry. So what do I do God? Move? I want to be here in the Pacific Northwest so bad. Have I let that cloud the call you've placed in my life? I had my profile submitted to a church by the ECC for a possible job— but what about my views on sexuality? How do I honor the church but also honor where you've brought me?

Is it wrong, God? I've asked so many times. Or is it an issue we have gotten too hung up on, and you just want us to love? I don't know what I should do. Before it was always so clear, but now it's not. Whenever I come in contact with someone who is gay. I feel the need to walk alongside them. I want them to fell loved. Is that because of what I've been through? Or is this part of my calling being shaped? It is something people need to have the freedom to wrestle with more openly. It's by no means a choice. Not all desires are good or should be fulfilled. But I've asked so many times what's so wrong about people loving you and loving each other regardless of their sexuality or gender identity?

God, I don't want to be careless with your word. When would you ever be disappointed in me for loving unconditionally? So that's what I'll do. Help me to do it well.

Tyler

Toward the end of October I finally got a job, at the Gap. When I walked in and told the girl standing behind the counter that I was there for an interview. I later found out that she was a transgender woman, and two of my three managers were gay. It was a very different environment than I had ever really been a part of before. *Maybe this was a good learning opportunity*, I thought. Maybe I could figure out how to be more comfortable with myself while the people around me so freely embraced themselves.

After the interview I went down to Portland for a few days because Bekah was going to be in town for a wedding. Boy, had I missed her. We had so much to talk about, and thankfully, she never got sick of processing with me.

October 19th, 2012

Am I gay, just flat-out gay and not bisexual? I wonder at times. I've NEVER let myself be even slightly okay with this part of me until recently, so it is a lot to take in. I want so badly to be okay with it, but I won't fully let myself embrace it. I'm taking steps. I feel passionate about being an advocate for those who identify somewhere on the LGBTQ spectrum. Is that my failed attempt at accepting myself? I say I'm okay with me, but deep down I'm not—is the closest I can get to loving me loving those who have fully accepted themselves? Maybe I don't need to end on either side. Or maybe right now, I am on one side and at some point that will all change. Bekah says I don't have to rush to a conclusion, that I overthink EVERYTHING—it's true though! I do!

Where are you in all of this, God? I heard you so much last year, and it seems like I'm not anymore. Do I have plugs in my ears? Am I choosing to not listen? Maybe I am talking too much? Remember that bridge? How is that coming along? Maybe it wasn't you speaking to me that night. Was it just a random coincidence? I don't want it to be. I want to see this awesome, immaculate bridge all done. To cross over it and see your work is so much better than I could have ever seen. Maybe I've gotten in the way or taken control.

God, I need you. Could you connect me somehow to some gay Christians? Thanks for the job. I pray for a work schedule that allows time for church, clarity, and discernment on how to love as you called. I'll say it here. Unless you give me reason to think/live otherwise, I will not speak out against homosexuality again. Instead, I will be a safe, welcoming place that connects people to you. If I'm wrong, then straighten me out.

Tyler

Though there were glimmers of hope that fall—spending time with Rebekah, finally landing a job—I was still trapped in fear. Sometimes I felt like I had become a zombie, staggering through life—a body that barely looked alive with nothing inside.

November 1st, 2012

Well God, here I am coming back to you after what seems to be a long time. I know you were always there. It was me; I walked away from you. I don't remember making a conscious choice to leave you behind. It must have been a gradual process. Here and there getting frustrated and hurt, which slowly saw me drifting away from you. I think seminary played a part in that, too. Knowledge and questions aren't bad, but I wonder if it began to disconnect me from your heart? I learned so much in seminary that I am so thankful for. At the same time, I really miss my old faith. The person who used to believe so easily and with excitement—how have I become so jaded? I think I know.

I saw a man die, I've wrestled with self-worth and love for myself, seen my friends go through crisis, been in crisis myself, wrestled with my sexuality, and tried to understand all that encompasses that. I've always been single, pulled and pushed to do things that I don't always want to, got my masters and now can't even find a job in ministry, and in the midst of all of it, you were there? It was part of your plan? That explanation used to work for me but no longer does. I want to know more. Why?

Why so much pain, so much hurt, so much confusion and frustration?

I want to serve you, love you, and be where you want me. But often, I feel like it is so hard to even know what you're doing. Why am I still single? I was just asked by a friend if it would be so bad to not have a spouse but instead have twenty plus people around me who will love and support me. My answer, yes, it would. At many points during my week I find myself alone and lonely. It seems everyone has someone. I love community and am so thankful for it, but I dream of having a home, wife, and children of my own to love and be loved by.

But that all being said, it's time that I just be with you. You are jealous for us, and I need to give myself to you once again. In the past when I've done something like this, it has been with the hope and expectation that it would end with me in some kind of relationship. This time it is different. I've seen how I have become so distracted in general and in faith. So I come to you with no time frame, no hidden motives. The only hope and expectation I lay before you is that I would be drawn into an even deeper relationship with you.

God, here I am. Bring me back to who I once was but in your own creative way. Incorporate the good ways I have grown and changed in the last few years. My heart is no longer any good. In a sense, it has become stone. I need a new one, God. There is still so much brokenness in my life, and I need your healing hand there. Help me to work through these things in my life. I'll search you out God; I may struggle with trust at times, so when I do, pull me back to you. I know I can't make deals with you, but what I really need is for you and your love to transform me. I want to be a pastor. Get me back to who I once was, but even better. These are my prayers God. I know they don't fall on deaf ears.

Carry me, hold my hand and comfort me as you break me down to be rebuilt.

Tyler

That November was big for me. Washington State was about to vote on the legalization of same-sex marriage. I began to reflect on the past ten years and all I had been through. In some ways I found encouragement in how much I had grown and learned about myself, but I was also saddened to see some of the same patterns of self-rejection and hatred repeating over and over. I wanted things to get better even though I didn't know what better would look like. I wasn't sure what I wanted or what would make me happy.

In my journals and prayers, I continued to beg and plead for answers and the Lord's help. I wanted healing in my life so that one day I could stand before the Lord. God would look at me and say, "Well done my good and faithful servant." How could God say that now with the stagnancy in my life?

But even in this darkness and confusion, I did something I never dreamed I would do: I voted in support of gay marriage. Even though I was still learning not to fight against myself, I felt enormous relief and joy for the people this change would affect. I was happy to know that people were free to love as they were created, to have human rights, and to not feel like second-rate citizens. In a small way, it felt like a big step in speaking up for myself.

As Christmas neared, my heart was still feeling broken. I felt trapped. I had a job at the Gap that hardly paid me anything and had nowhere to serve in church ministry as a pastor. It seemed like everything I applied for only ended in an informal letter of rejection. Why had God called me to Seattle? For this? Maybe I hadn't been called here, and I just came out of my own stubbornness. In the midst of these feelings of hopelessness, I continued to question again what God was doing. I normally loved the Christmas season, the joy of Christ's birth, the way that people come together and are more kind, but this year I just couldn't get excited. How could I celebrate when I hated myself so much?

Around this time, I had to make the difficult decision to move home to Olympia. I couldn't support myself financially long-term in Seattle on my part-time salary at the Gap. I already felt like a complete failure, and I was going to have to move into my old bedroom at the age of twenty-nine. If there had been any other option I would've taken it, but there wasn't one. I was depressed. I tried to admit again in my journal that I was gay. I succeeded for a few lines before I started to back track. I wasn't ready for that kind of commitment. Apparently, I liked being in the closet more.

Just two days before Christmas, I lashed out at my parents over something I can't even remember. I *do* remember that even in the midst of it I thought, *why are you doing this, Tyler?* But I knew the answer. When you don't love yourself, you need an outlet for your disappointment and dissatisfaction. This time, I took it out on my parents.

Although fighting is never fun, it opened up a fruitful if difficult conversation about how hard it was for me to reconcile my sexuality. With tears, I shared how much I hated myself for something I couldn't control—how I wanted more than anything for it to be taken away, how I believed I was created broken and a mistake. It was the first time I had talked about being gay with both of my parents in person. I felt like I had ruined Christmas yet again, but they assured me that I had not. I will never know how painful it must have been for them to see their child in such anguish. It ended with them praying over me. It was hard for me to let that happen because I was angry, tired, and to be honest, I didn't believe whatever they asked for would actually happen. I'd prayed for deliverance for years and not seen it; why would this time be different just because they were praying?

Back in My Old Stomping Grounds

Olympia, WA
Early Winter 2013
Age: 29

After about a month back at home in Olympia, I was hired again at Starbucks. It had been about five years since I had worked there, and I never thought I would go back, but it had been a good place to work. I got back into the routine quickly. But living at home was an adjustment. I was getting along fine with my family, but I felt a lack of independence. I needed to find something to do with my free time, so I got involved volunteering at my parent's church where I had once worked as an intern.

It was a little surreal going back as a volunteer. The students were great, and I enjoyed not being in charge for a change. But something was different. I felt I couldn't serve with the same passion that I once had. During my first few weeks, I was asked to share a bit about myself at youth group so the students could learn a little more about me since I would be volunteering with them.

As I sat down to write out what I was going to say, my mind went blank. I had no idea where to start or how to talk about myself without giving it all away. The difficult truth was that my struggle with sexuality had dominated my life for so many years—it was such an important, albeit burdensome, part of who I was. I didn't want to lie, but sharing everything was not an option. Without a real job in ministry, and without this struggle that had come to define me, who in the world was I? In the end, I put something together that had no depth. I saw again how living in secret robbed me of my joy in serving.

I wondered if I could ever find a way to serve in a church with my story being what it was. As I continued to wrestle with self-acceptance, I also began to notice something new about myself that I didn't like: I had become very critical of others—specifically other Christians. I couldn't pinpoint why. I knew it was likely for the same reasons I had occasionally lashed out at my family—because of a lack of self-love. But it may have also stemmed from a fear of rejection; if I rejected others before they could reject me, I was safe. Regardless of the reason, I didn't like it.

At first, being at home wasn't so bad. I enjoyed being at Starbucks far more than I ever enjoyed working at the Gap. But in March, I began to feel restless. I wanted to be doing so much more than what I was doing, and I felt like my talents were being wasted.

I met with a friend of mine who was working as a pastor and who wondered if God had brought me back to Washington for a season of rest. I had gone through such a tough year; maybe God wanted me to take a step back from full-time ministry in order to work on loving myself better. As I thought more about this possibility, it made sense. The whole time I was in Seattle I constantly kept myself busy. Maybe God wanted me to rest, so to prepare me for something, and since I wasn't doing that very well in Seattle, God removed me from that place, bringing me to Olympia where life moved at a slower pace. I'd have no choice but to rest. Was God preparing me for something else? Something that I was yet to see?

Regardless, living in Olympia sure didn't feel restful. At every turn it seemed I was seeing relationships that I admired and envied. Why couldn't I have that? I remember spending an afternoon with my grandparents, where I watched them help each other with things in their house. They were a team, and they loved helping each other out. I remember visiting them one afternoon. I asked them what they had been up to and they had both been struggling all day to open a jar from their pantry. They could have been upset but they just laughed about it. I wanted more than anything to be in their shoes one day—living with my spouse, struggling to do things but knowing I had my other half to support and help me when life was hard. Laughing through the triumphs in small victories—there was beauty and simplicity in that. *What a gift*, I thought.

One afternoon, I read through 1 Samuel and saw in the character of Hannah an example of someone I wanted to be more like. She wanted a son so desperately that while she was praying in the temple, crying out to God so passionately, the priest thought that she was drunk. Ultimately God blessed her with a son. What I wanted in my life may have been different from what Hannah asked for, but I wanted to learn to be dedicated like she was, not just so I could have a relationship, but just simply to be as dedicated to God as Hannah had been.

As the weeks passed, I felt cynical about this time of "rest" I was in and continued to get frustrated. Self-loathing and hatred coursed through my veins. I again wondered where God was, feeling like all of this was my own fault—that I was too sinful to be reached by God. I wondered if I was good enough to ever work in a church. I lacked direction and was unspeakably tired of not knowing. Never in my life had things been so up in the air, nor for such a long period of time. My faith felt like it was weaker than it had ever been, and I didn't know what it was going to take to fix it.

I wanted healing, but I no longer knew where to turn to find it. I had prayed. I had been prayed over. I had lamented. I had been anointed with oil. I had fasted. I had done conversion programs, sought spiritual direction and counseling. I confided in people and asked for help. But no matter what I did I felt like I was making no progress, and I again plummeted to rock bottom. Maybe I didn't even know the Lord and that was why nothing had changed. *Am I just a robot in my faith, going through the motions?* I wondered. I had an interview with a church in California that I heard had an opening. I thought that the interview went well, and on paper the position seemed like a good fit. But I had become so used to rejection that I expected the worst. I just kept marching along. It felt like I was living under a cloud.

Whenever I started to feel better, I would quickly feel pulled in the other direction. It was emotional whiplash. My sanity was at stake. I wanted more than anything to learn how to live my life just being me, not to change myself into something that everybody else wanted. I tried to take steps, and although I had gone back and forth to define my sexuality, I still couldn't face it.

I remember a brief moment of reflection in this impassable gloom, when I was honest with myself about one thing in particular for the very first time. *Deep down, I didn't want to marry a woman.* I had dreamed of it all those years, and thinking this for the first time felt like seeing another person's life, not my own. It felt foreign, unfamiliar, out of body. You'd think at this point, such a realization would have been easier to come to grips with since I had been going back and forth with how I thought about my sexuality for so long. But it was too heavy to hold onto for more than a moment. If I ventured into this future, this future where I didn't marry a woman, I wouldn't be able to serve in the denomination I grew up in. So many of my dreams for my life would go unfulfilled. I knew where the ECC stood on homosexuality, and I felt the hope of ever having many of my dreams come true slipping through my fingers like sand.

It frustrated me so much that the church was so unaccepting. Some would argue that they were just holding to their convictions, but this felt personal. Holding to your convictions should never make someone feel that they are not welcome to worship God or to be part of a congregation, especially for something over which they have no control. I didn't expect the church to be on board with everything right now—to just roll over and change their minds. But where was there room to discuss, let alone wrestle with the possibility of welcome?

I found myself feeling really turned off by anything related to the church. I remember going into a Christian bookstore and feeling so uncomfortable that I had to leave almost immediately. I sensed rampant consumerism on those shelves, and I felt like I knew what the people in there would think of me if they knew my secret. Things continued to get harder and harder and culminated with a journal entry during Holy Week of 2013, on Maundy Thursday.

Facing the Facts

Olympia, WA
Spring 2013
Age: 29

March 28th, 2013

This week has, like other weeks, happened with many unexpected upsets and new perspectives. It started Tuesday when I heard back from the church in Santa Barbara. I didn't get a second interview. I almost feel myself becoming angry as I write. I'm upset but also know that it is okay. I think I was more upset that I didn't know what to do or where to go next. Is this you closing the door for me and ministry? I cried in frustration and fear in the shower so my mom wouldn't know. Not knowing what this means. I had prayed for you to close this door if it was not the right fit or if you were calling me to something else. But what is the could you be calling me to? I feel as if I have been rejected so much.

Tonight as I walked the Stations of the Cross, I thought about how Jesus begged for you to take the cup from him, but still said that if it was your will, he will take it. Am I holding too tightly to my will? A few days ago Bekah texted me reminding me of how in the Chronicles of Narnia *Lucy wonders why Aslan doesn't come as he had before. His response: "Things never happen the same way twice." Bekah told me to reflect on the past to be reminded of what you have done to find hope that you will be faithful to work in my future. She said that she believes that you are doing a new thing in me, and we have no idea what it's going to look like.*

When I had found out that I had not received a second interview I asked Bekah if she and our friend Ellie could get together and pray for me. For direction, peace, discernment, anything. Today they met for a half hour over tears and prayed for me. They feel like you are preparing me for something big. What is that big thing God? Is it a youth ministry job? Something else? Does it have to do with my story? That would be a scary cup to take up. But if you call me I'll go.

I've been reading this book called Torn: Rescuing the Gospel from the Gays vs. Christians Debate. *It's about a man named Justin Lee and his coming to terms with his faith as well as his sexuality. He talked about how he had hoped things would change but came to the spot where he realized it won't. I realized that a small part of me has held onto the hope that I would one day change. I won't, though. You made me this way. You will use it. I can relate to many parts of his story on which I need greater reflection. But there are parts where I am different. I still have a small level of attraction to women.*

Is it enough to find peace in a married relationship? It's always been a dream and a desire for me. Is that to be let go of? I really have a hard time seeing myself in a committed long-term relationship with a man. Partly because I've thought for so long that it is wrong, and it seems so distant from what I have always wanted. That all being said, there is so much to be figured out. As I fear what is next, help me find hope in Jesus and in what he did for all of us! Thank you!

Tyler

Reading *Torn* was a little like looking at myself in the mirror. Whenever I had any free time, I would find myself with my nose in its pages, clinging to each story and feeling like there was finally someone out there to whom I could relate. When I finished the book, I reflected in my journal.

April 2nd, 2013

Last night I finished the book. It tells his story of growing up in a Southern Baptist home but also realizing that he is gay. As the book progresses, Justin shares about what it was like coming to terms with his sexuality and what his options are as a gay Christian. Stay celibate? Try to change his orientation? Or delve into a loving, committed relationship?

In the book he shares about the different experiences he had in the first two areas and ends with the conclusion that for him, he believes the Bible does support gay relationships and the Scriptures mentioning it are taken out of context by the church today.

As I read, I found myself in his story. The fear, pain, and hopelessness he experienced—I could picture in my own life. The questions he asked, too. One of the big things was when he talked about ex-gay ministries and how they really don't change people. People still are attracted to the same sex, and they are only suppressing their feelings. At first it may seem to work, and you get this great sense of hope, as if it's being put behind you. I remember this. Then at some point you crash. You slip up, and it's as if you are right where you began. That seems to bring a greater sense of hopelessness.

The book brought me to the realization that I did not just "struggle with same-sex attraction," but my internal wiring had me attracted to the same sex. How upsetting to learn. Especially being raised thinking it was an abomination. Then to realize nothing caused it, but instead, you made me this way. That is a tough pill to swallow and will continue to be.

In the book, there were often things I could not fully relate to. Justin seemed more confident that this was who he was. I didn't/don't all the time. How do I still have such a strong desire to have a wife and family? Why do I find some women attractive? I finished the book a little less hopeful, feeling as if my only options *were celibacy or a gay relationship that would lead to so much rejection.*

I don't know how to put into words what it feels like to think I may have to come to terms with the fact I may never have a wife or children. I sit here in this empty house and think how lonely and sad that would be. What about holidays or when I am old and don't have any family to take care of me? Is that really what you want/have for me? Or what about a gay relationship? What would be so sinful in that?

I want to agree with Justin, and part of me does. I realize that for other people I am okay with gay marriage, but for me I am just not sure. I need to do some real study. I don't want to live not honoring you or leading other people astray. I have a lot to pray about and think on. Help me to do both and to be fully invested. I've said it before and will again: I need your help and guidance with this one. Breathe truth into me, and show me where I'm called.

Tyler

As May rolled around, I was frustrated that it had been a year since I graduated, and I still didn't know what I was doing. But I was proud of the growth that I had undergone. I had two trips to Chicago planned for that month. The first trip would be for that year's seminary graduation, and the second trip was to help Bekah pack up and then road trip home—a good break for my mind.

Once I read *Torn,* I felt that there was so much to process and consider. I believe that although I had come out to myself over a year earlier, I quickly (and ironically) went into denial after reading that book. I was beginning to grieve the loss of the future I had always pictured. It was hard, but there was some comfort in coming to terms with this part of myself.

For so long I would say that I wasn't actually gay because I had never been in a relationship, but after reading the book I had a new perspective. I needed to face the facts. Orientation is always there. You don't become gay the moment you're in a relationship with someone of the same sex. You're gay because of how your heart was created to love. I didn't know why this was so hard for me to realize all those years. I had never thought about my sexuality this way. It was freeing as well as scary because, if this was true, I didn't know what it meant for my future in ministry. Was God going to call me to serve and just always suppress who I really was and live a lie like the ECC would force me to? Would I have to carry all the hurt I had for years, never feeling known by people around me?

At the beginning of May, after venting all about these things with Claudia, she encouraged me to talk to one of the professors from the theology school she attended, who also had a counseling ministry that dealt specifically with people who were in some kind of life transition. His name was Jon, and Claudia thought that he would be a great fit for me. I emailed him and set up a time to meet.

The first meeting was just to feel things out and see if it would be a good fit for both of us. As soon as I sat down, he asked me to tell him what was going on in my life. I let him have it. I held nothing back about my sexuality, underemployment, lack of direction, and inability to support myself financially. It wasn't hard to share. I was honest with him even at our first meeting that although I had just put it all before him, I had little to no hope or belief that he could be helpful or that things would ever get better. Laying the groundwork for what our time together would be like, I agreed to start meeting him on a bi-weekly basis. Unlike counselors I had worked with in the past, Jon always had homework for me. He also asked me to find three people who would commit to going through this with me by reading the things I wrote while in the process.

The first person I asked was Claudia. She had been there for so long and was one of the first people I ever came out to. We had been through so much. Next, I asked Rebekah. It was hard for me to picture my life without her in it. The third was my good friend and roommate through seminary, Sam. Sam always had answers that I could find peace in.

Though I didn't know what to expect, I was up for whatever. No matter how hard it was to swallow, I wanted to know who I was, who God had created me to be, and what it meant to live out God's call. I soon came to look forward to my sessions with Jon because I could be truly honest about everything I was thinking without fear of judgment. He asked me questions that were not easy and that always pointed me back to God. He also wasn't afraid to call me out when he felt I wasn't being honest—when I was trying to fool him or myself. It was in these first few sessions that it became clearer that I would need to come out publicly in order to find freedom from the pain. This meant a lot of things would have to change in order to prepare.

Laying My Dreams to Rest

Chicago IL—North Park Theological Seminary
Late Spring 2013
Age: 29

That spring I flew to Chicago for the seminary's graduation. I was really excited for my visit to Chicago as well as a little apprehensive. My heart was heavy. I was a little anxious, but I couldn't pinpoint why. Anxiety was such a familiar feeling that many times I just assumed it stemmed from nothing. I fell into familiar patterns, meeting up with students I had mentored and friends I missed, but something was different. It felt like I was in the early stages of grief, but for the loss of what, I did not know. It all came to a head on one of my first nights in Chicago, at my friend Hilary's apartment.

Hilary and I found common ground just after meeting each other in seminary, and she had always been there to make me laugh with quick-witted comments. Hilary made sure to let me know that I was always important and valued by her, and she was not afraid to share with me what she thought. She, like so many in my life, wanted to get to the truth of things, and was willing to fight for it. She had a huge heart and desire to care for and mentor people, and she was great at it. I had told her my story pretty early into my first year of seminary.

On that night, I was catching up with Cathy and Hilary before commencement. As they each shared what was going on in their lives, the pain in my heart started to surface. I felt as if my pain was going to boil over. When it was my turn to share, my eyes began to well up with tears. I shared all I had been learning about myself over the past year—that I was tired of fighting and that I was coming to terms with the fact that I was gay. I knew it would mean the end of me working within the denomination I had grown up in—a place that had always felt like home. *That's what the grieving pain was from*, I thought. Without realizing it, I had come to Chicago to leave my dream there where I started to take the first steps toward accepting myself just as God made me and to make room for something else—a new dream. It became very clear to me while talking to them that I had a few specific friends I needed to talk to while I was in Chicago.

That night we attended the seminary graduation and the reception afterward. It was far more challenging than I expected. I choked back tears, grieving the loss of this community that had once brought me such joy. I was sad that I would not be able to continue on in ministry within the ECC with these people around me in the context for which I had once hoped. I talked to two of the professors that I had confided in during my time there, and although it saddened them to hear that I was most likely going to have to step back from the ECC, they completely understood and supported me since the denomination was so close-minded on this matter. They offered both warm hugs and support. I had no idea my trip was going to be so emotionally taxing.

Before flying home, I sat down for coffee with my old roommate and close friend, Sam. I knew what his views on homosexuality were—affirming, progressive—and I wanted to be where he was. So I asked him to share with me very bluntly how he had come to that place. For the next hour my friend and I sat and talked very honestly with each other. We asked questions, challenged opinions, and bared our souls. As we talked, I was reminded that God was still building that bridge and that he had provided for me so many amazing friends. I know he delighted in the time Sam and I spent together at Starbucks—and in Sam for sharing his love in a way that was tangible—I felt like I could somehow grasp that love with my own two hands.

Once I was home, I fell again into a downward spiral that would take me to some of the most difficult places I had ever known or experienced. I only had a few weeks at home before flying back to Chicago again to help Bekah move back west. All the inner processing was exhausting. I knew that the baby steps toward accepting myself were good, but each one seemed to hurt so bad, like I was walking barefoot on broken glass.

I went hiking with my friend Cooper one weekend afternoon. When we first arrived at our destination, the fog was thick, and the trees looked so beautiful reaching through the mist. We knew where the trail was and what direction to go because we had done the hike together before, but the fog made it hard to trust that we were going in the right direction. It was exactly how my life felt.

I knew God was there, leading me, using the many amazing people around me to love and guide me. But the pain, doubt, and fear of disappointing God and those around me seemed to conceal the truth. Like the fog on our hike made it hard to follow the trail, the thoughts constantly running through my head made it hard to see the truth. After years of hiding in denial, it was proving to be more challenging than I had expected to accept my sexuality. I found peace knowing I'd soon be on a road trip with my dear friend Bekah. No doubt, we were going to have a lot to talk about.

Be Not Afraid of Who You Really Are

Chicago, IL to Olympia, WA
May 2013
Age: 29

I was in Chicago for less than twenty-four hours before Bekah and I embarked on our big adventure west. Before we left, we found some time to sit and talk with one of our professors about LGBTQ inclusion and the church.

This was the same theology professor I sat with during seminary, who challenged me to demand a blessing of God and told me, "I see God in you, Tyler." Boldly I shared how my views and beliefs were shifting. Regardless of any individual's view, I said, the church was handling this in a harmful, negative way. People like me were hurting, feeling alone, afraid, and finding more comfort outside of the church. It pained me that the church wasn't doing more to help—instead, Christians were more concerned about their reputation; they feared they would lose people if they came across as too supportive.

Instead of sharing what she believed on the matter, my professor asked me to answer a few questions. She asked what goods were found in a committed heterosexual relationship? We reflected on Ecclesiastes 4:9-12:"Two are better than one, because they have a good return for their labor: If either of them falls down, one can help the other up. But pity anyone who falls and has no one to help them up. Also, if two lie down together, they will keep warm. But how can one keep warm alone? Though one may be overpowered, two can defend themselves. A cord of three strands is not quickly broken." After reflecting on these verses I pointed out that there's accountability, a sharpening of one another, intimacy, and childbearing in a heterosexual relationship.

She then asked what goods can be found in a committed homosexual relationship. All my answers were the same, except for childbearing. She challenged that assumption, though, explaining that many heterosexual couples were unable to bear children and some choose not to, and that didn't make their relationship less good. She offered her thoughts on the need to broaden our interpretation of the passage to include child-*rearing*. As a part of the church, we are collectively called to look out for one another, including all children. I had never looked at things this way.

Then she asked a question that proved to be more challenging to answer than I expected: How is a committed homosexual relationship destructive to society? As I struggled to come up with a valid answer, I realized that every example that I could come up with was also true about heterosexual relationships. Where was I to go with that, I asked?

Smiling, she looked at me and said, "Wherever you end up, you need to find an argument that you're comfortable with and believe in and regardless, know that God loves you and that there is nothing that can separate you from that relationship." Good food for thought.

Our trip west was different than we expected, but it was good. I had said my goodbyes to Chicago and my community there a year ago, and although I had missed it, life away had become the norm for me. For Bekah, though, this was all new. I found myself feeling hopeless and burdened for a lot of the drive, when I should have been enjoying time with my friend while she was grieving the loss of her community in Chicago.

I was truly coming to grips with being gay, but after years of denial and suppression, it wouldn't happen overnight. I felt like I was being forced to choose between accepting myself and following God, as if the two couldn't fit together. As usual, Bekah breathed truth into the chaos of my thoughts, reminding me that our God cannot and will not be limited. God loves me, so why would I have to choose one or the other? She was right; I had so many people around me whom I loved, respected, and admired, all who had a deep faith, and all who told me that God made me this way, called it good, and desired for me to be at peace. Just the thought of accepting my sexuality was initially exciting, but then the crippling fear would set in and freeze me in place. Round and round I went in my thoughts until I had worked myself into a storm of anxiety and panic.

You would think that at this point Rebekah would have been fed up after the years processing this with me over and over, but I am still waiting for the day when Bekah asks to talk about something else. She looked at me, calmly told me to relax, and gently put me in my place, saying, "You try to force things so much. I really believe you need to learn to just be and trust that God is going to work it out. You don't have to have it all figured out right now. Just take it one step at a time."

I felt a rush of calm come over me. For the rest of the trip, we sang along to music, discussed TV show characters as if they were real people we were in daily relationship with, and made goofy videos of us singing songs from the musical *Wicked*. We still talked about tough stuff as it came up, but I no longer felt the obligation to come to some firm conclusion by the time we were back on Washington soil (as if that was even possible).

To this day, I am so very thankful for that trip, and of course, for Rebekah. I have always been able to be fully me around her, with no fear of judgment. It might seem silly, but it was in being goofy and singing along to one song in particular that I took another big step forward toward self-acceptance. It was a song I had heard many times. Bekah pointed at me with wide eyes, singing the lyrics, "Be not afraid of who you really are." All my life I had been terrified of who I was. That's what it all came down to. I had been taught over the years to be afraid of how God had created me. *How do I stop?* I wondered. I no longer wanted to be afraid. I wanted to live my life!

One of the best parts of our trip was the freedom to stop wherever we pleased. At Mount Rushmore while people watching, we both noticed a couple that intrigued us. There wasn't anything peculiar or flashy about them, but they had a unique style. Trendy clothes, hip glasses, and one was carrying an old retro camera. They were confident and cool. Bekah and I began to imagine together what their story was, knowing we would never know, both of us longing for a relationship and admiring what they had. We decided that they were on a road trip across the country, taking photos along the way to document their adventures. We watched as they interacted with people all around them, laughing and connecting with anyone who was willing. We were more than a little bit envious of what they had, affectionately calling them "the boyfriends." I found a great deal of hope in our image of them, and as I watched them get into their car together to set off for who-knows-where, I felt a longing for something like that. Seeing relationships like theirs continued to help me break the stereotypes I had built up of what gay relationships were like.

That night, we enjoyed one another's company while listening to music and watching lightning flash and dance across the sky in the distance. The ominous clouds we'd been chasing for the last few hours rolled in above us. We ventured deeper into the storm, and as the sun set, the lightning flashed, followed by loud cracks of thunder. It got darker than I have ever seen in daytime. Without talking, we watched in awe and wonder at the sky-show before us. The raging storm put into perspective how little we were in this world, that God had us, and no matter how much I tried to believe and think that I had control, I didn't. At one point, it was as if the floodgates were opened, and water came pouring down upon us, making it almost impossible to see. It was beautiful and terrifying all at once.

We reflected together about what we had just seen. The only word we could come to was "wonder." We later found out that we had driven through a tornado warning. Oops.

On the last day of our road trip, I felt anxiety creeping in once again as we approached home. While listening to a mix of Mumford and Sons and Need to Breathe, I was able to find much of what I was feeling in their lyrics. Music had always helped me put words to what I was going through. I was anxious because I had a pretty good idea where things were going in terms of my story as well as the next step. I just didn't know how to take that step or if I'd ever feel ready.

I was afraid of who I was, and I was gay. At some point, I was going to have to say something because keeping this secret was eating away at my core. The idea of living in that pain, in the lies, for the rest of my life was beginning to be scarier to me than any response I might get from anyone. I was sick of never feeling known by the people around me. Keeping this secret was so destructive, and even Bekah noticed the toll it was taking. I began to fear that I was losing part of me. But I knew I needed to continue to take it one step at a time.

Cracking Open the Closet Door

Olympia, WA
Summer 2013
Age: 29

When I got home, my mom asked about our trip. I told her about the highs and lows, the times of prayer and tears. The hardest part was this secret-keeping, I told her. I felt like a liar. She didn't quite understand why I felt that way, so I explained how it was hard to answer questions about why I wasn't in ministry, or about my dating life while briefly in Chicago. Beyond the questions in Chicago, in general when people wanted to set me up with their friend of family member, id have to find a clever way to deflect. I felt trapped by the life I had created for myself, living in secret for so many years. It was in that conversation that I told my mom I was going to have to come out at some point in the near future. I was afraid if I didn't, I would lose all of me. My joy had already been stripped, and each day seemed harder to get through.

My family was busy, and it was hard for us to find times to get together. My brothers and I and my sister in-law were home at that time to celebrate our parents for Father's and Mother's days. We found one day when we could all be in the same place to make our parents dinner. We took a nice photo of all of us—my brothers, me, and my sister-in-law, Heidi—and got it developed for them. Eric grilled while Heidi and I cut up vegetables for the meal.

Heidi and I had always gotten along well. It was hard to picture how a woman would fit in with our family of all boys, but she had figured it out. She was perfect for Eric, too. I had always hoped to have someone in my life—someone close enough that I would care about how they care for each other. Heidi was excited for the day she wouldn't be the only woman in the family; she didn't know that I likely wouldn't help her out in that regard.

In the kitchen that day, she asked me about different women we both knew and whether I had ever considered dating them. At this point, I was very good at deflecting, so I gave some quick and easy explanation for each. This one isn't my type, or that one isn't interested in me, and so on. Heidi asked me what my type was. I wanted to blurt out, "I don't know—guys," but that didn't feel like an appropriate or sensitive way to tell my siblings, even if it would have been funny. She was waiting for an answer. I didn't want to lie, so I just shot down the question. My mom was across the room, listening in. I had no doubt that she now understood what I had been talking about.

After dinner, we gave our parents the photo. I don't think any of us were expecting the reaction we got from my mom. You would have thought we had given her a new car. She began to cry as she and my dad looked at the picture with such delight in their children; they love us so much. For the rest of the evening I noticed that my mom kept going back to the photo and a big smile would stretch across her face as she looked at it.

I couldn't help but wonder if one day we would take another photo that included Timmy's and my spouses. If I got married and it was to a man, would my family be comfortable having that up on the wall?

June 27th, 2013

It has been a long time since I have journaled. I think with all the processing both internally and with the counselor, I run out of energy to do this. Or maybe it's just that there is too much hurt and frustration in my life, that it seems it would take forever to write it all down. But why the rush? You aren't going anywhere, and neither am I.

Yesterday at counseling, Jon told me he didn't think I was able to access my emotions very well. I may know and see when others are experiencing emotions, but when it comes to my story, I'm calloused. That's when I said, "I'm angry about so much." I then rattled off all the things I am angry about. It felt good, and I wonder if this might be a good practice for me to start doing on a regular basis.

Life is just so hard right now. I hate how I struggle. I'm angry that I don't ever get to feel known by the greater public. I'm angry that you would make me this way and make it so hard to understand if it's okay or not. I'm angry and feel trapped in this life, like

I never have a choice. I don't want this story, but it's what I have to work with.

I'm tired of fighting, of wrestling, of letting you down—tired of feeling less-than. Do I just have to live like this the rest of my life? Be alone? Not have a family of my own? What about my seminary degree? Why call me there? Was it to get the ball rolling with learning to love myself for who I am? Why do you seem silent always? Are you truly building a "bridge" in my life that is more detailed and immaculate than I could ever comprehend, or was that whole conversation at the night of worship last year a random coincidence that I overanalyzed to the point where it fit my particular situation?

I have seen a shift in the last so many months in how I see myself. Even last week I started to see myself letting go of my ideas of my sexuality being a sin. I mean, you did create me like this, and you don't make mistakes. Also, you don't make us sinful, but we are given free will. Is embracing my sexuality and its ambiguity wrong? What's so wrong about a loving, committed, same-sex couple? Aren't the same goods that are found in a straight relationship found in a gay one? If you're a God of truth, then you wouldn't call me to lie and hide who I am.

Furthermore, I think more damage has been done to me emotionally and spiritually, trying to change or undo this than would have been done had I always just loved myself and accepted me for me. If it's a sin or not, why has the church elevated it so much? I find more love and acceptance outside of the church than in it regarding this issue. I don't want to disregard all those in the church who are loving and affirming. There are so many friends in my life who are both believers but also affirming. Would you allow that into my life if you didn't want me to be okay with it?

I run in circles but am ultimately coming to the spot where I see the destruction, not in the relationship, but in the hiding, the lying, and the rejection. I don't need to be Tyler who is straight, bi, or gay. I just want to be loved and accepted as Tyler—your son whom you love and are well pleased with. You are, aren't you? Why is it so hard to find other Christians who are gay? Is it better for me to be alone in this for now? I just need help all around.

I'm scared to ask with confidence out of fear of only receiving silence. I'm wrestling, maybe like Jacob or maybe just like Tyler. He demanded a blessing, and I've done the same before. Maybe with expectations, but not today. I am a weary, scared, and broken fighter, Lord. I don't want to wrestle anymore. I'm mad about a lot. I'm hurt by a lot. I'm confused by so much. I'm ashamed and disgusted by so much. I don't know where my faith has gone, if it will come back to the way it once was, or if I'll ever feel at home in church again. But I want to believe those things can change—that I can find purpose, that I too will find love and a family, that I will tell my story one day with confidence, and it will help others draw to you.

Even though so much of my life is uncertain

I love you Lord. Don't let my heart become hard like Pharaoh's. Guide me, and give me hope, and although I feel so undeserving, I plead for your mercy on me as I try and figure these things out and ask for your blessing.

You're a God who doesn't take broken things and trash them and start over. You're a God who makes old things new. You're a God who works with your creation, not against it, even when they stray. So I ask that you do the same with me. Pour onto me your blessing, and give me peace to quit this wrestling match. You created me with a vision and purpose in mind. Help me become the Tyler you see, and help me to delight in this creation the way you do. Bless me, bless me, bless me, Lord. I humbly ask with a broken spirit and heart. Be now a peace in my life that passes all understanding, that washes away all guilt and shame. Help me to live more and more for you because I know lately I haven't. Now Lord, do your work in me.

Tyler

The release I had, both in my session with Jon as well as in my journal, felt really good, but it was only a temporary fix. Each day I woke up, and it was only a matter of minutes before the weight of the world would fall upon me. Each breath seemed like the biggest chore; I gave myself internal pep talks constantly. I set small goals for myself in order to make it through the day. "You can do it, Tyler. Just make it to your first break. Only a few more hours until bed, and you can sleep." Sleep was the best because I didn't have to think about all that was going on. I felt like a shell of who I once was. I was functioning but just barely, and that smiling face that once used to hide all the pain in my heart was no longer doing its job. People began to notice a difference in me, especially at work.

The normally cheery, upbeat Tyler was nowhere to be found, and I would speak only when needed, going through my tasks on autopilot. One day my manager, whom I had a great working relationship with, pulled me aside to see how I was doing; she had noticed something was different. I felt the tears coming, but I couldn't tell her what was really going on. So I just gave her the broad answer.

"I have depression, and it's gotten a lot worse than I've ever known it to be. I'll try better." She was supportive and told me to keep her in the loop about what I needed. It was good that she knew I wasn't purposefully not giving my best but that I really just couldn't. Had I been honest, I would have said to her, "Well, my depression is almost unbearable and seems to suck the joy out of any situation that could be positive. I hate my life, my story, who I am, and I want more than anything to change the very thing that causes me to hate myself, but I can't. I want to do what I am passionate about and be in ministry, but I can't because there is something about me that's not going to change, and it's enough for me to have a mark put on me that says unlovable, unacceptable, sinful, abomination. So no, I'm not doing very well, but if you have any suggestions of how I can fix it, I'll gladly take them." It was worse than even my first year in Chicago, and things were only getting gloomier.

I had no other option; I had to come out. All the secrets and the lies were eating me alive. There were still people close to me who didn't know, including my siblings, and I didn't want them to hear from other people. I needed to take the first steps to make things better. I found the desire to have the conversation with people stronger than ever.

I began to notify the friends around me who had been there for me all along that I was planning to come out. One of those people was my longest friend, Jenny. We met when we were really young at church, and she had always been like the sister I never had. I first came out to her in her bedroom after college. Sharing my sexuality then was unexpected but good. Crying, I told this person who had known me longer than anyone what I had been hiding. She was wonderful, and over the next few years, whenever we were in the same town, we would get together. She was always the one to bring it up, wanting me to know that she cared about me and supported me. That June over Skype, I shared with Jenny what I was afraid of as well as the excitement to not have to hide anymore. Jenny was joyful about things that I wasn't yet ready to be; she looked forward to me no longer hurting.

This was the beginning of many similar conversations, and on the fourth of July, while with some friends, I continued coming out, starting with my friend, Stevie. Stevie and I became fast friends. We are kindred spirits. She is artistic and finds beauty and potential in things that others don't. She is also a bleeding heart; she'll pick up any animal she finds wandering the streets to make sure it stays safe. Her heart is huge, and she longs for everyone to see the good in themselves. We were also always able to relate in our struggles; we'd both had our fair share. Sharing with a friend like Stevie would be easy, but I wasn't even planning on doing it that day—until I did.

A bunch of us were talking, and as I listened to Stevie talk about her frustration with people who aren't accepting of others, I felt this longing in my heart to tell her. I pulled her aside. "You know I wrestle with depression, but I feel it's important for you to know why. I'm gay, Stevie. And I have hated myself for years and have feared rejection and haven't wanted anyone to look at me differently, but I can't hold it in anymore and in some way soon, I'm going to come out."

Stevie gave me a huge hug and told me how special I was to her and that nothing changed. She was so excited that I was moving toward accepting myself. This is why whenever you've asked me if I am looking for a church job I have told you I'm taking a break from ministry, I told her. I want to, but there's no room for me to do that right now."

"You're so talented and gifted, Tyler, and people could be so touched by you and your story. Don't think that just because the ECC isn't ready for this that there aren't churches out there that are." I needed to hear that. People stay in the ECC like there is nothing better out there or that God can't be found outside of its Swedish walls, afraid to branch out from their long history there. I gave her a big hug and told her how great it felt to feel truly known by her—no more secrets. It almost felt like I had taken physical weights off of my shoulders that I no longer had to lug around. She gave me a hug and told me it was an honor that I would share my story with her.

A few hours later, I found myself in a similar situation with my friend, Kristen. We had met our freshman year of high school in math class. The truth is, I had a crush on her and made a point to get to know her with the hopes it would develop into something more. We never dated, but we became great friends. You typically wouldn't see one of us at school without the other. Our friendship was one that was very different than most of my friendships in high school. By my freshman year, I had already developed pretty tight bonds with my friends from church, so I never really hung out with any of my friends from school outside of the time spent there, except Kristen.

She knew from the beginning that my faith was very important to me, and at the time she had made it very clear that it was something she really wasn't interested in. But that didn't stop us from being friends or sharing our opinions with each other. Many times we would debate and not see eye to eye, but we always stayed close. Then, just before our senior year, Kristen started coming to youth group and excitedly told me that she had come to know Jesus.

We've gone on trips together, worked together, and always made a point to get together when we were home from college. Kristen was also never afraid to tell me how it was or to call me out when needed. The funny thing is, over the years the subject of my sexuality never came up. That changed on the night of the fourth, when I pulled her aside to talk. She knew that life was rough for me, but I had been vague about why.

My heart was heavy as I looked at her and said, "Kristen I have to tell you something that's really hard to say." She looked nervous. "I've always struggled with my sexuality. I'm gay."

She very calmly looked at me and said. "I know. Well I didn't know, but I assumed. I figured you would tell me when you're ready. But it doesn't change anything. Of course, I love you. We all have our stuff."

It was the first time I had heard that response and wasn't bothered. I typically hated when people told me they already knew. I always felt that it wasn't truth until I told you, but coming from Kristen, it was okay. She knew me so well, and we had been through so much. Sure, this was part of my story, but our friendship was built upon so much more.

I was feeling pretty good at the end of that night after coming out to both Stevie and Kristen, but I still had to tell so many others. *How was I going to do that?* I wondered. I wanted to do it right. *There was time*, I told myself. At least I was beginning the process.

Although things still seemed hopeless, God was looking out for me, providing just what I would need to light a spark in my heart once again for God and for ministry. I was going to spend the next week speaking at the camp I had grown up going to—the one where I said the sinner's prayer the summer after fifth grade and where I spent many summers as a boy as well as where I spent the summer working as a camp pastor alongside Bekah. I would be guest-speaking at the upcoming junior high camp.

Back at Camp

Yelm, WA—Cascades Camp & Conference Center
Summer 2013
Age: 29

Right before I got up to speak on that first night, my heart was racing. There I stood in the all wood amphitheater with a hundred-plus junior high aged girls and boys sitting around me. The fire in the pit crackled before me while the last bits of the day's sun made its way through the branches of the towering evergreen trees. Countless times, I had been in this amphitheater, sitting in the bleacher-like seats, but tonight I was front and center with all eyes on me. *I'm going to fail tonight. It's coming, I just know it.* But I didn't. My talk went better than I could have expected, and that was the theme for the entire week. Each day I went over what I was going to share with them that night, and each day I felt like I was going to fall flat on my face. But each night as my talks went well. Even with everything I was processing internally. I couldn't help but believe that God was there with me.

My first day of camp I got a small package. I was blown away when it was handed to me. What camp speaker gets mail? It was from my sweet friend, Kelly, with whom I had gone to seminary. I opened the envelope, and inside was a handmade card for each day of the week, giving me encouragement. She had to have planned ahead to get them done and sent in time to get to Washington from Chicago. *What a wonderful friend*, I thought. Kelly is one of the most generous, creative, and thoughtful friends anyone could have. We had many talks about life and my sexuality during our time in seminary and Kelly always offered a safe space and unconditional love.

So to get these notes from her was very special. It was another reminder that God was looking out for me. Throughout the week, different friends surprised me and came to hear me speak, including one of my old youth leaders from high school, and I felt so loved.

My talks that week all revolved around the things I had learned over the years as I wrestled with my sexuality. I found creative ways to talk about what God had said to me without flat-out saying that I was gay. I was worried it wasn't going to go over well, but throughout the week, campers came up to me to tell me things they identified with that I had shared. A few of the staff even told me that what I said was exactly what *they* needed to hear.

The last night at camp, I had the opportunity to talk with a boy who wanted to give his life to Christ. It was a special and holy moment. After we parted ways, I remember sitting under the stars in wonder at how big and good God was, thinking, *Why would you use me this week if I was embracing this "sin" in my life? Wasn't I going against you?* I wish I could say I heard a voice. I didn't, but I did feel as if God was looking down on me and that God was proud of me.

The week was just what I needed. I was afraid to go home because I didn't want to go back to what I had been doing. I wanted to be doing more. I knew the depression was only lifted temporarily, but I wanted to remember what that week was like and use it as a springboard to whatever was next.

You Have to Choose to Be Well

Olympia WA—My Home
July 2013
Age: 29

In the weeks following speaking at camp, I reflected back on the time spent there and what I had shared. I found that in many ways, I was preaching to myself. The previous summer while at CHIC, the youth conference in Tennessee, I had heard my friend and pastor, Judy, preach on John 5, and I had taken notes. A lot of what I wrote down still resonated with me, and I incorporated many of the same ideas into one of my own talks during that week at camp.

Judy was the campus pastor at North Park University while I was in seminary and has touched many lives over the years, including mine. She was affirming and supportive of me whenever I would go to her office to process my struggles with sexuality while in seminary. Little did we know that years down the road, the ECC would fire Judy from her position for officiating the wedding of two men. They were gearing up to draw a hard line in the sand against LGBTQ-affirming pastors and to use Judy and many others as examples, but that's Judy's story to tell, not mine.

Judy is a gifted preacher, quickly drawing those around her into whatever she is speaking on, which is why I pulled from the talk I heard her share the previous summer for one of my own messages. It was from John 5, which was a story about a man who was paralyzed and who wanted to be healed. This felt like a particularly important message for me to absorb. Confidently, Judy preached this message while surrounded by thousands of high school students who were at the conference.

In the story in John 5, there is a paralyzed man who wants to be healed, lying by a pool. Jesus went to the pool, knowing that there would be people there who wanted to be healed. He went with the desire to meet with and spend time with these people. This story shows us that Jesus sees us in our place of brokenness, comes to us, and asks, "Do you want to be well?" He knows it and understands it and meets with us in it. Jesus makes it seem so simple; it's a matter of making a decision and living into it.

Making a decision to be well may seem so simple, but most of the time we make it complicated. I am so good at making excuses. That one thing that I wanted to get well from seemed so hard because I had built up walls—I had made it nearly impossible to accept my sexuality and to love myself in order to be well. For so long, I was afraid that people would find out my secret. I would put up a front, fearing how people would respond. Would I still be accepted by those around me? What if

I regretted sharing it?

But I also clung to my secret in some ways. I had grown so comfortable with the pain that I couldn't really picture what it would look like to live life apart from it. It had become the norm for me, and I just accepted the pain I felt as how things always would be. Sometimes just the unknown can be scarier than being unwell because at least the unwell was familiar. Jesus could make me well, but he wasn't going to force me.

In the story, Jesus asks the paralyzed man if he wants to be well, and the man gives him excuses for why things haven't gotten better. The man believed his destiny was to live on that mat. The mat in my life was the fear, pain, and shame. But when we step into Jesus's light, he will clear the way for us to get up like the man in this story did and move forward. The key part is that we have to decide that we want to be well and get up!

One of the things I had grown to love about this story was that Jesus tells the man to take up his mat and walk. He doesn't tell the man to leave his mat and walk away, but to take it with him. This man had been bound to that mat for his entire life. People with physical limitations like him in that time were seen as almost subhuman. The mat was a symbol of that. I'm sure he hated that mat and couldn't wait to get rid of it. It resembled the life he lived before Jesus healed him, and he no longer needed it. But Jesus gives him a very clear command: "Get up! Pick up your mat and walk."

I believe that Jesus told the man to bring the mat with him because he knew that when people saw him with it, they would ask him why he was carrying it. That mat did represent a part of the man's story, but it no longer defined him. He had chosen to be well and was healed. The man may have been ashamed of the mat and may not have wanted to be associated with it any longer, but Jesus was never ashamed of the man. When we choose to be well and move on, we need not be ashamed of our past. We have to carry that "mat," whatever it is, so that we can share about what God has done in our lives. It's a reminder of where we've been, but it doesn't have control over where we're going.

In the Old Testament, it says, "Cursed is the man who dies on the tree," and in the New Testament, God sends his son Jesus to die that very way, on a tree. God is constantly creating good out of bad. That's what he was doing with my story.

In my study and preparation for my talks at camp, I learned about these specific kinds of trees that are found in Yellowstone that can only release their seeds at a certain temperature. So each year, when wildfires spread and the trees begin to burn, their pinecones open up and release seeds that plant new forests. It's a natural process—God creating something new from something old and dying.

No one can make you stay well once you've made the decision to get well. You have to make the decision to live well each day! Remember what God has done and what God has brought you through—what you have learned—and share that by carrying your mat.

The amazing truth about Jesus Christ is you can be made well even if you're not healed in the way that you hoped. This was something I was coming to learn as I came to grips with the fact that my orientation was not going to be changed. I always had in my mind the best outcome based on my understanding of life. But maybe being made well looked a little different than I originally thought or anticipated.

I had always seen my story as less than good. For so long, I wanted to be changed so I could forget about what had taken place and move forward. Now God was taking that story, not getting rid of my sexuality, but redeeming it and making it new so I could share with others about what I had been through—not hiding what had gone on before in the hopes they would seek the Lord because of my story.

The type of "well" I am talking about is not just a physical wellness, and it doesn't always mean that it takes away what unwell thing is happening in your life. It is a wellness that comes from being loved by God and from experiencing the grace that can only come from God—living well and being reconciled to God in our present situation, no matter what the outcome. It is taking life's circumstance and finding God's hand in it. During my talk I pointed out that it's not a prayer you say, and things magically get better. Instead, this wellness comes from finding God in the midst of life's trials. I have to choose joy in those situations and get excited for God to use my "mat" to change the lives of others around me and give them hope.

It's like breaking a bone. When you break your arm, you have to wear a cast until the bone is healed. When it's all healed, your arm looks fine, and unless you knew that it was broken you wouldn't be able to tell. In some cases, that bone may be stronger where the break was; if it were to be broken again it wouldn't likely break in the same place. Although it may appear that it is no longer broken on the outside, you could see in an x-ray that it had once been broken and made well again.

My brother Eric is a great example. Since he was really young, he has always sought out adventure. When he was in fifth grade, he broke his arm from falling out of a tree at our church and had to get a cast. This didn't stop him from climbing trees. He didn't let fear hold him back from something he loves. Today he's an awesome rock climber who does stuff neither my other brother Timmy nor I would like doing; we aren't big fans of heights.

When Eric was in eighth grade, he was into BMX biking and would go on ramps and do jumps—he was pretty good at it. One time he fell and landed on his handlebars and bruised his pancreas. He almost had to have it removed because of the damage. Later that year, while riding and going off a jump, he fell off his bike and somehow knocked his helmet loose. His head hit the concrete, knocking him out. He was rushed to the hospital. He ended up being okay, but the accident left permanent damage. Because of the impact, he destroyed the optic nerve in one of his eyes, and since then, he has been legally blind in that eye. There is no way the ability to see the way he once did will ever come back. But he is healed, he is well, and he still lives his life searching for his next adventure. He just has to be aware of the limitations in his sight.

That is being made well. It doesn't mean that there will be no trace of my past. It means I jump back into life, living with joy as someone who has embraced and moved on from the pain in my life.

The night I shared this talk I challenged the campers to ask themselves what the "mat" was in their life. What held them back from being made well? I knew what mine was. Although the hardship was going to have to continue for a little bit longer, I was in the process of getting up and taking that mat with me.

While I prepared and shared my talk on this passage, I was convicted in new and unexpected ways. I believe this was the beginning of the fundamental change I now see today. But things were going to have to hit one more major low before they were going to start going up.

Rock Bottom

Olympia, WA to Seattle, WA
Late Summer
Age: 29

August 11th, 2013

*Pathetic. That's how I feel, Lord. I'm hurting
so bad, Lord. I have no idea what I should do. Things
feel and seem so hopeless. My heart aches and yearns to
do something more than what I am doing, but I don't
know how, where, or what it is I am to do. I know
making people feel loved is something I care about doing.
I hate to think of people not loving who they are, who
you created them to be. This all stems from the fact that
I claim to love me. I am trying to, but in reality, I think
I am running away from me, if that is even possible.*

Also, as I was at camp this weekend, I

watched as many of the camper staff prepared to go back to school, start internships, or something else, and what was I doing? Moving back home at the end of the weekend to continue working at Starbucks. Pathetic. All in the midst of it, I loved their company and the community I found there, and I found myself longing for many of them to like me. Then to think of all the people who are yet to know my story and wonder if they would stick around? Hopeless.

I desire to get a job in ministry in some context, but I am afraid I'll have to be silent about my story and will only be able to love if it's in a way that honors the opinion of those around me. Hopeless.

Will I ever find a love of my own and get to be special to another person? Hopeless. For so long I have said, "It's okay, God's doing something. I am just trying to trust him." But now I fear that there might not be something better—that I've been placing my hope in an idea or misspoken vision. Maybe I am just too selfish because I can't bring myself to apply to work in a ministry that would call me to be celibate. Am I, Lord? I feel like that's so unfair. Not that life is always fair, but I feel like it is one of my biggest desires to have someone else, and I fear I never will. Not to mention the loneliness, but what about the desire for physical intimacy as well as spiritual? What to do with that?

God, I surrender. I don't know how I do that or what it looks like, but I'm waving my white flag. I CAN'T do this myself. I am desperate and depressed. I find myself tired, irritable, and easily frustrated. I was once someone full of so much life, someone that people expected big things from. Now this seems to be life in the desert. I find myself trying to find what would be the best way to find freedom from all the variables for the many directions I could go, and the only one that comes to mind is death.

I don't want that, but it seems to be the only option. I won't do anything, but it scares me that this has not come to mind just once but many times in the last week. Surely this is not what you had as a plan for me, right? You spared my life in the car accident for this? You delight in this? God why are you so silent? Will I ever hear you again? Have I done something wrong? More than ever I need you.

I said it, I surrender. I need you to take control of my life and take me where I must go. Develop the character in me that is needed to share your love. Don't let me forget this time, Lord; I want to understand those hurting even when my life seems to have turned around. People need your love; they need you; I need you and your love. Guide me, and direct me. I feel so lost. I am stubborn, and I'm sorry. But you knew that before I did, and you chose me. Come alive in my life in a way I haven't seen. I'm scared, but I'm trying to trust.

Tyler

During that time I went through moments where I was afraid for my life. The more I hid things, suppressed accepting myself, and let any kind of real love in, the more my hope of a better life vanished. I was functioning purely to get through the day, and thoughts of taking my life would pop up in my most hopeless moments. *Was I becoming suicidal?* I wondered. It wasn't that I *wanted* to take my life. I didn't have a plan. I just didn't want to hurt anymore, and it seemed like the only option—a horrible one but the only thing that would end the constant suffering. The thoughts would come most often when driving. I'd be driving and thinking about what I could do to make things better, and I'd start to think, *I could just turn my wheel really hard into oncoming traffic, and it would all end.* Or, *if I turned my wheel here I would just go off this bridge.* But as quickly as the thought came, I would snap back to reality and realize that wasn't the answer, terrified that the thought had even come into being.

I remember a specific drive up to Seattle while driving north across the Ship Canal Bridge. I could almost see myself driving off the side, falling the one hundred and eighty two feet to the water below. *Would I feel anything?* I wondered. *Would it hurt?* The questions seemed to come so quickly. Was I going to follow through with this? As scary as the prospect was, it would be a relief. I wouldn't have to hurt anymore; I'd have to trust that God would forgive me.

What kept me from taking my life was knowing the pain it would cause my family and friends. Plus, I didn't really want my life to end. I knew my life could be good, and I had seen that. But I couldn't live like this anymore.

As I saw it, I had two choices: I could live my life, constantly denying this part of me, every day struggling to get by, dragging myself through the day. Or I could stop fighting and open up my heart and mind to another perspective, seeking God in the midst of it. Sure, many would think I was wrong and sinful, but the life I was living was not a life God would want for anyone. It was a lot to process, but I was pretty sure I knew what decision made the most sense. In many ways, I felt like the decision was being made for me.

Glimmers of Hope

Olympia, WA to Seattle, WA
Late summer 2013
Age: 29

The next week, light and hope began to seep through the cracks in the years of pain in my life. I was in Seattle at my friends' Kaylin and Blake's, helping Kaylin make dinner and sharing with her about my week at camp. I downplayed the pain I was experiencing, but Kaylin saw right through it. I began to cry and told her how much I hated everything about me and that I felt hopeless.

She stopped what she was doing and looked at me and said, "Tyler, you're being so hard on yourself. Can't you see that you are beating yourself up day after day about something you can't control? There is nothing wrong with you, and you have people left and right telling you how great you are and how you've touched their lives, but you can't believe it. Do you think that when Marie, Alex, Blake, myself and others tell you that we love you just the way you are and that we believe God does too, we're lying? No. You assume that these things will never get better and that you will never have love in your life. I think you are limiting yourself too much. What if you were to let yourself think for just one minute that you could meet an awesome guy just like you who loves God? It would be no different than what Blake and I have or Marie and Alex or any of the other couples in your life, and I would love to see the day you bring him over here and we all just have a blast together as we all do, and it won't be weird that you two are men." She made many good points and it's going to be tough, I though. But I really need to let this soak in.

In the coming weeks, I slowly allowed myself to imagine what that would look like, and what I found was surprising. I found peace and even small moments of excitement of what could be. One late summer afternoon while driving in my truck, country music playing with the warm summer air blowing through the windows I began to imagine myself with a family—a husband, a few kids, and a dog—maybe even serving in ministry. As I looked in the rearview mirror, I noticed a big smile on my face I hadn't known was there. Sure, it was only just daydreaming, but it was the birth of a hope for a better future.

The next week my friend and roommate from seminary, Sam, came to visit with his friend, Adam. Sam had become one of the main people I went to when I was grappling with how my sexuality fit into theology since our time as roommates. You would think he would get frustrated at having to tell me time and time again that I was good and on the right path—but he never did. With patience, grace, and conviction, he continued to work through it with me. He reminded me of the parable in the

Bible where Jesus talks about how good trees produce good fruit, and that's how you know they are of God.

"Beware of the false prophets, who come to you in sheep's clothing, but inwardly are ravenous wolves. You will know them by their fruits. Grapes are not gathered from thorn bushes nor figs from thistles, are they? So every good tree bears good fruit, but the bad tree bears bad fruit. A good tree cannot produce bad fruit, nor can a bad tree produce good fruit. Every tree that does not bear good fruit is cut down and thrown into the fire. So then, you will know them by their fruits," Matthew 7:15-20.

He challenged me to look at my life over the years and see all the good that was coming to be through the ways I had cared for others while serving in ministry as well as through my friendships. There was an abundance of good fruit in my life. "You are good, Tyler. A good tree can't bear bad fruit," I remember him saying.

In one of our many conversations on this Sam told me he was feeling that he needed to be more vocal about his support of gay marriage and the ordination of gay people within the ECC. He figured if I was going to be penalized for who I was, and he felt the same way as I did, he deserved the same outcome, even if he wasn't gay. What an incredible ally.

During his visit, we spent the week hiking, hanging out in Seattle, and drinking tons of coffee. Together with Adam, we discussed the topic of homosexuality and the church in person for a change, and Adam heard more about my story and what life had been like for me. He was yet another person who was loving and affirming. *When was God going to send me friends I respected to tell me I was wrong and venturing into sinful territory?* I wondered. At that point, I had told many people, and a few had shared some concern, but the majority told me they were there with me and were already celebrating who God created me to be.

In June, Marie, Alex, Kaylin, and Blake had gone to the Pride parade after church. I had no idea they were going. I asked Marie why they had gone.

She looked at me and said, "We went to support you. You are not able to fully see how great you are and be proud of how God created you, so we went because we are already celebrating who you are. Since you're not at that point yet, we went in your place."

I was almost brought to tears. I hoped I would one day be fully content with who I was. But it was a journey that I had released all control of; I was on a train car that had broken loose, spilling down a hill in the opposite direction of the engine. There was great freedom in this—I went careening in my own direction, no longer pulled along to some predetermined destination. I was, for once, wild and free.

At the end of August, I sat down and had lunch with a man who was on the ECC denominational leadership team. He was someone who would check in here and there to see how my search for a church job was going. I needed to talk to him about my life—all the pain I had been feeling as well as this new drive to come out when the time was right.

We sat down for lunch, and knowing we only had a limited time to talk, I laid it all before him. Each time I shared about my sexuality and my story, I still never knew if I was going to cry or not. On this day, the tears were free flowing. To the best of my ability, I used the words I could conjure to explain what it was like for me to live with this struggle all of my life. Once I dreamed of being a youth pastor, and now I was pretty sure that it wasn't going to happen.

Although what I shared was heavy and something that takes time to know how to respond to, he replied with grace. He was kind, pastoral, and empathetic. It's what anyone in my situation would have wanted. I felt heard, not just listened to. I knew his heart was breaking for me. I didn't expect him to tell me the denomination's stance was going to change. *But what was I supposed to do?* I wondered. Each time a church calls or someone suggests a church job I should apply for, I had to find a way getting out of it—it was clear I was hiding something.

I left our lunch meeting feeling cared for, heard, and loved. Before parting ways, he offered to connect me with a spiritual director in the area. He thought it would be a great way for me to process all that was going on in my heart and to seek God's discernment for sharing my story.

All at once, things began to happen that didn't make sense. Things that went against the way I had always thought. God was not going to let up until I saw and believed that he loved me and saw me as good. Nature had always been a place of serenity and peace for me, and while reflecting on some pictures of trees and plants I had taken on a recent trip into the woods, I had this thought: *Trees and plants are all so unique and different in how they look and work, but the one thing they all have in common is they give us oxygen and life.*

As I thought about this, it was as if I felt a voice inside say to me, "Look at the beauty of my creation and how they are so unique in how they look and act, but they still serve the same purpose. Why would you think that I would limit my creativity in how I created you and the way you love? You need to be you and love people the way I am calling you, and this means loving yourself for how I created you."

But God, I thought. *Being gay is wrong and sinful, and the church collectively will think that I am sinful and have strayed from you if I embrace who I am and talk publicly about it.* I felt the voice again. "Do you serve me first or the church? Does their opinion matter to you more than mine?" It was a lot to process, but I still wasn't fully on board. *Speak a little louder, in a way that won't let me question quite so much,* I remember praying.

Around this time I had just hit my six-month point at Starbucks, which meant it was time for my review. Going into it, I wasn't particularly worried. I knew that I was a good worker but had room to grow, and encouragement toward that was forthcoming. As I sat there, my manager worked down through each section of the review, telling me how I had excelled at not allowing my struggles with depression to get in the way of my work. She also shared where I needed to grow, but I sensed heaviness in her. That's when she began to tear up and shared something that she had no idea would be profound to me.

She knew about my depression but not what the root of it was. With tears in her eyes, she looked at me and said, "Tyler, I'm so glad you came to this shop to work. You're so loved by everyone here and by our customers. I just wish you could see how great you are. I know you have had a lot of pain, but I wish you could just be you and see that it's enough."

Where did that come from? I wondered. She had no idea that my greatest struggle was to be me, fully me. This had nothing to do with my job. It was as if I had stumbled upon a burning bush like Moses that God spoke to him through in the book of Exodus. I felt like God chose a very unlikely person to speak to me in order to get the point across, and I had to hold back tears while I listened.

As always, as quick as these profound words washed over me, skepticism began to creep in again. I couldn't fully believe it was God until I had shared it with Sam, Claudia, and Rebekah and got their thoughts. They would help me make sense of it. They could show me if I was reading too much into it. But all three of them encouraged me to embrace it. I wanted to believe it was God and that it was truth, but skepticism had taken ahold of me. But then that same message kept coming in places that I would have never expected.

Thirty, Flirty, But Not Quite Thriving

Seattle, WA
September 2013
Age: 30

On September 6, 2013, I turned thirty. This birthday felt different than the others—thirty seemed so old. Bekah came to visit the night before, and we spent the whole Friday together doing whatever I wanted. We got up and made breakfast together, read from a devotion that we both loved, and talked about life over coffee on my parents' back porch under the warm, late summer sun. Throughout the day, my phone was constantly buzzing with texts and notifications of well-wishes from friends—all of them important and special. One message in particular both encouraged me and left me longing even more to come out. It was from my dear friend Ellie.

Dear Tyler,

I am beyond blessed to know you and have you as a friend. I know how it feels to sometimes struggle with

254

knowing, truly knowing, that I am worthwhile and valuable. I am sorry that you sometimes feel that way too, but I want to affirm a few things in you that you can look at when you might feel not as great about life or yourself or your calling:

1. You are HILARIOUS. I feel like I laugh so much around you. It is restful!

2. You listen really well and listen without judgment. It is refreshing because most judge and give advice. You listen and affirm people's personhood.

3. You are better at being with people in pain than almost anyone else I know. Maybe it is due to your own pain, but whatever the reason, you let people grieve in healthy ways, and that is a gift.

4. You offer hope to people struggling with faith. You listen, offer grace and experience, and you let them know that you love them anyway. I can't think of a better way to show God's love than that! I feel like that is how Jesus would do it.

5. You let people be themselves. I know that I can say whatever and be whatever in front of you, and you accept me. Wow.

6. You are a really good mentor. I can't tell you how many times I have randomly run into (not literally) someone you have mentored, and they mention you with such awe and thankfulness for you. You rock!

7. Your honesty is so much more what God calls us to

than trying to cover up our struggles. I know your
honesty with those close to you and those God calls you
to share with makes God really happy. All in all, you
rock. And I know God loves these things about you too.
So. Cool. HAPPY BIRTHDAY!!!!!

With peace,

Ellie

Ellie is one of those people that everyone is drawn to. People just want to be around her because of her peaceful, welcoming, free spirit. She loves nature and typically is singing because of her excitement for what God is doing. During my last semester in seminary Ellie had become one of those safe places for me to wrestle, so I was so grateful to have her by my side.

Ellie and I had talked in May when I was in Chicago for graduation. Over a Chipotle burrito, I told her about feeling hopeless, not knowing what was coming next—how my heart ached because of something I had no control over. So much had happened since then, and it was good to hear from her on my birthday.

Bekah and I spent the rest of the day in Seattle, drinking more coffee and talking about life. We specifically went to Capitol Hill in Seattle. The Gayborhood. The same place I had been basically one year earlier after returning from Europe and felt so out of place. This time was different. While sitting in a coffee shop talking to Bekah, I found myself distracted by a guy a few table over.

He was probably around my age with short, styled dark

hair and light blue eyes. He was dressed in fitted jeans and a patterned V-neck t-shirt. We kept catching eyes, then looking away quickly when the other noticed. I whispered to Bekah, "Help, that guy keeps looking this way. What do I do?" "Well, my love, you smile back and suck in the joy that comes from being noticed because you are something special," she said to me. Although I had come a long way, I was not yet ready to start dating. I still needed to come out.

From there we left and drove south to Tacoma for dinner, where I sat in the middle of the long table in an Italian restaurant, surrounded by friends. Many friends who knew my story and celebrated it.

It was surreal, As I looked around I was surprised by how many people I had told, but even more at how affirming and supportive everyone had been. Not everyone there knew my story but the ones I was closest with did. Before I went home that night, I told Marie and Kaylin I had a feeling that thirty was going to be a big year. I knew in my heart that it was the year I was going to come out. I just needed to figure out how.

This is Me

Olympia, WA to Seattle, WA
September 2013
Age: 30

The following week, I had my first meeting with my spiritual director, a middle-aged man who was just a little bit taller than I am. Which is to say, rather short. He seemed kind and gentle. We sat across from one another in a room next to very large windows overlooking Puget Sound and the Olympic Mountains. Once seated, like my spiritual directors in the past, he lit a candle to represent Christ in the room.

For the next hour or so, I shared everything that was going on in my life—all the pain, the struggle to love myself, and my fear of going against God. The truth that I walked away with that day was that God offered me peace, and that when things got stressful, I needed to take a step back and rest in God's presence. My director challenged me in those stressful moments to imagine myself holding a small bird in my hand—to remember that I would need to take calm slow breaths so it wouldn't be frightened away. In that practice of slowing myself down it was his hope that I would be able to find a way through those anxious times. "God offers us that peace, and we need to accept it," he said—like a little bird climbing quietly into our hands. I went away feeling refreshed.

About a week later, on a warm summer afternoon, while walking around one of the lakes in my hometown, I came out to a close friend of mine. I had no fear going into this conversation. I shared about the pain and the longing for God to bring someone into my life like me that struggled with their faith and sexuality so that I wouldn't feel so alone—someone I could relate to. No longer expecting that person to randomly appear, I began to wonder out loud while talking with her what it would look like to be that person I was hoping for—to come out myself. She just quietly listened as I poured out my heart, processing out loud the things I was excited about and the things I was scared of. When we came to a break in the conversation, I looked over at her and watched as tears filled her eyes. That's when she opened up and told me that she could relate to me more than I expected. She too had been waiting for someone to share their story of wrestling with sexuality so she could finally feel safe sharing that she did as well.

For the next few hours, I listened to her story and offered some of my own perspective from coming out to close friends and family. For a little over ten years, I had been slowly coming out to those around me as well as going back and forth with coming out to myself. I had been in and out of the closet so many times, I swear if I did it again the hinges on that door would have fallen off.

While we walked and talked, I could see in her so much of the pain I carried. The worry of being unloved by God—the fear of rejection. But I didn't believe those lies for a minute. There was no doubt in my mind that God loved her. As I encouraged her, mentioning these things, I was able to see how much I had grown as well. It was further proof for me that I had to go public with my story. I wanted to be a resource for people who wanted to share their stories. But there were still a few people I really needed to talk to. My brothers and sister-in-law didn't yet know.

I didn't have the same fear I once did as I prepared to tell my siblings. Most importantly, I wanted to make sure I did it in a way where they all felt equally valued and important, since I had told many others before them. I originally had wanted to find a time to tell them before Timmy went back to Chicago for school, but that didn't work out. So I decided I would have to send them all an email. That way they would all get it at the same time and have the chance to process what I shared before responding. It's not every day you get an email like this from your brother.

I'd be lying if I said I wasn't nervous. Eric is only two years younger than I am, and I respect him a great deal. He had been a missionary and knew more about church tradition, history, and theology than I felt like I did, even after seminary. What was he going to say or think when I told him this?

Timmy, our baby brother who was no longer a baby but halfway done with college and taller than me. He has one of the biggest hearts I had ever seen. He could never say a bad thing about anyone. He always saw the good in people, even when I vented my frustration. Would he be able to see the good in me?

I'm the oldest and always hoped I could be a brother that they both looked up to, but would all that change after I told them? I was finally being honest with them about who I was. Aside from the pain of keeping the secret, it was getting to the point that it seemed almost unbearable to continue holding my story to myself.

Then there was Heidi, who fit so well with our family. I admired her boldness as a teacher, and as a woman working with other women who were being trafficked in Belgium. She went into environments that weren't safe for her, hoping to show others that they were worthy of so much more. I was pretty sure that upon sharing with her, I would be a recipient of that same love.

So late on September 13th, I said a prayer for honesty and for boldness, and I sat down at my computer to write my siblings a letter.

I started off by telling them it was one of the hardest letters I had ever written. Over the next three or so pages, I came clean about my sexuality and detailed all the pain I had been through in hiding for so long. I made sure they knew that I was aware of the church's perspective, and I struggled to put into words how painful that had been for me. I also wanted to make it clear that it was not a choice I had made. It was that type of thinking that led me to believe that I was a mistake, begging and pleading for God to change me for years.

As I continued, I shared how this had been a journey and not something that happened overnight—it was through years of wrestling and most importantly through the Lord's guidance. *God doesn't fix things that aren't broken*, I said, and this would become a mantra for me as I gathered the courage to come out publicly. I'd grown up hearing this phrase, "freedom in Christ," but I'd never fully understood what it meant because I always felt so trapped in my life because of the things I was taught by the church. But freedom in Christ didn't mean hiding each day, lying about who I was. It meant being open about the story God had written in my life and celebrating that story.

I knew there had to be other people out there who were hurting like I had been, needing people with whom they could feel safe and to whom they could relate. I believed God was calling me to be that for others. God had showed me that I was just as worthy of love, that I wasn't flawed and unworthy of grace. I was just like everybody else.

I was finally in a spot I never dreamed I would come to—no longer ashamed of my story, and neither was God. The Lord had written it and called it good, and I wasn't going to listen to anyone that would tell me otherwise anymore. I needed the freedom to be me, to be the Tyler God created me to be— fearfully and wonderfully made.

I finished my letter by thanking them for hearing what I had to share. I made sure to explain that I understood it would take some time for them to come to terms with this and that I was willing to wait. I concluded by saying that *this is just a small part of me that has been hidden away for far too long. Things are rough now, but I don't need you guys to be worried about me. I've made it thirty years, so I think I am going to be okay.*

I let out an enormous sigh of relief after clicking send on that email (after re-reading it around one hundred times). But just as quickly as I hit enter, I felt this panicky feeling of, "Wow, now it's out there," rush over me in a cold sweat. No turning back. But the responses I got from them were better than I could have hoped. They all made it very clear in their responses that I was loved just as I am.

Tyler,

I love you so much, and like you said, nothing has changed. You are still the same brother I grew up with. We could talk more when we are together, but I think this is the theological issue of our age, and I can see God is calling you to lend your voice. Maybe not right away, but when you are ready. Thank you for sharing, and I am sorry I could not help carry your burden.

Eric

Tyler,

I love and care about you so much. I ditto Eric's words. I support you :) I just read it now because I'm still at work, and the kids left a little bit ago. I'm so sorry you had to deal with this so long. The cool thing is more and more people are ready to hear these things, and it doesn't need to be so shocking or scary. I know it still is, but you have a bigger support than people even a couple years ago. AND it will only get better.

LOVE YOU!
Heidi

Hey Tyler,

Just want you to know I read the email. Of course it is a shock and will take some time to fully grasp. Like you said, though, nothing has changed, and nothing will. You are still the same person, and I still love you the same. I am incredibly impressed by your decision to let it be known; I don't know if I could have done that. I just hope everything goes well for you. It's hard, but I am looking forward to moving on from the initial surprise and having it be very welcomed. I love you.

Timmy

Once I had heard back from them, I felt as if the thousands of pounds that I had been carrying for years had been lifted off of my back. *If it felt this good to tell my siblings, I wonder what it will feel like when I share this publicly with everyone*, I thought. People around me began to notice a difference about me; they said I seemed lighter. One of them told me I seemed more like Tyler than she had ever known me to be. It was a welcomed observation after so many years of being told it was clear I was carrying a heavy burden.

Towards the end of September, I was contacted by a church that thought I'd be a good fit as their youth pastor. I was skeptical but wanted to hear them out and spend some time with their students. As I listened to the head pastor talk about the position, I was surprised to hear that it might actually be a good fit. But when I talked with some of my friends about it, they reminded me that although it seemed like an interesting opportunity, it sounded an awful lot like another closet—the very thing I was trying to break free from. Although I hadn't officially come out, I was finding more and more peace and freedom as I accepted myself. I couldn't be working at a church, knowing that in the not-too-distant future I'd be coming out. God calls us to a lot of things but does not call us to be hidden.

Around this time, I had my second spiritual direction meeting. As I drove and reflected on the previous weeks, I realized I had been more at peace than I had experienced in a long time. I had found freedom, even if just a glimmer. I had been practicing being more still. I was seeing the beginning of what coming out would do for my emotional health and I liked what I saw.

I told my spiritual director when I arrived that I had been thinking about coming out publicly on social media. As we caught up on what had been going on in my life since our last meeting, I shared with him a photo from the previous weekend. "It's me on a hike from last weekend. While I was eating lunch this little bird landed on my hand after I calmly offered it," I told him. I noticed his eyes light up and a smile spread across his face. I knew why he was smiling. During our last meeting, he had encouraged me to picture God's peace in my life like a little bird in my hand. *Hmmmm*, I thought. *Coincidence? How had I not made the connection?*

I told him how conflicted I was about pursuing the ministry job. Three of my friends had come to the same conclusion that I needed to make sure it would be a safe space to be me. "I'm so sick of never being known by those around me," I told him. "That's not freedom, and I don't believe that God is calling me to continue to live in secret." The will to come out continued to grow in me, overtaking the retreating fear. So much good could come from doing this, I thought.

My spiritual director then asked what I had to do in order to get the bird in the picture to land on my hand. "I just had to offer what I had, and it came. Actually, so many birds came, my friend and I had to run away!" In response, he asked if sharing might be what God was calling me to do. Offer me and my story, and trust that God will take care of me and bring the right people into my life.

Freedom was the word of the day. Christ offers freedom, and I had to ask myself how I was living into that currently. I shared the conclusion I had come to that God doesn't fix things that aren't broken. I believed the only broken part of me that God wanted to fix was all the hurt and self-loathing I had experienced. I left that meeting excited for what was next, with a challenge from my director. Having mentioned that I would be visiting a friend in Eastern Washington that coming weekend, he challenged me to sit in silence on the long drive and ask God what it was I was being called to do.

Before I left for my trip, I was asked by the church I had been talking to if I would come meet their leadership team. I couldn't hide it anymore; it was time to tell them the truth. I wanted to be a person of integrity and tell the pastor about my need to no longer be hidden. Before 1 left for Eastern Washington, I emailed him a letter so he could have some time to process before we met.

Time to Make a Decision

Western to Eastern Washington
September 2013
Age: 30

The drive was about six hours, and it wasn't until about four hours in while driving through the rolling hills of Eastern Washington, that I finally turned off the music and began to pray. The sun was beginning to set behind me over the wheat fields while they danced in the gentle breeze, making them glisten copper and gold, and I just rested in the peace I experienced more and more each day. As I prayed and asked about how to come out, ideas immediately filled my head. I needed to write it all out. Not in a social media post, but something different. I needed to write a document or book of some kind, I thought.

As I drove, prayed, and thought, it was as if I saw the whole thing written in my heart. I knew what I needed to say, how to put things, and what the flow would look like. I wanted it to sound like me, telling my story. It was going to be no easy task, knowing it would require me to look back over everything in my past—all the pain and heartache, the confusion and hopelessness. It was a lot, but my mind was made up. Now I just needed to find time to sit down and do it.

Even knowing the pain I would face, my heart was filled with an excitement and urgency to start writing; I was done carrying secrets. I had a taste of freedom in the times I had shared with friends. I prayed for whatever it ended up being and kept it tucked in my heart until I could set aside some quality time to start writing.

I couldn't help but reflect on the fact that just over a year ago, I was driving the same stretch of highway but in a very different spot emotionally and spiritually. God had not given up on me. I worried so much that things would never get any better. Now life was far different than anything I would have ever dreamed or planned for myself. God really had a plan, I believed. Maybe this was the beginnings of that bridge being built? It sure looked nothing like what I would have planned for myself and yet it was good.

"Being confident of this, that he who began a good work in you will carry it on to completion until the day of Christ Jesus" Philippians 1:6.

The weekend away was a much needed break. Everything would be waiting for me when I got home. On the Sunday morning before I drove back, we visited my friend's church. It had been a long time since I had gone to church. At the beginning of the summer, I had begun spending my Sunday mornings in solitude, reflecting in my journal, praying, and processing life over a cup of coffee on my parents' deck.

I no longer felt safe at church, and my heart was cynical. I didn't believe I could be fully accepted if I were to share who I really was. I had sat in church services at my parent's church where from the pulpit I heard encouragement from the senior pastor I had known for years and worked with to vote against gay marriage. I remember him claiming that it was our jobs as Christians to vote against this "assault" on traditional marriage and on Christianity. How could I worship in a place that was against me? It was too hard for me to be there, and it felt as if God was calling me away, reminding me that he dwells in my heart; I can spend time with him anytime, anywhere.

Sitting in church that morning, I found myself a little nervous, but I prayed for an open heart, and it ended up being very life-giving. The pastor that morning was a messianic Jew. He shared about how we are all first born into God's kingdom. Listening to him reminded me of my Old Testament class in seminary. He challenged us to spread God's love and values by the way that we live. I agreed completely. It was what I was trying to do each day with how I loved people around me. *Would talking openly about my story be helpful for others or cause more problems?* I wondered. As he continued to preach, he spoke about God saving the Jews from Egypt for a purpose. He concluded by asking us what the Egypt was that God was saving us from, and what was the message we were being called to proclaim in that freedom. The sermon rested heavily on my heart the whole drive home. So much so I had to stop at a Starbucks to journal about it.

September 29th, 2013

> *Today while driving I found myself excited at the prospect of writing my story into a book. Prepare my*

heart, mind, and hands as I begin this process.

I am being saved from my "Egypt" for a purpose. If asked what I thought my Egypt was, I'd say the closet of my silence. Even just a few weeks ago, my manager at work told me she wished I could see how awesome I am and just love myself and be me. That was so unexpected. It was a burning bush moment, and I am only just now making the connection of this and the message at church today. I've felt oppressed, and you offer freedom. I pray I would learn to trust that you have me—that you're taking care of me and will continue to do so, that you have good things for me.

Give me ears to hear what you're saying to me, where you're calling me. Silence the destructive voice that waits to pull me back to where I once was. I think I am okay just the way I am. Help me to believe it. I open my hands and heart and offer me, all of me. Use my story and most importantly your great love for people in a mighty way. I am ready for the journey, no matter how scary. You won't leave me. Make your presence known. Cast out my fear of what the outcome may be. Use the voices of those around me to speak truth and love, and help me open my heart and receive it. You're so loving.

Tyler

What a change from where I once was. So much peace had come over me. I frequently found myself dreaming about what life could be like for me and excitement about who I was.

The next weekend I went and stayed with my brother

and sister in-law. It was the first time I had seen them since I had sent the email in which I came out to them. We went out for beers with our friends, Chad and Jodi, who were in ministry with my brother. Jodi, not knowing what kind of answer she would get, asked what my perfect ministry job would be. Well, here goes nothing, I thought.

For the next hour and a half, I shared with them what life had been like for me. With more excitement and purpose than ever, I shared my hope and desire for the church to be more open to wrestling honestly with human sexuality, as well as with many other subjects. The pain it had caused to not feel safe for so many years had led me to feel like death was my only option.

I'm sure it was hard for Heidi and Eric to hear these things, but they made sure I knew that no matter what happened, they loved me and were by my side. They wished I had told them sooner, but they understood that it was only out of fear, not out of a lack of desire to be known by them. Jodi and Chad were great, too. We didn't discuss whether or not it's a sin, but rather how the church needs do a better job loving people who are wrestling with their sexuality. LGBTQ people weren't being loved and accepted, and the church was losing people because of it. Something needed to change, and now was as good a time as any. I needed to start writing.

An Unexpected Author

Olympia, WA to Seattle, WA
October 2013
Age: 30

On October 8, 2013, I sat down and started writing what you have in your hands today. I knew that my story had the ability to change so many lives. I was so excited about sharing it, and I wondered if I would even wait until the book was done to come out publicly.

I never dreamed that I would write this. The one thing I had kept hidden for so long was going to be open to whoever was willing to take the time to read it—pages full of my experiences, thoughts, confessions, hurts, and triumphs. That night I only wrote an introduction, but it was a good start, and I was so excited to continue writing, not knowing how long it would take, when it would be done, or even how long it would be. But it felt right.

October 8th, 2013

> *I pray that this story will share of the redemption that has taken place—that is yet to come. Protect me from writing things that are not helpful and help me trust that your Spirit is flowing through my fingers onto the paper. If even just one person reads and is able to relate and feel like they have someone who understands, then this is worth it. You're so good. Draw me to you, Lord!*

Tyler

Once I started writing, I couldn't stop. Whenever I had free time, I would pull out my computer and flip through past journal entries in order to tell my story as accurately as possible. Although riddled with sadness and pain, I was thankful for those books I had poured so much of myself into. There were so many reminders of how bad it once was as well as how things were getting better.

In the months of moving toward acceptance of my sexuality, I realized that I had a deep-rooted, twisted, and internalized homophobia from all I'd been through. I had held onto stereotypes of what gay people were like based on what I had seen and been taught. It was unfair. Friends had encouraged me to broaden the people I had in my life and put myself in an environment where I could observe and see that people are just people and their sexuality, although part of who they are, does not dictate their actions. During my weekly trips to Seattle, I would frequent different coffee shops on Capitol Hill and people-watch while working on this book. I would wonder what life would be like when I was no longer in hiding and even pretend that I was out while sitting in these coffee shops filled without, queer people. As I put each word on paper, I could feel the slow process of healing beginning; small pieces of shame began to fall away. It was hard at times—I shed a lot of tears—but with the sadness came laughter as well.

Each day, I expected anxiety or depression to begin creeping back into my life, but I found it happening less and less. Sure, I had hard days, but I was always able to find a silver lining. Writing my story out was a way of spending time with the Lord, and while I was reflecting on the journey I'd been on, I felt like I was living into my calling more than I ever had. It was as if God was sitting behind me, shining down on me, smiling at me, and encouraging me, saying, "Keep going; this is good!"

That being said, not all days were easy, though. On one Sunday morning in particular, I could feel a heaviness in my heart as I sat down to write.

October 20th, 2013

>*This morning's time with you came as a greater blessing than I expected. I was looking forward to it, but I was in somewhat of a funk last night before bed. I was confused about my story. Worried I had it wrong—not able to see clearly and lacking trust in where you were taking me. But I got up today and didn't turn the TV on. I wanted the first thing I did today to be things that would bring reflection. Most importantly, I needed Sabbath. I decided to listen to a sermon titled, "Peace," by Rob Bell.*

>*I was drawn to that word. I needed peace. You know that I needed it. I began to draw on my iPad as I listened. I started drawing two cliffs like I had*

pictured years before, symbolic of the distance I felt from you because of my story. As I drew for the first time in a long time, I was impressed by my God-given talent. I was not tempted to be a perfectionist.

As I listened, I was challenged and refreshed. "I am a sacred child of God." "I can't find my worth in what I am doing, how I am being used, but only in remembering I am loved by God and that's why I serve." "If I am feeling angry or passionate about something like an injustice, maybe it's because of a deeper calling. What will I do with my energy from this calling to bring shalom (peace) to the world?" Was I created for something more, and I am not using all I have? Everything I was hearing seemed so applicable to where I have felt you calling me.

Before I began to accept that this is who I am and that it might be okay, depression would come and go, sucking away all my joy. My anxiety was overwhelming. I felt hopeless that I could ever be happy or that things would ever get better. I somehow felt I deserved all the pain in my life, and I was one of my own biggest critics, bullies, and judge. Worst of all, thoughts of taking my own life as an escape from my "life" started to appear. This was not living, not surviving, not even coping, but slowly dying—not freedom in Christ, but bondage. But when I began to see that maybe I was a good creation, not a mistake but fearfully and wonderfully made, unique and full of potential, dearly loved by God, things began to change.

Once I began to accept and love how I was

created, my depression and anxiety began to subside, and I began to find hope that things could get better, that it was okay to dream and look forward to good things in my future, even blessings. I went from being a bully to my own spirit to becoming a hero and someone who would no longer let my own words of destruction and self-hatred exist. Most importantly, I went from wishing for an end of life to experiencing excitement for the story that was being written, with a feeling of urgency and determination to create a space for others to share, wrestle, and come before you Lord.

Before, I hated part of your creation and would not call it good. But you already had called it such. Hating myself was saying you didn't do a good job, and it no doubt had an effect on how I saw you, served, and shared your love. Thank you for revealing this truth to me.

Tyler

The morning was so good and gave me the courage to keep going forward with my writing no matter how hard it got. It wasn't for the faint of heart. There was so much to go over, and I had to somehow figure out how to put it all into a format that was understandable, relatable, and well balanced. Often, I was scared of what it meant for me to share this. But song lyrics provided helpful encouragement like they had for so much of my life up until that point.

Sara Bareilles came out with a song earlier that year called "Brave." I related to it immediately. In this anthem, Bareilles challenged her listeners to be themselves and share their truth. I found out later that it was written for a friend who was thinking about coming out. For years, I would whisper to myself that I was the strongest person I knew because of all the fighting I had been through. Looking back, I no longer see that as brave. I was living out of fear and self-hatred. Now, writing my story and sharing my truth? *That* was brave.

The biggest motivation in all of this wasn't a song lyric or a pat on the back from a loved one. It was God. Whenever I have felt like I was getting discouraged and doing the wrong thing, or the weight of it all got too heavy, it seemed God would send something or someone into my life to remind me to keep going. God's eyes were on me, and God delighted in what I was doing.

Toward the end of October, on my way home from a day trip to Seattle, I caught up with my friend, Alex, on the phone. Midway through the conversation, he told me that he had started reading a memoir by a man who was both gay and Christian. He shared with me his frustration as he read. He was angry, knowing that when I came out, some people weren't going to listen to my story but just tell me how I needed to live so they wouldn't be uncomfortable. It meant so much to me that he was not only angry about the things going on around us but that he'd taken the time to read the book in order to understand me and my story better. Encouragement, just when I needed it.

A week or two after that, while driving to meet a friend of mine whose children had been in my youth group, I felt the familiar nudge to tell my story. I wasn't sure how she was going to receive it or how to even bring it up, but I wanted to follow where I felt I was being pulled. Before going into the coffee shop, I prayed God would prepare the time and space, and I took a deep breath as I went inside. While telling my story, I noticed a woman near us in the coffee shop who seemed to be eavesdropping on our conversation. As I was talking, she got up to leave. I hadn't been talking very loudly, but maybe she heard something she didn't like. I shrugged it off. A few minutes later, she came back and stood off to the side, as if she had something to say. After she didn't move for a minute or so, I turned to her and asked if I could help her. She uncomfortably smiled and said, "Sorry to interrupt, but I heard what you were talking about, and I wanted to say thank you." She then handed me a folded-up paper and left. When I unfolded it, inside was a list of LGBTQ organizations for youth in Olympia with her name and email. At the bottom was a note that said, "Thank you for being the change our world needs to see so bad." Again, encouragement just when I needed it. I showed my friend and told her how things like this had begun to happen to me more frequently. She listened and was kind, but I could tell she wasn't supportive of where my journey was taking me.

Writing my story was on my mind at all times. When I wasn't working or sleeping I was pouring through my journals, praying, and typing away on my laptop. For the most part, I was excited, but one day while on a break at work, I found that familiar condemning feeling begin to creep in. I worried I was wrong in what I was doing and prayed again that God would give me encouragement to keep going. A half hour later, I felt my phone vibrate in my pocket. We weren't supposed to have our phones on us while working, and I had forgotten to leave it in my bag. But I was curious about who had texted me, so I went to the back and snuck a look at the text. It was from one of my friends. "Thinking about you and your story a lot. You're inspiring, man." *Wow God, you work quickly*, was my initial thought, but skepticism took over just as quickly. *Maybe that was just a coincidence*, I thought. I had just talked to him the other day, so maybe it's just fresh on his mind.

But God was persistent, and not long after that, one of our regular customers came in—an older woman who always ordered a decaf iced espresso. She had a bag in her hand and told us she didn't have time to come in the day before on Halloween to give us treats. She pulled out of her bag a piece of chocolate for each of us. Before leaving, she reached into her bag again and pulled out a pencil. She handed it to me and said, "I don't know what you're going to do with this here at work, but take it and go and write something good." She then smiled, grabbed her coffee, and left. If the text wasn't enough to convince me to keep writing, this sure did. She had no idea that I was writing a book. I carried with me a big smile the rest of the day.

Reflections on the Closet

Olympia, WA
Late Fall 2013
Age: 30

I am where I am today because of the voice of truth God has shared through the many friends mentioned in these pages as well as so many others not mentioned but who have lent their hearts, prayers, and support to me over the years. We hear a lot about how the church is the scariest place for people who are gay, and in many ways I agree, but I have also seen another side. If only the church focused less on what it perceived as wrong and was more willing to wrestle with new ways of thinking. Some people have little hope for the future of the church on this matter. But I know so many people who have risen to the challenge to love me well.

So what now?

Writing this book was something I never dreamed I would do. For years I've heard stories of how people ran from God for a long time when they were being called into ministry. I never really understood this and thought that I was different. I was excited about serving in ministry. But I've come to realize I have been running, too. I believe for years God had been reaching out to me, trying to tell me that I was okay and loved just the way I am. In my mind, there was no way God would make me this way and also say that who I am is good or okay.

Now, after all I've been through, I don't see how I could have possibly thought that way. Coming to a point where I would share the truth about who I am hasn't been easy, some may wonder how I can say that God made me this way, when in their minds, being gay goes against God. But it really isn't that odd for God to do something that makes no sense to us. We have tons of examples of this in the Bible.

Look at Abraham. He and his wife prayed for years for a child, and when they finally had Isaac, what did God do? He asked Abraham to sacrifice his son—murder him. Or what about God asking Noah to build a boat and make room for two of every animal because a worldwide flood was coming? What about Mary? For a young woman in her time, to become pregnant outside of marriage was grounds for stoning. But when the angel told Mary she was pregnant with the savior of the world, Mary welcomed the news and accepted the honor of being the one to carry Jesus as her son. Those are just a few of the many times in the Bible we see God act in a way beyond our ability to comprehend or understand. I don't believe God stopped working even after the bible was finished being written.

The other reason I share this is because I know how tiring it is to live a life wrapped up in lies. Not only have I lied by acting as someone I wasn't in order to keep my secret safe, but I also asked friends who knew that I was gay to lie for me. For that, I am sorry. I learned growing up that we serve a God of truth, and Christ calls us to live in freedom: Up until now, the way I have lived has been anything but free. I have been living in bondage to fear. I have been living in a secret hopelessness. The Bible says in 1 Peter 1:16, "Be Holy, because I am Holy." Our God is a God of truth, and our God is Holy. I have to believe that being honest about all that is going on in my life is one step in the direction of holiness.

I am no longer ashamed of my story, and neither is God; God never was. Therefore there is no need for it to be a secret any longer. Step into the light, and the truth will set you free. God's light is shining on me, and I am ready to tell the truth. I'm ready to be free of all the stress and shame that comes with keeping a secret for so long. "Therefore, there is now no condemnation for those who are in Christ Jesus" Romans 8:1. I need not fear condemnation because I have Jesus in my life.

A friend of mine recently sent me a video about stress that was eye-opening. In it, the speaker talks about what our body does when we enter a stressful situation. When you encounter an evident threat of some kind, your hypothalamus, a small part in the base of your brain, sounds an internal alarm in your body. When this happens, your body releases two hormones, adrenaline and cortisol, and certain functions regulated by that part of the brain temporarily stop so that your body can react accordingly. When the threat has passed, things go back to the way they once were. But not for someone who is living in constant stress. When someone is under stress constantly, these triggers do not turn off and that person's body lives in fight or flight mode at all times. This can and does have long-term effects. Our bodies were never meant for overexposure to these hormones that disrupt our system. As I researched it more, I found that chronic stress has been known to cause anxiety, depression, heart disease, digestive issues, sleep problems, weight gain, and memory and concentration issues. I had experienced most of these symptoms.

Keeping my sexuality a secret and trying to change myself caused me to live in a state of chronic stress. I came to accept the stress, often not knowing where it was coming from or why. But in the few months after I began to accept my story and share my truth, the stress that was once such a regular part of my life began to subside. I wasn't really living. I wasn't surviving or even coping. I was slowly dying.

But what was I to do? I was sinful and I hated that part of myself. I had subscribed to a phrase I was raised hearing everywhere: "Hate the sin, love the sinner." This idea initially made sense to me. It still calls for love, doesn't it? But it's the first part that I have a hard time with. Hate the sin. How can you honestly love someone if you hate something in their life, or worse, something fundamental about them? Sure, if it's an action you don't like, I guess I could get on board with that, but in this case, what you hate is not something I've chosen; it's just part of who I am.

Who I am as a gay man has been part of me from the beginning, and when I hear that phrase, what I hear is, "I love most of you Tyler, but there is a part of you that I hate." "Do not judge, and you will not be judged. Do not condemn, and you will not be condemned. Forgive, and you will be forgiven. Give, and it will be given to you" Luke 5:37-28.

Reading through the gospels, I have seen that Jesus loved those around him and cared for the marginalized. I see the church constantly position itself to care for others, but then Christians get fixated on something they disagree with and before long, that's all they see. This kind of thinking has caused people who are gay and many others to feel that they are less-than, bad, deviant, and unclean. But God has already called me and others good, and said no one can say otherwise.

We see this in Acts 10 and 11, where there is a story about a man named Cornelius who is a Gentile; he wasn't seen as a member of the chosen people of God. In the story, Cornelius and his family are devout, God-fearing worshipers, and God tells Cornelius to send for a man named Peter. Cornelius then asks a few of his servants to bring Peter to him.

The next day, while on his roof praying, Peter is given a vision from the Lord. What looked like a big sheet is lowered down from heaven, containing all the kinds of foods the Hebrew people saw as unclean—food they weren't supposed to eat. Peter hears the Lord say to him, "Get up, Peter. Kill and eat." But Peter tells the Lord he can't because he has never eaten anything impure or unclean. The voice speaks to him and says, "Do not call anything impure that God has made clean." This happens three times before the sheet is taken back to heaven.

While Peter is trying to figure out what the meaning of this vision is, Cornelius's servants arrive at his house, and God tells Peter that he has sent them and to not hesitate but to go with them when they invite him to go back with them. So Peter welcomes them into the house as his guests.

The next day, Peter and a few people from his own community travel back with the visitors, to Caesarea, where Cornelius is expecting them. Peter lets it be known that he typically would not associate with Gentiles because it goes against Hebrew cleanliness rituals. But God had given Peter the message to not call any person unclean that had already been called clean. Peter asks why they have sent for him. Cornelius then shares about his encounter with God where he was told to gather his people together with Peter in the presence of God to listen to everything the Lord has commanded.

At this point, Peter begins to speak, saying how he has come to realize that it is truth that God does not show favoritism. God accepts anyone who knows him and does what is right. They all knew about Jesus's life, ministry, and his death and resurrection. They knew that Jesus appeared to those chosen by God after he was raised, and they all knew the command to preach of these things, believing that Jesus is the one whom God appointed as judge of the living and the dead.

In the story, while Peter was still speaking these words, the Holy Spirit came upon all who were there, and the circumcised believers who had come with Peter were blown away that the gift of the Holy Spirit fell even on the Gentiles, hearing them speaking in tongues and praising God! Witnessing this, Peter acknowledges their receiving of the Holy Spirit and orders them to be baptized in the name of Jesus Christ.

In Acts 11, when Peter gets to Jerusalem, having heard that the Gentiles had received the word of God, Peter is criticized by his fellow believers for associating with Gentiles and going into their homes. So Peter explains to them in detail what happened. "'As I began to speak, the Holy Spirit came on them as he had come on us at the beginning. Then I remembered what the Lord had said: "John baptized with water, but you will be baptized with the Holy Spirit." So if God gave them the same gift he gave us who believed in the Lord Jesus Christ, who was I to think that I could stand in God's way?' When they heard this, they had no further objections and praised God, saying, 'So then, even to Gentiles God has granted repentance that leads to life'" Acts 11:15-18.

You may think that I am sinful and wrong because of what I shared, but no one but God has the right to call me unclean or impure, and God hasn't done that. At the end of this story, I find what seems to be a parallel to the church today. The other Hebrew Christians were frustrated with Peter and could not believe that he had been associating with Gentiles; they struggled to believe that the Holy Spirit actually could be with them based on who they were. Sound familiar?

I have heard many people say they don't believe someone can be gay and Christian, as if somehow this small part of someone is great enough to limit the work and love of God. I believe this type of thinking makes God a lot smaller. I have Christ in my heart. Just because I am now coming out does not mean this hasn't always been true about me. The difference is I am finally laying it out in the open! As my friend Sam has encouraged me, the test of Godly things are fruit. I've been told there is fruit in my life, in the ministries I have been a part of, and that fruit comes only from God, who is in me.

I haven't gone to church on a regular basis for many months because I no longer felt safe or welcome to be me. My sexuality has been a secret for most of my life. It breaks my heart that while in these hard times these past few months I have wanted nothing more than to be able to go to church—to be honest with God and worship. But I feel there aren't many places for me to do that. I am limited with only a few churches that will welcome me as I am, but those aren't necessarily the worship style or tradition that I would choose. Then the churches that I would like to go to say they want to be an open place for gay people, but I believe they say that with the expectation that people like me will come and be changed and turn from our "sin." What does the Bible say? "Let everything that has breath praise the Lord" Psalm 150:6.

So how do we handle this "issue"? How can I serve in the midst of coming to grips with the truth about my sexuality? I have a few suggestions. First, please allow me and other Christians who are gay our humanity. We are not issues to be solved and figured out; we are people. All that Jesus ever called you to do was love. "By this all men will know that you are my disciples, if you have love for one another" John 13:35. It has not been easy to hold onto my faith while facing the truth of my sexuality, and when I am treated as not fully human, but just as some hot-button issue, I feel like I am robbed of my humanity. It creates wounds that are difficult to heal, and for some, those wounds can be fatal.

The current climate of the church breaks my heart. There are people out there who are wrestling with their sexuality. Many are feeling like their greatest hope for relief is to take their own life. They should be able to find solace in the church, where they could be heard and loved. But instead, they fear judgment. This is appalling. It's a tough reality to face, and there really is no easy way around it. It's so important that we figure out a way to be more open to hearing stories before more lives are lost.

We allow our fear and lack of understanding to get in the way of welcoming people from all different walks of life in our churches. The church was never meant for those who had it all figured out. Everyone has a story that needs to be told and heard, and people should not feel ashamed when they seek healing and guidance from God. Its sad that many feel safer outside of the walls of the church rather than in.

I also want to talk about shame and how we can avoid burdening our children with it. Our children are actively shaping their vision of the world based on what we say and do. Shame held me back for years. Shame isn't something we're born with. Instead, it's learned from our experiences with condemnation, denigration, and rejection.

I had my first lesson in shame when I was in kindergarten. The daycare I went to had many fun toys and clothes to dress up in. In one of the toy boxes was a bright red, shiny silk skirt. I had seen many children, both boys and girls, play with it, and one day I decided to put it on and spin in circles, not because I wanted to pretend I was a girl, but because I wanted to see what it would look like when it fanned out and sparkled. I was teased by my classmates because I was a boy wearing it, and I was embarrassed and ashamed. I never went near that skirt again. I didn't understand why it was only for girls. I still loved playing with dinosaurs and adventuring out in the woods, but those parts of me were negated by the fact that I had once put on a skirt. I was curious, and I discovered that, sometimes, curiosity wasn't allowed.

My next lesson in shame came in the third grade. At the time, the movie *Aladdin* had just come out, and I really loved it. The main character went on adventures, riding on his magic carpet, fighting thieves and other villains with a sword. He even had a genie and his best friend was a monkey! I thought he was the greatest. One day, a friend and I played with some new Aladdin toys he had just gotten. One was Aladdin, and the other was Jasmine. I thought they were pretty cool, and I wanted an Aladdin for myself. I saved my money and asked my parents to take me to the store to get one.

My excitement changed to shame when my parents realized that the Aladdin toy I wanted happened to be a doll. The thought never crossed my mind. It was just like any other action figure I had played with. I remember them trying to talk me out of getting it. They were from a generation where gender roles were more structured, so it was hard for them to understand (not that it is any excuse). In the end, I did buy the toy, but I was never able to fully enjoy it because of the shame I felt the day I brought it home.

Then, in fifth grade, shame showed up again. I love professional basketball, and I had the dream of one day playing in the NBA. I knew I wasn't going to be tall, but there was a player on the Charlotte Hornets named Muggsy Bogues—I mentioned him earlier—who was only 5'3". If he could do it, then so could I. At one of my school basketball games, I was sitting on the sidelines and I had my legs crossed. I didn't put much thought into it, but an adult told me not to cross my legs like that anymore because boys don't sit like that. I was embarrassed and worried others had seen me sitting this way. For years afterward, even until very recently, I would catch myself starting to cross my legs and instead shift into a more "masculine" position.

Fortunately, I have had friends who have been willing

to help pull me up out of my shame. Even as I write this book, I'm relieved—to be known by those around me and proclaim this truth. A truth that no longer brings me shame like it once did. I would never have gotten to this place if it weren't for people willing to love me and help me to carry this burden.

God delights in his children working together in community. "Carry each other's burdens, and in this way you will fulfill the law of Christ" Galatians 6:2. I know there are people out there who have little hope that things will change, but I have not given up hope. What you have before you is an account of how I have been able to share my burdens. It happened because I was given the freedom to be me, to be raw and real, without a label.

Our society loves labels. Gay, fat, thin, athletic, religious, liberal, conservative—these words are loaded with prescribed meaning and context, but they don't tell someone's story. When we give someone a label, it takes away the opportunity for them to tell their story, and it removes from us the opportunity to hear and dwell in the easy and the hard parts of someone's story in order to understand them. I challenge the church to do a better job at listening to queer people of faith's stories and invite us into the conversations rather than talking about us without us present.

My favorite part of Bible school was the time each day where someone would share their story. It was in hearing those stories that I was able to get to know people on a deeper level. I love to ask people their stories and hear where they came from, what they have been through. There are stereotypes out there for virtually everything—I have used them too. I thought I knew what gay meant because I had seen it in movies, on TV, and I had heard pastors speak about it at Christian events. Rarely did I see it presented in a way that was not extremely flamboyant, in your face, and hyper-sexualized. This did not line up at all with who I was, making things more confusing and hard for me to understand my identity—as if your sexuality would always determine how you dress, talk, and act.

I know people have assumed that I'm gay, and when I have asked why, the reasons make no sense to me. "Well, you're just so nice and sensitive; there was no way you could be straight." Or, "You're more fashionable than most guys." Some of these things might be true, but I am not sensitive or stylish because of my orientation. Perhaps, I am more aware of hurt around me due to the fact that I have experienced pain myself. And I am particular about how I dress because it's a way to express myself—I have always been artistic, and this is one of the many ways I can show that. (My mom also has a great eye for fashion, and I was fortunate to inherit that eye from her.) I think the only assumption I heard that even remotely works was that I must be gay because I had never been in a long-term relationship with a woman. I can't argue with that one.

To people on all sides of this "issue," I ask you to broaden your perspective. Take some time to get to know people who are gay. It would not be fair to assume I understand all straight people from what I hear about spring break trips to Cancun. And while we're at it, take some time to get to know people who are Christians. They're not all awful people who hold up terrible "God hates fags" signs. Every person has a story to be told, and we can all choose love.

I would also like to ask Christians who struggle to fully accept their gay sisters and brothers to stop fixating on sex acts when it comes to gay relationships. We act as if sex is the only signifier of who is and isn't human. Sex is an important part of our humanity, but there is more, including a desire for love, companionship, family, and commitment. Some people hear that someone is gay and feel there is no need to hear anymore because they already know what that means. Those Christians think that gay people are an abomination or that there is no way gay and Christian can be in the same sentence. It's this kind of thinking that scared me away from facing myself. I was afraid of the labels, and I didn't like how it felt to be forced into a box of who I was allowed to be based on who I was attracted to. To know that when I met people, some would've already made up their minds about me is sad and discouraging and painful.

When a friend or family member comes out, the stereotypes tend to fade away—the person who was always there, in living color, is so much more than the label. At least, that has been the case for me. It's what you are accomplishing by reading my book. You have taken the time to hear my story, and you have allowed me to be known and heard by you. I believe that if you were to spend some time with me, you would find the same Christ in my life that you have experienced in your own. I know my family and friends would all attest to this.

My faith and my relationship with Jesus Christ is so interwoven with who I am that trying to separate it from me would likely destroy me. It's been a fight to keep my faith over the years, but I have come this far and I have no expectation of that changing anytime soon. Recently I heard someone say, "Do not close the door that opened the heart." I believe the Lord has opened my heart, and I see people differently than I once did. With each opportunity to talk with someone, I desire more than ever to understand them, to love them, and to hear their story and their truth without judgment.

Over the years of coming out to friends and family, I have learned a lot about what was helpful and what wasn't for me—some things that I think are important to share. It's practical advice for those who are trying to support or encourage someone who is struggling with their sexuality. I have four things that I think are best to avoid, and four things to try.

First, avoid reacting. Instead, respond. It may seem like there is not much of a difference. When someone reacts, it is almost always defensive, emotional, and reckless. Responding, on the other hand, is more about logic than emotion. It's about engaging and asking questions in order to better understand. When people around me have reacted instead of responding, I've had a hard time confiding in them again. When they have had the presence of mind to *respond*—to calmly ask questions and offer encouragement—I have taken great hope from that. When someone comes out to you, it is most likely not a decision they have come to lightly, so remember to try to understand the truth they are sharing with you.

Second, avoid telling someone who comes out to you— or confides in you about struggling with their sexuality—that you already knew they were gay. You might think it's helpful to do that—to say, "I already knew that, and I still loved you"— but this, too, can be hurtful. It's *my* truth to tell, not yours to surmise. I'm not gay until I say I am. It's not true until I tell you it is. I can only speak from my own experience, but this was a big one for me. Particularly when I had not yet figured it out but was merely reaching out for a shoulder to lean on, people thought it might be helpful to rush me out of the closet. But it only made things worse to feel like I was outing myself unintentionally—that people thought they knew more about me than I did. I wrestled with this day in and day out for much of my life. How could you know before I did? A good way around this is to just hold your assumptions to yourself. Ask questions and offer support, and wait for the person to come to their own conclusions in their own time.

Third, when someone confides in you, don't assume it's okay to tell your partner or spouse. I understand that to hear this news can be very challenging for some, but I believe that information given in confidence is precious, and if a person is not out yet, you have a great responsibility to keep that confidence. I've had people tell me after I came out to them that they told one of our mutual friends—often a spouse or partner—because they needed to have someone to talk to about it. But if there is anyone you need to process it with, it's the person who has shared it with you. If a tough secret is shared with me, I don't go to someone else and share with them in order to get clarity. That's betraying trust. Like any secret you might share with a friend, if you wouldn't want it shared elsewhere, then give the person coming out to you the same respect.

Lastly, avoid throwing Scripture at someone who is coming out. You may have heard the verses in the Bible on homosexuality referred to as "clobber passages," and for good reason. They're used to break people down—to shut them up. You are of course free to disagree, and there will be time for that, but whenever that time comes, never use Scripture against people. Especially if you're concerned that what they share could be detrimental to their faith. You're not helping if you attack them spiritually. In fact, this is how you push people away from their faith. Regardless of your interpretation of these texts, I don't believe that God would ever want us to use the Bible to hurt people. It took me years to understand that the Bible is not a rulebook, but a narrative. It's God's story.

As for things to try, first, when someone comes out to you, try asking questions. Let the person know that you want to better understand and that you need to ask questions in order to do that. Then, once you're given permission, ask away, and keep asking. When friends asked me questions, I was reminded that I was not alone and most importantly, that my friends cared and were on the journey with me.

Second, try reminding this person that they are okay. Don't just assume that a person who comes out to you knows what you think of them. Tell them. I have so often questioned whether I was good, and it was very healing to be reminded that I was and my friends were sticking by me in it. I still have friends today whom I reach out to, asking for encouragement when things are hard.

Third, get educated. Take the time to learn about the LGBTQ (lesbian, gay, bisexual, transgender, and queer) community. Learn what the words mean. Go there with your friend or family member. By doing this you are investing in them and in something that is a significant part of their life. Do your research, and talk to the person in your life this pertains to. But be honest. If it's hard, let the person know that it's hard, and that it will take time. Give them the freedom to say they need to take a step back if necessary. This isn't just a topic; it's their life. Communication should be one hundred percent open.

Finally, and most importantly, be an ally. I can stand up for myself until I'm blue in the face, but people can just say that I'm biased because I have an agenda or I want to justify my "sin." When straight people speak up on behalf of their gay and lesbian sisters and brothers, I believe it carries greater weight.

My friend, Rebekah, once told me that when she hears people use language like "gay" in a derogatory manner she pictures me, and it cuts her deep. She feels that if she doesn't speak up she is somehow saying that it is okay for me to be treated that way. She can't be silent. So speak up. Don't let people use words like gay and fag! It's never funny or okay. Help people who don't fully understand see that people who are gay are people. They are people with feelings, and they are fully human. Be an ally.

I know this is easier said than done, and it will no doubt bring its fair share of consequences. Some people may see you differently or may, unfortunately, lose respect for you, but when you step out and speak up for the marginalized, you are doing exactly what Jesus modeled for you to do.

I have been beyond blessed by the people God has brought into my life to walk through this time with me—people who have been willing to ache with me as well as celebrate have made the hard times so much easier.

For anyone who may have come across this and can relate in any way to my story, I want to encourage you that as scary as it might be, when you are ready, find at least one person that you can talk to. You are not meant to carry these burdens alone! I always wished there was someone else out there like me to whom I could relate, who would come out so I could have the courage to do the same. It's my hope that sharing this will encourage others to come to me and confide in me so that I can offer them the love and grace that was offered to me and that I so badly needed.

Remember as you prepare to share your story with anyone, your truth is yours and yours alone. No one can tell you otherwise. They have not walked where you have or experienced the pain that you have. Tell it without shame because God has never been ashamed of you. It can be petrifying to share your story, but the freedom that follows is so worth it. I feel today like I can breathe more freely than I ever knew was possible. We need people to share, so others can feel the freedom to do the same.

Living in shame is no way to live. You were not meant to live in the closet. No human was. When I was in sixth grade, I had two parakeets. I loved those birds, but when they got out of their cage it was always so hard to get them back in. They didn't want to be confined by bars. As much as I loved them, I always felt like I was limiting them by keeping them behind bars, making them prisoners in that cage. In the wild, birds can come and go as they please. They were never meant to live in cages, and neither were people. God cares about us and will provide for us—we have to trust that. I am reminded of the verse in Matthew:

"Therefore I tell you, do not worry about your life, what you will eat or drink; or about your body, what you will wear. Is not life more than food, and the body more than clothes? Look at the birds of the air; they do not sow or reap or store away in barns, and yet your heavenly Father feeds them. Are you not much more valuable than they?" Matthew 6:25-26.

For too long I have allowed myself to be confined to a cage, watching as other people lived free. I was not meant to be there, and I am ready to knock down the gate that has been holding me in. I am ready to fly free, to trust in God's provision, and to be a voice for those who are still in the process of breaking free.

Thank you for taking the time to read and hear my story. I'm only one person, but I know that there are many more out there waiting to have their stories heard. Be open and willing to hear someone's story. Cry and wrestle with them. We are all human, desiring and deserving of love. Don't let your fear and lack of understanding get in the way of experiencing all that the Lord can do.

Epilogue

Pacific Northwest

2013 - 2020

Originally, my plan to come out was to self-publish this manuscript and just share it with little explanation, letting the story take on a life of its own. But the deeper I got into the story, the bigger I realized it was—kind of like an iceberg. It looks big when you see what's sticking above the water, but once you dive down, you realize you've only seen a tiny bit of its mass. That's how my story was, something that continued to get bigger the deeper I dove, full of sharp, cold edges, holes, and cracks, with a hard icy exterior.

When I realized this wasn't going to be how I came out, I began to ponder what would be the next best way. I could have my friends' just share for me when people asked about it from time to time, but that didn't feel right. For so long I had hidden this part of myself in shame. It was important for me to share as an act of pride and courage. "This is me, so take me just as God made me." I also felt that since I had such a long history working in ministry, that if I were to let people share on my behalf, the story could get twisted. I didn't want that. I needed a way to share that wouldn't require me to have to keep telling people over and over again. At the time, blogs were really gaining a lot of attention, which seemed like the perfect venue. I could write up my thoughts and then share them via Facebook and just let it spread as it would naturally. If the story got twisted, there were always my words to go back to.

In December of 2013, I felt that I was finally ready. I was still living in Olympia, my home town—the last place I wanted to be when I came out. I was afraid of how people from the church I once called home would respond, so I did what I always had when I didn't know what to do. I prayed. I first thanked God for all that I had been through over the last few years—the pain as well as the relief, the uncertainty and the hurt. Seattle still felt like the perfect place to be. Especially since I had spent so much time there over the last year. I prayed specifically that God would provide a job and a way to move there come January. I honestly didn't expect much, but I figured it didn't hurt to pray about it, so I continued to pray like this for the next several days. Not long after, I heard from a friend in Seattle whose coffee shop was about to open a new store, and they were hiring baristas. I applied, interviewed, and was given a job. Best of all, I needed to be in Seattle ready to work on January 2nd. I could see the big exhale coming!

I began to create my blog. The tagline across the top read, "Longing to be Heard: Perspectives in the Midst of Struggle." I didn't want the tagline to give away what my post was about. Once that was all put together, I only had one thing left to do: write my post.

The first write-up was long. My dear friend, Sam, helped me edit and consolidate. I decided the day to share would be January 8th. There was no significance to that date; it was just my first day off from work. So I sent an email to my close friends who had been on the journey with me, asking them to pray for me and to monitor my post for people who said unkind things. I was scared and excited the night before. I had the blog all set up and ready to go live on my computer, so all I would have to do the next day was click "post." I went to sleep, reflecting on my life. Somehow I had gone from wanting to hide this secret away for my whole life to now being filled with excitement to share and be known.

On the morning of January 8th, I got up and read over my post one more time, got down on my knees, bowed my head and said a prayer. Then, taking a deep breath, knowing that what I was about to do could not be undone, I exhaled and clicked post. I closed my laptop and went and jumped in the shower, my mind and heart racing. Should I run back and delete it? Had I made the right decision? Was it too late to turn around? No, I thought. This was the right thing to do. I felt a mix of exhilaration, relief, and a bit of apprehension as to what responses I would get. I couldn't believe my eyes when I opened my laptop after getting dressed and saw that many people had already liked it, commented on it, and even shared it. It felt like an out-of-body experience.

When I shared it to Facebook, I didn't title it anything that would jump out and tell people I was gay. I wrote, "Here is a little bit about what God has been doing in my life. It's scary but also exciting. If you think it would be helpful for others to read, feel free to share it!" The post itself was titled "Time to be brave," as I had been very inspired in the months leading up to coming out by Sara Bareilles' song "Brave".

Here's what the blog said.

Hi, my name is Tyler Krumland. I am the oldest of three boys, born and raised in Washington. I love being in the woods, photography, coffee, and deep conversation, and my relationship with Jesus Christ is the most important thing to me. Growing up I was typically seen smiling, having fun, enjoying every experience in life, but deep down I was carrying a pain deeper than anyone really knew. My smile masked years of self-hatred, pain, sadness, and hopelessness. For years I kept the source of the pain secret, but I'm done hiding, it's time to be brave and that's what this blog is an attempt at. You see the thing is, I am a paradox. I am a Christian, but I also happen to be gay.

For some this may be shocking whereas others may have had their assumptions. Some may have tons of questions while others are in the process of getting down on their knees praying for me in fear that I am on a fast train to hell. Whatever it is you as a reader are experiencing, before you jump to any conclusions, let me attempt to put into words how I have come to where I am today. It's a place that only the Lord could have brought me to.

Each day for the last twenty plus years, I have woken up with what felt like the weight of the world on my shoulders, knowing there is something about me that is different; something that automatically made me wrong and bad and if shared publicly would cause me to be seen as sinful, disgusting, and in some people's eyes an abomination. Words can't explain how painful it is to sit with people you care about and respect and hear them say things like this, not knowing they are in fact talking about you. Each one of their words ripping and tearing your humanity away from you until you have become nothing more than an issue to be figured out and overcome; many claiming to be acting in love. But it didn't feel loving. Although it hurts to hear them say these things, the thought of losing them is equally painful and scary.

For a long time, I tried to change; I tried everything—therapy, fasting, praying, dating women, being prayed over, and even anointing with oil. Nothing worked. I refused to give up the idea that one day I would be "healed"; I would become straight. Then this last summer I came to a breaking point. The years of lying, failed attempts at change, and self-contempt had all caught up with me. It breaks my heart, but I had come to the point where it seemed the only hope I had at finding peace was death. Was I going to have to take my own life in order to find freedom? I didn't want that, but I also couldn't bear hurting any longer.

So I cried out to God and begged and pleaded for answers, asking why he wouldn't change me, fearing I might do something that could not be reversed. What I heard was the opposite of what I expected:

"I don't fix things that aren't broken. The only healing that needs to happen in your life is how you see yourself.

I have already called you good, so quit allowing those around you to tell you what good looks like. I make no mistakes; now go be who I created you to be, and be the change this world needs."

As I began to accept that this was who I was and how God created me, I saw something start to happen. The depression that had been with me for most of my life, that robbed me of my joy daily, began to diminish. Anxiety and worry that were part of my daily routine became almost non-existent. I began to have an excitement and a hope for my life that was not there before. Most importantly, I found my relationship with the Lord growing. Who God was and how vast his love for his people began to manifest itself in my life, and I felt I could not hold back from sharing it with others. I began to see each person I came in contact with as someone with a story deserving to be heard, and I wanted more than anything to offer them the love of God. For years I heard about freedom in Christ and thought that I knew what it was, but I was quickly realizing that my understanding of that freedom had been limited.

Freedom in Christ does not call someone to lie each day about who they are and play some role that will cover up a part of themselves. I was not living in freedom but in bondage. Freedom is what came when I finally began to accept myself as a good creation and stopped telling God he had made a mistake when I was created. I am his beloved, loved just the way I am. There are tons of stories of how God spoke to me and brought me to where I am today, but I'll save that for later posts.

So what does this mean for me? I act and do things the way I do because I am Tyler. Yes, being gay is a significant part of my story, but it is not the only noteworthy part of who I am. There are tons of other things about me that are far more interesting:

The fact that I love dinosaurs today maybe more than I did as kid. Or that one of my favorite ways to relax is over a cup of coffee with my Bible and journal by myself. Discussing theology with people brings out the nerd in me I never knew existed. I love photography and feel at peace when in nature capturing its beauty with my camera lens, and my favorite is when I get to share it with people I love. Spontaneity and adventure are things I wish I had more of in my life. I love music of all styles, believing that for every season and setting there is music that fits it beautifully—even pop music has its place in the soundtrack of life. Falling asleep to the pouring rain is one of the most soothing sounds, and I also still long to have a family of my own. Most importantly, though, I am a follower of Jesus Christ. All these other things that I find joy in are out of a response to the relationship that I have with my Maker. All those things are outdone by this truth. It may be hard for some to see how I can in the same paragraph acknowledge I am gay and a Christian, but it is possible. I am that paradox.

In sharing this with you, I ask just a few things. First, no one wants to be forced under a label, and I am no different. Just as straight people come in all shapes and sizes, with a plethora of interests, the same is true of people of the lgbtq (lesbian, gay, bisexual, transgender, queer) community. So before you force a label on me or anyone else and expect to see me become some caricature you have seen on TV, take the time to have a conversation with me. Hear my story; get to know me—the me that has been in hiding—but also the me that is ready to be brave.

Last fall I asked the Lord how he wanted me to share my story, and I had this idea of a book come to mind almost immediately, so I sat down and began to write. In just over a month, I had written a book all about my story. I will soon be self-publishing it in hopes of offering a greater perspective of what it has been like to be a Christian who has struggled with his sexuality. I have no doubt that you will find the same God you know in your own life at work in mine.

Another request, please don't call me sinner. My name is Tyler. I understand that everyone has their own perspective and understanding. But if you feel it is your calling to make me aware of my sin, I am uninterested in having that conversation or argument with you. I have been fighting for years, and I am tired and done. All that brought me was to one of the most hopeless places I have ever been, and I have no interest in venturing there again.

If you want to talk with me in order to understand my story better and have a conversation, then by all means get in contact with me. That's the reason I created this blog. In the coming days and weeks I'll be sharing more of what this has been like for me. I am more than my sexuality. It's my hope it will be a place for connections and that I can be a safe place for people who are struggling. I am not searching to be fixed but simply heard. That's what anybody wants and deserves. Hear people's stories, truly hear them, and never presume to understand where they have been, what they have been through, or where they are going. In assuming, we belittle both the joys and great pains that they have experienced.

Thank you for taking the time to hear my story. I couldn't ask for anything more. I don't fear what might be said to me because I have an arsenal of people who love me and love the Lord that will not sit silently while hurtful things are said to me. They will jump to my defense. They were already there defending and celebrating my personhood before I was, and I thank God for that.

I know that my journey is not going to be easy, but I have hope that life no longer living in the closet will bring a new hope, excitement, and wonder about truly living. Things won't change overnight, people will continue to say hurtful things, I will still struggle each day to believe that I am actually worthy of God's love, and at times I will get weary. In those moments I will just look to the Lord, where my hope comes from, get excited about the work God has started and will no doubt faithfully complete, and choose to be brave!

Tyler

That day was a blur. I spent it with my friends, Marie and Katie, and their children, which was just so great. Marie and Katie were two people who had been with me for most of the journey. I was overwhelmed by the amount of support and messages I received via email, Facebook, and by text that day. I got so many that halfway through the day, my phone died. The freedom I felt was exactly what I had always hoped for, and that night I slept better than I had in as long as I could remember—without the weight of the world on my chest.

In the coming weeks and months, I found myself subconsciously hiding who I was, as I had done for so long. I would sometimes dodge questions at first and then remember that I didn't have to. I was out, and I was able to take that deep breath all over again. The kind messages continued and with them came some of the not-so-helpful or encouraging ones.

One in particular came just a few weeks after coming out, from a woman from the church I grew up in. When I received her message I wasn't surprised. It was brief—just a note that said, "Thought this was interesting" and an article attached, written by a man who had once been openly gay but had since left what he called a "lifestyle" and is fully supportive of conversion therapy.

As I read the article, the anxiety that I hadn't felt in some time began to creep up on me. It ran through my veins like poison until I was almost shaking. The anxiety that had loomed over me for so long rose back up in me like a swelling tide. I was both terrified and angry. Why did she do this? Why can't she just mind her own business, I wondered? I sent back a message that said, "I appreciate your concern, but I have to ask you to let me be. All my life I have read articles and blogs like this, making me feel like the worst of all people because I have made some kind of 'choice.' I will always be my own worst critic. Messages like this bring up old feelings of self-hatred that led me to begin to consider self-inflicted harmful actions. I know you care, and that's why you sent this. My spirit is fragile and tired. If you want to support me, then all I ask is that you love me for me. If that's too hard, then I'm sorry we can't talk about this anymore. God is my judge. He's the one I'm in relationship with, and I'll continue to seek him and follow as he leads, regardless of other people's perspectives." She wasn't one to let things go so easily, so we went back and forth for a bit before I stepped away. I knew that friendship was something best left in the past, as it wasn't giving me life.

I wish I could say this was the only negative reaction I received, but over the coming months I had to weather plenty of push-back—from subtle tweets about me from past students, to article after article showing up in my inbox, to negative comments on any post I would share on Facebook. I was even unfriended on social media, which we all know means people are serious!

That June was my first LGBTQ Pride month in Seattle. I had gone to a Pride parade one other time in Chicago while still in the closet, but this time I got to be fully me. Everything was a new experience. Toward the middle of the month, I posted an image of myself on Facebook. It was in black and white, and I was wearing a black shirt that read #betrue printed in gradient rainbow, the only color in the photo. My post read, "I don't normally post things like this, but it being LGBTQ Pride month, and five months since coming out, I thought it would be a good time for reflection. For most of my life, I thought God made a mistake when he made me. Whenever I saw a rainbow, I thought there is no way I'll ever be proud of who I am. For years I lied about who I was and felt terrible, but coming out and being true to who God made me has brought me so much freedom. Today I can say that I am proud to be a gay Christian man. Life is still hard. I struggle. I make mistakes. I wrestle and doubt, but I'm learning each day, more and more, about who the Tyler who doesn't have to hide is. God makes no mistakes, and God knew what he was doing when he made me just the way I am. Never be afraid to be who God made you to be!"

Most of the feedback from my post was positive except one message I received from a woman from my home church. (I'll call her Brenda.) She, like the other woman I mentioned earlier, was very conservative and felt compelled to thrust her opinions and beliefs on others. She sent me an article about how God doesn't actually call us to be true to who we are without any further note or explanation. I honestly didn't give it much thought. I hardly knew the woman and wasn't sure how she found the post, as we weren't friends on Facebook. I engaged in a bit of back and forth, with little movement toward understanding. I was done. It was a weird role reversal, where I was having to ask adults I to be kind.

As these things continued to happen, I slowly became more and more disenchanted with church and with Christians in general. I felt like in many ways I was no longer a person but a controversy to be discussed. I had been raised to believe Christians were people who offered unconditional love, but that wasn't what I felt or experienced a lot of the time.

And yet, strangely, I understood where they were coming from. In their minds they *had* to do this. They thought they were looking out for me. But that didn't change the hurt and damage that it inflicted. For the first time, I saw what it was like to be on the outside of the Christian bubble, and it didn't feel good. It made me wonder, in what ways had I unintentionally caused pain in people's lives in the name of Jesus in the past? While processing all this, I took some time away from church on Sunday mornings to refocus and heal. I still loved God, but I was so conflicted with how I saw people act who claimed to follow Jesus. It didn't align with who I thought we were called to be.

I was taught, growing up, to follow God wherever that God might lead, and when God started to lead me in a direction that the people around me didn't understand, feel comfortable with, or agree with, I had to make a choice: follow God, or follow where these people say I should go. So I stepped away for a while. I knew God was with me, and I needed a break.

Unfortunately, the way I was being treated in God's name had made it increasingly hard to go before God. Some of the old thought patterns returned—I started telling myself that it was my sexuality that caused this distance, not other peoples' reactions. My anxiety began to rise again, and it was easy to trigger me. I asked God to help me find peace again. I knew these patterns no longer served me, but they weren't going to stop overnight.

You might wonder if I regret coming out, and to that I say, *hell no*. It was necessary in order for me to live. I don't know if I would be here today if I was still living in the world of suppression and self-denial that was my day-to-day for the majority of my life. No, I don't regret it—in fact, I feel lucky that I had to do it.

Coming out is a big deal for anyone who has to do it, and I now feel that it is one way we as LGBTQ people are a little more fortunate than straight people. Being gay forced me to really look into my life and figure out who I was. When it came time to come out, I had to overcome all the fears of rejection and realized it was more important that I was confidently me than to be liked by everyone around me. It's funny, because over the years I saw LGBTQ people portrayed in the media as weak, wimpy, lacking depth. In my opinion, they're some of the strongest people I know. They have had to go up against all the odds to make it known who they are. And it doesn't stop there; coming out, I've learned, is a process that continues for the rest of your life.

So where am I today? As I sit and write this it's been almost five years since I officially came out. I met and married my husband, Stephen.

(Update: In the spring of 2022 Stephen and I made the difficult decision to end our marriage. We both remain people that care deeply for each other. The following information about Stephen still remains true!)

As I processed things over the years, I always said that I would know God was okay with this if I met a man who loved God, too, and that is Stephen. He is gentle, kind, compassionate, artistic, and he makes me so much better. So much more Tyler.

As you might expect, I carry a lot of hurt and anger with me today. Whenever it's about to boil over, Stephen is there to dial me back. He grew up in a home where he never struggled to believe God wouldn't love him for being gay; in fact, he learned the opposite—that God loves all his children, period. No exceptions. It has been with him that I have begun to see God again in new ways.

For the past few years, we were part of an ECC

congregation in Seattle that loved us for us. They're one of many churches within the denomination who are pushing back against the leadership that is trying to limit how pastors care for LGBTQ congregants. We weren't a social experiment for them or a token—we were Tyler and Stephen. We got to go to church and talk about more than our sexuality. We've had the opportunity to speak during our Sunday school hour, work with our junior high and high school students, and I also preached for the first time since coming out.

Although the church was good to us, I still struggle with triggers that may be there for the rest of my life. To this day I feel uneasy whenever I hear any of those "Christianese" sayings that used to be common in my own vocabulary. Whenever I stumble across someone reading the Bible in public, my initial feelings are to run, followed by annoyance and disgust assuming they would judge me. I felt guilty about this for a long time. Like I didn't like the Bible or God. But I have since realized it's a coping mechanism, and when those triggers go off, telling me to prepare to defend myself, I take in a deep breath and remind myself that these people are not those who have harmed me in the name of God. I've endured years of spiritual abuse by some who have used the Bible to make me feel worthless so that I would fall in line with their theology. It's no wonder I feel this way when I'm around things like this. It also reminds me of the person I once was—a person who inflicted emotional and spiritual abuse upon myself. I now need to remind myself when this happens that not everyone's the same. They're not my abusers, even if their actions remind me of the abuse I endured, and it's okay to want to distance myself from these things. God is bigger than this and is everywhere, so I can't run, and I don't need to.

My faith is growing, shifting, and changing. I find more comfort living in the in-between. I don't need to have all the answers like I once did. Love is a great place to start, and in my opinion, the best guide for navigating life. I still pray and journal when I need to quietly reflect. For a few years I had a very long commute to work which gave me time to get through many books and podcasts, and I have found that there are many other Christians like me who have been burned, but who still hold onto their faith in Jesus. It's cathartic, healing, and refreshing.

I no longer identify as an evangelical because I can't get behind what they stand for anymore. I especially no longer want to be called a Covenanter, the term for someone who is a part of the ECC. I grew up proud of the church I was from, but I no longer carry that same pride for the place I dreamed of serving as a pastor for my adult life. Now I find myself feeling much different.

In the years since I came out, I have watched as the denomination has kicked out entire churches because of their welcoming stance of LGBTQ people in all capacities. They have fired friends of mine for their inclusive stance. They have even removed a long-standing campus pastor from their university—one who helped shape me and multitudes of others—because she officiated the wedding of a few LGBTQ students of hers. They seem to only want to control how their pastors serve, going as far as punishing pastors for praying at an LGBTQ wedding.

I said my final goodbye to the ECC in June 2018. I was asked to go as a delegate from our church in Seattle to the denominational annual meeting that was taking place in Minneapolis. This was important as they were voting on a new president, and the candidate that was being considered was very conservative and had a problematic past. He even had past experiences partnering with a conversion therapy group. I had little hope for the ECC at this point, but I felt it was important for me to go to this final event for closure—to speak up for Tyler who had been silenced by them for so long. Fortunately, I was going with Ellie and others from my church who were friends and allies. They had my back.

On Friday afternoon, June 22, 2018, hundreds of delegates from around the country took their seats in the large auditorium. Before we voted on the president, there was the opportunity for questions from the delegates on the floor. I knew I had to be the first one to ask him a question—to start things off. I couldn't care what all the people around me would think.

Just that morning there was a vote from the floor on whether the ECC should create a space for people to process together if they were wrestling with their conclusion on the topic of LGBTQ inclusion. It was going to be a verbal vote. The moderator asked for all those in favor to speak up and say yes. There were a good number of yeses which was encouraging. Then it was time for those opposed. Like daggers, resounding noes pierced the room. There was a couple behind me whose voices stuck out over the others—that's because they were familiar voices to me. It was a couple I had grown up with, friends of my parents. They were the same two I had run into in high school after seeing *Brokeback Mountain*, which caused me so much shame at the time. It was the same woman who had once taught me that I can't trust my heart, and it was also the same woman who sent me a painful article after I had come out.

I channeled that hurt and frustration from the noes as well as the pain I felt from that couple behind me, and when the moderator opened up the floor to questions for the presidential candidate, I jumped up to the closest microphone and was called on first.

I was shaking as I stood there in front of the hundreds of other delegates. Most of which would not agree with or like what I had to say. Wearing my black Nike shirt with the rainbow #betrue logo across the center. I took a deep breath as my face appeared on both of the large screens of the auditorium. *Here I go*, I thought. It's time to take my voice back. It's time I get the last word and show everyone here that I am not ashamed of who I am or how God made me. Many here want to silence me, but God has given me a voice, and I need to use it.

Making eye contact with the president on stage, I took a deep breath and said, "Tyler Krumland from First Covenant Church Seattle and North Park Theological Seminary grad. Mr. moderator, this question is for the president elect. In the early 2000s, you were a pastor at First Covenant Church in Portland, Oregon, which had a strong relationship with Portland Fellowship a ministry promising transformation and freedom from same-sex desires. A Christian leader with ties to such a ministry is a red flag to many LGBTQ Christians who have endured terrible abuses in similar programs, and to their friends and families who love them. As a Christian who happens to be gay, this is very concerning to me personally. I, like many queer people of faith, have unfortunately been involved with these ministries promising to offer freedom from something we never chose. During my time in one of these online programs, through mentors claiming to act in Christ's name, I was taught to hate myself and how God made me. When the program didn't change me, I lost hope and wondered if taking my life was the only option even though that wasn't what I wanted. It made me feel like I must not love God enough, that I didn't pray hard enough, and that my twenty-five-plus years of trying to change weren't enough. My time in this program has caused lasting anxiety and depression, and today I still struggle with trying to believe God loves me. So please explain your previous relationship with this organization and how your views may or may not have changed."

I tried not to be phased by those shaking their heads in disgust with me, and I took a step back from the microphone and stoically stared down the candidate for president, waiting on his response.

With a smug look on his face he began, "Well thank you so much for asking that question, and I just want to tell you that Jesus loves you, I love you, and you are welcome in the Evangelical Covenant Church, and I want to say I'm sorry to you for how the church has mistreated you in the past. Now I'd like to address your question, and it really is a two-part question. First, let me talk about reparative therapy, and then I will take some time to chronicle the relationship between Portland Fellowship and First Covenant Church Portland where I was a pastor. So I share your grief and pain over the abuses of reparative therapy, and my heart goes out to people who have endured this abuse. I stand in a place of lament with them and with you and with your families and with your friends. I agree with Preston Sprinkle who said no one should force another person to change their orientation. If someone should seek reparative therapy, they need to be the one who desires it, they need to be realistic about their expectations, and Mark Yarhouse who's an expert on this topic, in his book, *Homosexuality and the*

Christian in chapter four presents an outstanding summary of the various approaches to counseling and their implications, and as a segue to talking about the relationship between Portland Fellowship and First Covenant, let me just say that in Portland Fellowship's newsletter dated April 2015, Portland Fellowship advises parents if you have a child who has embraced a gay or lesbian identity, forcing them into therapy to change their sexual orientation will only cause deeper pain and confusion. Now I'd like to address the relationship between Portland Fellowship and First Covenant Church in Portland. I served as the pastor of First Covenant Church in Portland, Oregon, from 1999 to 2006, and in the early 2000s, First Covenant Church gave minimal financial support to Portland Fellowship. First Covenant Church appears in a Portland Fellowship newsletter from 2004, thanking the church for financial support. Portland Fellowship's spokesperson preached at our church on August 20th, 2000. On April 18th, 2001, and April 28th, 2004, a spokesperson from Portland Fellowship taught our youth group for about forty-five minutes each. According to our youth pastor at the time, the presentation was informative, compassionate, enlightening, and non-judgmental. I met with the Portland Fellowship interns for ninety minutes in 2002 and ninety minutes in 2004, and I taught this group of young leaders how to prepare and deliver a talk, and my name appears in two letters in December of 2002 and December of 2004, thanking me for teaching their interns. I did not serve on the Portland Fellowship board, I have not been in contact with Portland First Fellowship for twelve years. Thank you."

I went and sat down, purposefully avoiding eye contact with the couple I once considered friends, who were sitting behind me. I was thoroughly disgusted by his response but not surprised. He didn't even fully answer my question. He told me

I was welcome in the ECC, yet the denomination had just fired a beloved campus pastor for officiating the wedding of two Christian men who happened to be gay. They were also in the process of removing a historic church there in Minneapolis because they had decided to become open and affirming. *Where was I welcome?* I thought. He also quoted two people in his response, calling one an expert on the topic of homosexuality. They were both straight people—talking about LGBTQ people without bringing us into the conversation. So typical and not surprising. It was frustrating, but I felt relief because I had stood up in front of those hundreds of people and told them with my words and actions that their opinions and approval no longer mattered to me. Their opinions had shaped me for years. But now I sought the approval of God alone.

I thought that was the end of things with me and the candidate until I saw him in passing in the lobby a few hours later after he had been officially voted in as the new president. Taking a deep breath, I approached him and asked him if he had a few moments.

He responded with a friendly, "Of course I do," until we locked eyes, and he realized who I was. His expression immediately changed to frustration, as he crossed his arms, showing me how closed off he truly was to this discussion and to me. "Today I asked you a question, but you never really answered; you said you don't think anyone should be forced into conversion therapy, but you believe it's okay if they decide to go themselves. Is this true? I put myself into an online program, and it was still just as damaging." His eyes darted around the room, almost as if he was searching for an exit plan, hardly listening to me, but he had to be careful because we were in the main lobby surrounded by delegates, mingling. He needed to keep up appearances.

He quickly reiterated what he had said earlier, wanting to end the conversation quickly, and then without warning he said, "It was nice to talk to you," and then began to open his arms to give me in a hug. It felt like slow motion. Initially, I felt like it was the right thing to do to reciprocate this hug even though I didn't trust the man, didn't like him, and definitely didn't want a hug from him. In that instant, I thought of all the brave woman in my life who have had a situation like this happen but spoke up and said, "No," and I realized, I don't have to hug him back. As his arms began to come around me, I pushed my right hand forward into his chest and said, "No, thank you". He immediately recoiled with eyes as big as saucers, hands up as if he had just committed a crime, as he realized people all around had just witnessed this. He awkwardly backed away into a group of men in suits, and that was the last I saw of him.

My adrenaline was racing. I couldn't believe I had just done that. I spoke up for myself to the top of the ECC. No change would come from that moment, but I could leave the annual meeting with my head held high. I was going to be okay, and I didn't need the ECC. God was bigger than this messy denomination and was going to be with me wherever I went.

That night, there was a small dinner—a get-together for allies and LGBTQ people at the church nearby that was in the first steps of being removed due to its inclusive stance. Before dinner, the pastor asked if I would want to pray for the groups. At first I said, "That I wasn't comfortable," but as I thought about it, I realized this was likely my last time doing any formal pastoral act for a group, so I changed my mind and prayed for the group, the meal, and the future of the ECC, knowing full well I was done after this weekend.

The weekend ended with a church service at that church led by a dear friend, Pastor Judy, who had recently been fired. It was my last time of excitement worshiping with all these ECC people I had spent so many years of my life with. I was okay though because I knew that those friendships would carry over, and they did. Following the church service, Ellie, myself and a few other friends walked the few blocks to the Twin Cities Pride Parade. The perfect way to end the weekend and my time in the ECC. A denomination I believe is becoming more known for who they're against rather than what they stand for.

Growing up, I believed there was a war between good and evil in this world and that the church was always on the side of good. Now I see that the church often fights what it's not comfortable with, but I believe that's true for all of us. Fear of the unknown causes us to close off, shut down, and put up walls, which is why sharing our stories is so important. It is in the sharing of stories and listening to them that lives are changed and walls are torn down. Jesus did this, associating with all the people he wasn't supposed to, and that's how I want to live my life.

I originally wrote this book with the hope that those who disagreed with me would have no other option than to believe I am okay just how God made me—that they would no longer be able to argue against how God had been at work in my life. But now I see that I was doing this for the wrong reason, for the approval of people, not God. God had already called me good, so that was all the affirmation I ever needed. For so long, I was searching for human approval, and I'm done doing that.

I don't know what's next for me, but I know that there will still be days when I will struggle to believe that I am okay, days when I'll fear that I am going to hell, but as time goes on, those wounds are healing, and I am finding it easier to live in the peace that I find with Jesus. I will still ask questions that won't have answers. At times, I'll still miss so many of those friendships I lost when I came out.

It makes me sad that I don't feel safe at my parents' church or any other church within the ECC, a place that once gave me so much joy. I pray that things will continue to change and that LGBTQ people will feel the freedom to come out. I pray that the greater church community will open its eyes and hearts to these incredible peoples' stories. I hope that people who may not understand what it's like to be gay will read this and that it will give them a glimpse of how to care for those around them that might come out just like so many did for me. Most importantly, and like the example set by Richard, I hope my story shows people how to love them well.

ACKNOWLEDGMENTS

This isn't just a story about my coming out. It is a compilation of the stories of the people around me who were patient, kind, supportive, and loving; who encouraged me along in the process of unlearning toxic theology and who created space for me to learn to love myself just how God made me. This book only includes just a sampling of the many who have made a permanent impact on my life. For that love I am eternally grateful to all of you, those named and unnamed.

To Karen Quinn, who helped edit and clean up the first very messy draft of this story that I wasn't even sure was worth more than a quick glance: thank you for your hard work, dedication, and excitement to work on this project with me. I am grateful for your encouragement, reminding me that it was good and needs to be shared.

To Judy Peterson, Ellie VerGowe, Glenn Palmberg, Pete Hawkinson, Paul Corner, and Steve Elde, who have pastored me so gently after coming out: thank you for reminding me that I am good and loved. Thank you also for standing up for me when others were unkind. You created a safe space for me to share my fears, hurts, doubts, and hopes. You've all been lights in my life.

To my professors in seminary Michelle Clifton-Soderstrom, Phil Anderson, Jay Phelan, and Richard Carlson who were a safe haven for me to be honest, doubt, and ask questions. I don't believe that I would have made it through seminary without you. Thank you for providing a safe space to be me while in an unsafe space.

To the many who donated money to help make this book a reality: without you this book wouldn't have happened. Each time one of you offered support, it was encouragement to keep working even when things were hard. Thank you for sharing so generously and believing in me and this project.

To anyone still in the closet wanting desperately to come out: I see you. I know how hard and scary it can be. I hope you can find some encouragement in these pages, glimmer of hope which shows you that even though at times it may feel as if you're alone, you aren't. Never underestimate your story; it is valid, good, and worthy of being told.

To my family: I know that it was painful and difficult for you, in many ways, when I came out. There were many tough conversations, but I believe we are all stronger because of this. I am so lucky to have you, knowing not all LGBTQ people are fortunate enough to have family who remain faithful to love them after they've come out. I love you.

ABOUT THE AUTHOR

A writer, occasional speaker, and artist, Tyler's greatest love is being with people and hearing their stories. Whether walking with them through pain or celebrating, he is passionate about investing in relationship with others.

Tyler is happiest when he's able to get out into the mountains among the towering evergreens—he's a Pacific Northwest native through and through. He can often be found exploring Portland, Oregon. From food trucks & Willamette Valley wineries to exploring Mt. Hood and the coast, he's always up for an adventure.

Tyler holds a BA in communications from North Park University and a MA in Christian Formation from North Park Theological Seminary.

Follow along with Tyler at
Instagram: @TyKrumland & @TylerKrumlandart
Twitter: @TylerKrumland

Printed in Great Britain
by Amazon